GRAMMAR
FOR
JOURNALISTS

GRAMMAR FOR JOURNALISTS

REVISED EDITION

E. L. CALLIHAN

Professor and Chairman
Department of Journalism
Communication Arts Division
Southern Methodist University

CHILTON BOOK COMPANY
Philadelphia   New York   London

To My Wife Lillian

WITHOUT HER HELP THIS REVISED EDITION
COULD NOT HAVE BEEN PUBLISHED

Foreword

It is a good thing that Lee Callihan does in the pages of this book. Someone should worry about the writing behavior of both practicing and student journalists. He does it well.

My own distant background badly needs revisiting. And, I suspect many of my colleagues will welcome this completely revised edition of GRAMMAR FOR JOURNALISTS as a reference book for the media as well as a textbook for students.

In these moments of constant news developments, it is imperative that newspaper and broadcasting practitioners write clearly, concisely, interestingly—and correctly. In the related areas of magazines, public relations and industrial journalism there is the same obligation.

We assume that the journalism graduate comes properly equipped when he enters the professional field. But the assumption is not always correct. We find ourselves conducting newsroom "classes" and refresher courses in elementary grammar. And we patiently wonder whatever happened to spelling books.

Professor Callihan advises that his meticulously programmed

book "is intended only to help cure 'grammaritis,' which journalism employers rank as the No. 1 ill of journalism graduates and other beginners in journalism." Further, its flexibility makes it serviceable in the classroom and laboratory in any number of courses.

But most important for those of us already out in the field, the new edition of GRAMMAR FOR JOURNALISTS is so devised that self-instruction is easy. A new feature is the use of short quizzes at the beginning of most of the chapters. By taking these, the practicing journalist may be surprised to find how much he needs a thorough review, at least, of grammar.

The author has numerous exhibits of poor grammar, spelling, punctuation and sentence structure—all taken from newspapers, magazines and broadcasts. He graciously apologizes for his invasion into the professional field and then pricks our hides with the comment that the examples "indicate that even the professional journalist's knowledge of grammar leaves something to be desired."

Over the years it has been my privilege to work with many of Professor Callihan's products. Many have graduated to the staff of my newspaper. I have always found the same qualities in the Callihan product. They do know how to spell. They do know how to structure a sentence. They do know the basic rules of grammar.

The author does not waste words in presenting the elements of grammar. He starts with the journalist's chief tool, the sentence, and moves through the parts of speech, the framework of the sentence, the correct use of verbs, nouns, pronouns, verbals, adjectives and adverbs, prepositions and conjunctions, etc. Part II is devoted to unity, emphasis, coherence or clarity, and variety of expression in sentence construction, and Part III has important chapters on punctuation and spelling. Mr. Callihan's approach is brisk, anything but boring.

One very valid point is made in the presentation. It is to be assumed that the aspiring journalist is attracted to writing and has a certain facility with words. The desire and the interest is there—but can he put it together?

Actually, writing flows at a swifter, smoother pace if the writer does not hesitate to ponder the rules of grammar. It gives the confidence that leads to real creativity in writing.

So, thank you, Lee Callihan, for a contribution. It shall be on the shelves of this newspaper's library. Or, better, on the City Desk!

Felix R. McKnight
Co-Publisher and Editor
The Dallas Times Herald
President (1961–62),
American Society of Newspaper Editors

Contents

PART II

Sentence Construction

PART III
Punctuation and Spelling

Introduction

In view of the nature of many journalism curricula today, with their emphasis on the ability of students to report and interpret the American environment, complete with all its problems, it may be unfashionable to point out that students must learn the rules of grammar—and how to apply or, if necessary on rare occasions, to disregard those rules for effective communication.

And yet, sadly enough, some students with good minds and a flair for writing still enroll in journalism programs although they lack a firm grasp of grammar and, yes, spelling as well.

What to do about these students? One solution which numerous educators have adopted is to place in their hands E. L. Callihan's fine book, GRAMMAR FOR JOURNALISTS, the first edition of which was published in 1957. Many reporting and editing instructors require that all their students—both those weak in grammar and those with few problems in that respect—master the materials in the book.

This completely revised second edition of GRAMMAR FOR JOURNALISTS, brought out by a new publisher, is a natural supplement to the usual texts in reporting and editing. Because the entire book is slanted to the beginning newsman, with illustrations taken from actual copy, students quickly grasp the relevance of the rules to their own needs. Motivation to learn is high, and discussion and tests may be incorporated with little difficulty into normal course procedures.

Exercises, which appeared in the first edition of GRAMMAR FOR JOURNALISTS, were eliminated from this streamlined edition. The exercises—all taken from newspapers, magazines and television-radio broadcasts—will be updated and published in the future in an inexpensive paper-back edition, probably along with grammar and spelling tests that have been developed over a ten-year period by Dean Wayne A. Danielson of the University of Texas at Austin, and Dean Harold L. Nelson of the University of Wisconsin.

It is a truism to assert that the first criterion for all writing is grammatical competency. Words should be spelled correctly, sentences should be complete and well structured, and punctuation should be incorporated to provide clarity and occasionally a more dramatic impact. One may not expect a student to write with beauty, grace and crystal clarity, but one can expect him to handle his language with grammatical competence.

Unfortunately, grammar does not appear to be taught as effectively in many high schools today as it once was. Grammar has been a casualty of student-motivated learning. As one college English instructor commented:

"It has been difficult to establish adequate motivation for study of grammar. . . . The effort is unrewarding in an educational era when student interests dominate curriculum. Teaching of grammar has bogged down. . . ."

Overcrowded conditions in many high schools also have reduced the number of writing assignments and spelling and grammar drills, as well as attention to individual student weaknesses.

Compounding the situation is the appearance, as Marshall McLuhan has pointed out, of a generation of young people who have grown up in the television age and whose communication skills appear to be more oral- than writing-oriented.

Consequently, college journalism instructors often wind up teaching basic grammar—and spelling too—as a part of beginning reporting and editing courses. With this completely revised and up-dated edition of GRAMMAR FOR JOURNALISTS as a supplementary text required for all such classes, they can accomplish this objective and help produce students equipped to handle any writing or editing task successfully.

Dr. Warren K. Agee
Dean, Henry Grady School of Journalism
The University of Georgia
President (1958–59),
Association for Education in Journalism
President (1956–57),
American Society of Journalism
School Administrators

PART 1

ELEMENTS OF GRAMMAR

1
Advice for Journalists

Either you are preparing yourself for a career in journalism, or you already are working on a newspaper or a magazine, in public relations or advertising or in radio-TV, or perhaps free-lancing.

No matter what area of journalism you plan to enter or in which you now are working, you certainly must have a certain facility with words and you like to write. But also—quite probably—you make your share of mistakes in grammar and spelling!

"What are the greatest weaknesses of men and women who are entering the broad field of journalism today?" This question put to the editors of 100 newspapers throughout the United States brought the reply: grammar, spelling, punctuation.

The journalist who aspires to reach the top in his profession cannot afford to ignore the warning and the advice offered by these editors, who are representative of thousands of editors who hire—and sometimes fire—young men and women entering journalism.

Advice from these editors boils down to this: Get a good

foundation in grammar and spelling if you want to go far in journalism. Get it, preferably, while you are still in school. Don't wait to acquire it the hard way—after you go out on your first job.

GRAMMAR FOR JOURNALISTS is not a panacea for all the ills from which journalism students and practicing journalists suffer. It is intended only to help cure "grammaritis," which journalism employers, as well as journalism school directors, rank as the No. 1 ill of journalism graduates and other beginners in journalism.

This book deals with the fundamentals of American grammar. It does not go in for subtleties but aims at being plain, explicit and useful. The standard of correctness in the book is not academic but journalistic; in other words, it is the standard of most good editors.

As the author pointed out in the first edition, there is no quarrel with ending a sentence with a preposition or with splitting an infinitive or a verb phrase. It is now considered proper to end a sentence with a preposition or to split an infinitive phrase when such a construction makes the sentence clearer or more emphatic or more natural.

However, in this revision of GRAMMAR FOR JOURNALISTS the author is more permissive than he was in the first edition. Although language usage in most newsrooms and magazine offices remains fairly conservative, we must accept certain changes in use, although we don't have to go all the way in using *Webster's Third International Dictionary* (1961) as our Bible!

We must be more permissive, for example, in accepting the use of *will* for *shall,* and perhaps in the abandonment of most distinctions between *should* and *would.* We must recognize that *further* is rapidly replacing *farther,* but we also must realize that many editors will still insist on the use of *farther* in referring to distance or space. Certainly we must yield ground on the use of *like* as a conjunction in place of *as,* particularly in the fields of advertising and electronic journalism.

In regard to the television-radio field, we have recognized in this revision of GRAMMAR FOR JOURALISTS that there is a distinction between spoken language and written language. The electronic journalist, therefore, must be granted more freedom than newspaper reporters in the use of colloquialisms. For example, the weather forecaster on television should be permitted to say that "the temperature tomorrow will be *around* 80 degrees," and the newsman to quote the newly elected mayor as saying that he "would *try and* live up to the great responsibilities of the office." Whereas, the newspaper reporter probably will be required by his editor to make it "*about* 80 degrees" and "*try to* live up to."

In other words, the newspaper editor must insist that his staff members cannot write it "just the way they talk" because they are working for a printed medium, rather than for a speech medium, and the *written* word is much more permanent than the *spoken* word. Therefore newspaper editors, and most magazine editors, must insist on good *written* English usage, which must be more precise, formal and literary than the colloquial language of the electronic journalist.

Whatever medium you work for, you should always strive to use "good English," which is not necessarily "correct English," as advocated by the strict grammarians. Let your chief objective be to write carefully, precisely, logically, directly and clearly—and you will find you are writing *correctly!*

This book, the first edition of which was published in 1957, was the first grammar written specifically for journalism students and practicing journalists. Most of the examples used in the book to illustrate common errors in grammar, spelling, punctuation and sentence structure were taken from the columns of various newspapers and magazines and from radio-television newscasts. Some changes were necessary to conceal names of individuals and of publications.

This book is planned for flexible use in any journalism program. It will be serviceable in any course in newswriting or reporting, in editing and in feature writing—as an auxiliary textbook and/or reference book. In the near future a paperback workbook containing exercises and tests based on GRAMMAR FOR JOURNALISTS will be published, to sell as a package to college students or practicing journalists.

Exercises in the first edition of GRAMMAR FOR JOURNALISTS, which have been omitted in this edition, will be updated and published shortly along with tests that have been developed and tested in several universities for many years by Dr. Harold L. Nelson, Dean of the School of Journalism, University of Wisconsin, and Dr. Wayne A. Danielson, Dean of the School of Journalism, University of North Carolina. Dr. Danielson left North Carolina to become Dean of the School of Communication at the University of Texas this past summer.

The practicing journalist should find this second edition of GRAMMAR FOR JOURNALISTS suitable to refresh his knowledge of grammar, spelling, word usage and sentence structure. The journalist should think of himself as "continuing student" of our language. Any time which he spends on this book will pay for itself handsomely.

When he finds himself getting beyond the "depth" of this book, the student or practicing journalist should refer to additional works of reference, especially to the most modern guides to English usage and style. The two best guides, which have been most quoted in this new edition of GRAMMAR FOR JOURNALISTS, are: Theodore M. Bernstein, *The Careful Writer: A Modern Guide to English Usage* (New York, Atheneum, 1965) and Roy H. Copperud, *A Dictionary of Usage and Style* (New York and London, Hawthorne Books, Inc., 1964). Although the author regards it as being far too permissive, Rudolf Flesch's *The ABC of Style* (1964) will be worth adding to your library.

Henry Ward Beecher, an outstanding pulpit orator of the last century, used to boast: "When the English language gets in my way, it doesn't stand a chance." Mr. Beecher could afford to speak as he pleased as long as he was interesting to his audience, but a reporter cannot adopt the same attitude. The reporter is working with raw material—the news—which must be made not only interesting but accurate. To make the news accurate, the reporter must use sound grammar, unless he is quoting certain persons whose slips in grammar are characteristic of those individuals. And certainly there is little excuse for the writer to use incorrect spelling and punctuation.

Imagine what confusion would result if a reporter made a grammatical blunder like this one:

"When six years old, my Grandma died,"
A freshman wrote today.
Do you suppose Grandma's playmates cried
When Grandma passed away?
(From *Word Study*.) *

A newspaper editor would see no humor in it. Nor would he like the remark of the journalism teacher who said that "some students believe that learning spelling and grammar is pointless since newspapers have their own rules."

It is true that newspapers have their own rules, but these rules deal largely with what is called *newspaper style* and are concerned primarily with such mechanics of writing as capitalization, abbreviations, use of figures and use of titles. This book, then, is not too much concerned with so-called newspaper style. Instead, it treats the fundamentals of expression which cannot be handled in the ordinary newspaper style book —fundamentals which an editor will expect you to know before you join his staff.

And if you are tempted to cut corners in studying this book, or if you begin to think the subject is of minor importance, simply recall the words of one distinguished editor: "Journalism graduates are more concerned with news-gathering than anything else. This is necessary, but if they do not know grammar and spelling, all is lost. *There is no other foundation upon which they can build.*"

* Used by permission of G. & C. Merriam Company.

2
The Journalist's Chief Tool— The Sentence

Journalists do not manufacture facts, but they do manufacture sentences which go into building news stories, feature stories, feature articles, editorials and advertisements. Almost anyone can make sentences, but journalists are expected to be experts in such work. Putting words together to make good sentences—sentences that can be read with maximum profit and pleasure—is the basic job of the journalist, and *grammar is simply the correct use of words in sentences.*

Our logical starting point, then, is a brief overview of what the sentence is and what it is not. Can you tell the difference between a whole sentence and a fragment of a sentence? Can you tell the difference between one sentence and two sentences run together? Fundamental knowledge for the journalist is to know unerringly whether a group of words is a complete sentence; to know the various forms of the sentence; and to know how to avoid errors in sentences and how to keep his sentences varied in form and pleasing to the eye.

To test yourself on these important questions, why not take the short quiz that follows? You may take the quiz either by rewriting the sentences, making all necessary corrections, or by using copy-editing marks. Don't forget to look for errors in punctuation.

Quiz

1. "Orange Juice" Simpson hesitated for a split second, then he reversed his field and went 68 yards for a touchdown.
2. The team of 24 Americans, 16 Canadians and 12 Australians were soon developed into a highly effective unit.
3. Herbert Asbell of Brooklyn, as well as two unidentified South Vietnamese, were killed in the skirmish.
4. Harkey's injured knee has failed to heal completely, therefore he may see little, if any action against Notre Dame Saturday.
5. Both owners finally relented and sent their animals to the country. But still no ordinance against livestock, so Mrs. Bilbeck brought in the eleven pigs.
6. It is not my problem, it's yours.
7. The sister as well as the two brothers have been charged with the murder, however the police are still seeking a man who boarded with the Smiths until a month ago.
8. After all, Cavan is only a sophomore, so don't expect him to make the all-conference team this year. Although he appears to be the most promising candidate in years.
9. Rain, hail and wind, along with the recent tornado, has caused an estimated $22-million damage to crops and livestock.
10. When two of the jurors became violently ill, the jury of eight men and four women were discharged.

Turn to the end of the chapter to see how many errors you missed.

WHAT A SENTENCE IS

A sentence is a group of words that expresses a complete thought.

A sentence is made up of words, and words are classified as

parts of speech. There are eight parts of speech: *nouns, pronouns, adjectives, verbs, adverbs, prepositions, conjunctions* and *interjections.*

Remember that grammar has only two main divisions: the parts of speech and the sentence. The sentence is simply a combination of words (parts of speech) expressing a complete thought. To make sure that you have a thorough knowledge of the sentence in all its variations, it is necessary to review the kinds of words and the relation of each word or group of words to the others in the sentence.

Study these examples of sentences:

Deputy Sheriff Charles Player shot the fleeing robber.
The Rev. Carl Duck will be the principal speaker.
Halt!

SUBJECTS AND PREDICATES

A group of words which expresses a complete thought has two essential parts: a subject and a predicate. The *subject* of a sentence is what is spoken about. The *predicate* of a sentence is what is said about the subject.

To test whether a group of words is a sentence or not, find the predicate first. The predicate is a verb, of course. Then ask a question by putting *who* or *what* before the predicate.

Deputy Sheriff Charles Player shot the fleeing robber.

Shot is the predicate. Who shot? The answer is: Player shot. Then Player is the subject of the sentence.

To make a second test, repeat to yourself the whole group of words: Player shot the fleeing robber. Ask yourself, "Does this group of words make sense standing alone?" Since the answer is that it does, you know that this group of words is a complete sentence.

You should recall at this point the difference between the complete subject and the simple (or essential) subject, and the difference between the complete predicate and the simple (or essential) predicate. You need to identify them unerringly if you are to avoid making errors in grammar. Note these sentences and see if you can find the errors, which were made by reporters who could not distinguish between complete subjects and simple subjects.

The Southern California coach, as well as the players, were elated over the 24-7 romp over Northwestern.
A group of Cuban-trained insurgents are plotting an overthrow of the government.

In the first sentence above, the complete subject is *The Southern California coach, as well as the players;* the simple subject is *coach.* Since the simple predicate must agree in number with the simple subject, the simple predicate should be *was,* not *were.*

In the second sentence, the complete subject is *A group of Cuban-trained insurgents in a nearby country.* The simple subject is *group,* which is a collective noun, and collective nouns may be either singular or plural, depending on the meaning which is to be expressed. If the collective noun refers to the separate individuals composing the group, it is regarded as plural and takes a plural verb. If the collective noun refers to the persons as acting or thinking as a unit (in unanimity), it is regarded as singular and takes a singular verb. In the sentence you are considering, the insurgents are thought of as acting together as a unit, and the singular verb *is* should be used. The error was made because the prepositional phrase contains the plural noun *insurgents.*

Always remember that the *simple subject* is the essential noun or pronoun, or its equivalent, that tells what or who is spoken about in the sentence, and that the simple predicate is the essential verb or verb phrase which says something about the subject.

A reporter has no difficulty in writing a simple sentence like this: Gerald Smathers is dying. This sentence consists of only the simple subject *Gerald Smathers* and the simple predicate *is dying*. But more words usually are added to both subject and predicate, like this:

The frail, 70-year-old Gerald Smathers, together with his two younger brothers, is dying of malaria in the tropics.

When a writer adds words like this to the simple subject and simple predicate, he may run into grammatical trouble unless he keeps in mind the simple subject and makes the verb agree with it in number. In the sentence above, the simple subject, stripped of all its modifiers (the adjectives *The frail, 70-year-old*), is *Gerald Smathers*. The phrase *together with his two younger brothers* is parenthetical. Hence *is dying* is the correct simple predicate.

The *complete subject* is the simple subject together with all the words grouped about it which modify it. The *complete predicate* is the simple predicate and its modifiers. Until you can distinguish unerringly between the complete subject and the simple subject, and between the simple predicate and the complete predicate, you will have difficulty in constructing sentences that are grammatically correct.

KINDS OF SENTENCE ERRORS

There are two common sentence errors that the journalist must avoid making: fragmentary sentences and run-on sentences. The ability to recognize complete sentences is the first step in writing correct sentences.

Fragmentary Sentences

Fragmentary sentences are either *phrases* or *dependent clauses* which should not stand alone as complete sentences.

A phrase is a group of two or more associated words not containing a subject and a predicate.

A phrase does not make a complete statement; it is only a

part of a clause or a sentence. A phrase is never a clause, and certainly it is not a sentence.

The following example from a newspaper shows how a reporter made the error of writing a phrase as if it were a sentence:

One body was recovered last night. That of T/Sgt. William G. Seymour.

The first construction is a sentence. It passes the first sentence test. The verb, or predicate, is *was recovered*. What was recovered? *One body* was recovered. *One body* is the complete subject; *body* is the simple subject. The second test proves that the construction is a complete sentence, since the words make sense standing alone. But what about the second group of words, *That of T/Sgt. William G. Seymour?* It contains no verb. As there is no verb, there can be no subject. The construction is only a phrase—a fragmentary sentence. Both the reporter and the copyreader must share the blame for this error getting into print, but the reporter will be held chiefly responsible.

A clause is a group of related words that form part of a sentence.

A clause must have a subject and a predicate. There are two types of clauses: *independent* (or *principal* or *main*) *clauses* and *dependent* (or *subordinate*) *clauses*.

Study this sentence from a metropolitan newspaper:

Rex never won a round on the United Press score sheet. Although he fought on even terms in the first session.

In the first construction, you see that *won* is the verb—the predicate. Who won? *Rex* won. Is it a complete sentence? Yes, for it makes sense standing alone.

Now test the second construction. The verb is *fought*. Who fought? *He* fought. The pronoun *He* is the subject. Is it a complete sentence? No, for it does not make complete sense standing alone. It seems to be suspended in air. Apparently it depends on something that has gone before to make complete sense. This group of words is a dependent or subordinate clause punctuated as if it were a complete sentence—another form of fragmentary sentence. This is an error which the journalist must recognize and avoid.

An *independent clause* is one which can stand alone. It makes a complete statement or asks a question or gives a command or makes an exclamation. An independent clause, therefore, can stand as a complete sentence, but it may be combined with one or more dependent clauses or with one or more independent clauses.

A *dependent* or *subordinate clause* does not make complete sense. It cannot stand alone as a sentence. It depends on an independent clause which precedes or follows it for its meaning; it is subordinate to the independent or main clause.

Most editors frown on both forms of the fragmentary sentence and consider it a serious error for a journalist to punctuate either phrases or dependent clauses as if they were complete sentences. An ace reporter or columnist may occasionally be allowed to use a fragmentary sentence, but until you reach top rank on a newspaper staff you should refrain from turning in copy with phrases and clauses used as sentences. Most editors will assume you made the error through ignorance.

Bob Considine, an outstanding reporter and columnist, wrote the following:

Queen Mary stays active and alert in her eighties. Likes a sherry or so before dinner and a cigaret after.

You recognize the second construction as a fragmentary sentence. You may contend that the subject *she* is understood; however, this is not a complete sentence.

The following is considered to be a complete sentence:

Halt!

This sentence gives a command. Its subject is *You,* understood.

The beginning reporter will do well to use a subject in every sentence he writes, except exclamatory sentences, until he has an established by-line, like Considine. Certainly most editors would not permit such a fragment as the following to appear in their papers:

When Alan started acting it was in radio doing 20 programs a week. Now making "One Woman."

The second construction should read something like this:

Alan is now making a picture titled "One Woman."

Don't forget that the threat of libel hangs constantly over both the reporter and the editor, and libel can be committed in the use of a fragmentary sentence. Consider the consequences if in this sentence a typographical error had been made in the spelling of *is* as *as*:

He maintained the woman is a prostitute.

Try testing the following two constructions:

The turtle's name is Big Boy. Although it is neither big—nor a boy.

RUN-ON SENTENCES

The second type of sentence error is two sentences written as one sentence with only a comma to separate them or with no mark of punctuation between them. The following sentences appeared in a big-city daily:

The Fountain of Youth is not in Florida, it's in Russia.
Some liberal Democrats are advancing Ted Kennedy for the 1968 nomination, however, most Democrats feel that Hubert H. Humphrey is sure to be nominated.
As our estimated landing time approached we began wondering what was going on so I went forward to the crew's quarters.

The type of error committed in the first two examples above is what many English teachers call "the comma blunder." In these two sentences some mark of punctuation other than the comma was needed between the two complete statements.

In the third example not even a comma appears, although a comma before *so* would not make the construction correct in the eyes of most editors.

The sentence error called "the comma blunder" occurs when a writer runs together two independent clauses or sentences with only a comma between them or without any punctuation mark at all. The comma is not sufficient unless a coordinate conjunction is used to join the two complete statements, thus:

The Fountain of Youth is not in Florida, but it's in Russia.

A better form, however, would be to shorten the sentence by reducing the second clause to a phrase, thus:

The Fountain of Youth is not in Florida but in Russia.

Another correct form would be to use a semicolon between the two statements, thus:

The Fountain of Youth is not in Florida; it's in Russia.

But remember that unless the clauses are rather closely related, it is always correct to make two separate sentences of two complete statements, like this:

The Fountain of Youth is not in Florida. It's in Russia.

To avoid the comma blunder, remember that a comma placed between two independent clauses is not sufficient unless a coordinate conjunction also is used to join the clauses. You are likely, then, to commit this error as long as you fail to recognize the coordinate conjunctions. There are six simple *coordinate conjunctions* commonly used to join two independent clauses. They are easily remembered in the following rhyming form:

and, or, nor,
but, yet, for

Note the correct use of a comma before the coordinate conjunction in each of the following sentences:

The tabulations will be made available to any groups wishing to use them, and the council itself will provide the speakers.

In the past we have considered the diversified farm as necessary, but we must look at this idea now in the light of today's conditions.

Commissioner Dirksen abstained from voting on the question, for he had not had time to read the petitions thoroughly.

Most editors recognize one exception to the rule of using a comma before a simple coordinate conjunction that joins two independent clauses: If the clauses make a *short* compound sentence, no comma is needed.

Hunter threw the ball 34 yards and Ranager caught it.

It is always safe to use the comma, however, even with short clauses. If there is any possibility that readers may misunderstand the meaning of the sentence, use the comma before the conjunction.

When the conjunction is omitted, it is always safe to use a semicolon between the two independent clauses. If the two clauses will make more sense if they are completely separated, punctuate them as two complete sentences.

Either a semicolon or a period should precede a *connective adverb* which connects two principal (independent) clauses:

Some liberal Democrats are advancing Ted Kennedy for the 1968 nomination; however, most Democrats feel that Hubert H. Humphrey is sure to be nominated.

Some liberal Democrats are advancing Ted Kennedy for the 1968 nomination. However, most Democrats feel that Humphrey is sure to be nominated.

Connective adverbs are discussed more fully in Chapter 10, but you will do well to memorize the following words and phrases which are often mistaken for conjunctions when used between two independent clauses:

accordingly	however	so	at last
also	indeed	still	at least
besides	moreover	then	in fact
consequently	nevertheless	therefore	of course
hence	otherwise	thus	

Note that the connective adverb *however* is the only one in the list that is always considered parenthetical and hence always requires a comma after it.

"I think I'll pitch Briles; however, I can't be sure he'll start," the Cardinal manager surmised.

Look again at the third example of sentence error (Run-on Sentences) on page 15. If the reporter had placed a comma before *so*, many editors would accept the sentence as correct because they consider *so* a conjunction. The majority of editors, however, class *so* as a connecting adverb that requires a semicolon before it.

As our estimated landing time approached we began to wonder what was going on; so I went forward to the crew's quarters.

The use of *so* as a conjunction should be sparing, and a semicolon should be placed before it. Do not overwork *so* as a conjunction; the result is monotonous writing. In almost every instance, you can get a much stronger construction by tossing out this word.

Variation in the use of *so* can be obtained by using *so that*.

The two men will take along rifles so that the party will be protected.

You can say the same thing, however, in less space with little change in meaning.

The two men will take along rifles to protect the party.

To obtain variety in writing, you may use *so* modified by a dependent clause.

The injured girl had bled so much that they had to give her two transfusions.

The dependent clause beginning with *that* modifies *so*. This is a much better construction than: The injured girl had bled profusely; so they had to give her two transfusions.

If the use of *so* as a conjunction to join two independent clauses were eliminated from the journalist's writing, better copy would result.

Some editors might go even farther and recommend the elimination of such connecting adverbs as *accordingly, also, consequently, hence, indeed, nevertheless, thus, in fact* and *of course*. They are used too often by many writers.

Five Ways to Avoid Writing Run-on Sentences:

Study the following incorrect sentence and note the three ways given below to correct the error.

Dry climates are good for persons with tuberculosis, doctors often advise tuberculars to go to New Mexico.

This sentence error can be corrected in any one of three ways: (1) by using a semicolon in place of the comma; (2) by using a coordinate conjunction like *and* following the comma; (3) by using a period after *tuberculosis* to make two sentences.

However, there are two other ways to avoid this sentence error and to achieve stronger sentence construction: (4) using a phrase in place of the initial independent clause: (5) using a subordinate clause in place of the first independent clause.

Dry climates being good for tuberculars, doctors often advise patients to go to New Mexico. (Phrase)
Because dry climates are good for tuberculars, doctors often advise patients to go to New Mexico. (Subordinate clause)

CLASSES OF SENTENCES

In reviewing the sentence briefly, you should recall that sentences are classified in two ways: (1) as to use; (2) as to form or structure.

CLASSIFICATION AS TO USE

1. A *declarative sentence* tells something; it states a fact or a possibility.

The jet fighter pilot died in the crash.   (Fact)
The jet fighter pilot may die.   (Possibility)

The declarative sentence ends with a period.

2. The *interrogative sentence* asks whether something is a fact or not a fact.

Is the pilot a Jordanian?
Is he not telling the truth about the crash?

The interrogative sentence ends with a question mark.

3. The *imperative sentence* gives a command or an order or makes a request.

Don't enter that room.
Please help me with this problem.

The imperative sentence usually ends with a period.

4. The *exclamatory sentence* expresses strong or sudden feeling or emotion. It may be written with or without an interjection.

My God! The plane is falling!
Oh, I can't move my leg!
Ouch! That hurts!

The exclamatory sentence ends with an exclamation mark. Don't use the mark in sentences which are not really exclamatory. If an interjection is used in the sentence, it may be followed either by a comma (as *Oh,* above) or by an exclamation mark (as *Ouch!*). Note that the use of an exclamation mark after the interjection makes it necessary to capitalize the next word. Remember that every sentence begins with a capital letter.

Some interrogative sentences and some imperative sentences may be considered exclamatory, in which case it is correct to end them with exclamation marks.

Is your mother injured!
Sock it to him!

CLASSIFICATION AS TO FORM

Sentences are classified into four groups according to their structure or construction.

1. A *simple sentence* consists of one independent (or main or principal) clause which contains one subject and one predicate and which expresses one complete idea, thought or meaning.

The plane fell.
The plane fell into the Pacific Ocean.
Every pilot in service will receive a bonus from the government.

Although the simple sentence has only one subject and one predicate, either the subject or the predicate or both may be compound. Two or more nouns or pronouns tied together form a *compound* (double) *subject,* and two or more verbs joined together form a *compound predicate.*

The pilot and the co-pilot died in the crash. (Compound subject)
The private *stopped and saluted* the general. (Compound predicate)
The pilot and the co-pilot both *lived and died* together. (Compound subject and compound predicate)

Each of these three sentences is a simple sentence.
Not all simple sentences are short sentences. Both the sub-

ject and the predicate may have many modifying words and phrases, and these words and phrases may also have modifiers. For example:

> Over the past few weeks, the once-liberal regime of Alexander Dubcek, the party first secretary and leader in the "socialist commonwealth" reforms, has bent to the Russian will by restricting travel and by sharply curtailing freedom of the press, including suspension of the party's official weekly, *Politika,* and the journalist union's magazine.

This sentence contains only one subject, *regime,* and one predicate, *has bent.* The subject is modified by the article *the,* by the adjective, *once-liberal,* and by the prepositional phrase, *of Alexander Dubcek,* used adjectivally. *Alexander Dubcek,* object of the preposition *of,* is modified by the long appositive that follows *Dubcek* and which is set off by commas. It is a double appositive, *party first secretary* and *leader. Leader* is modified by the prepositional phrase that follows. The predicate, *has bent,* is modified by the prepositional phrase *to the Russian will.* The verb is also modified by the compound prepositional phrase: *by restricting travel and (by) sharply curtailing freedom of the press.* The prepositional phrase is used adverbially, answering the question, "*How* has the regime bent?" Within the long phrase is a shorter prepositional phrase, *of the press,* used adjectivally to modify *freedom.* The sentence ends with a long present participle phrase, *including suspension of . . .* Within that phrase is a prepositional phrase, *of the party's official weekly,* Politika, *and the journalist union's magazine.* The phrase is used adjectivally to modify *suspension.* You might note that *of* has two objects, *weekly* and *magazine.*

Most good journalists use simple sentences often and to good effect in their writing. You are urged to do likewise. Use but don't abuse the simple sentence. Don't use it exclusively. Other kinds of sentences serve definite purposes and give variety to one's writing.

2. The *compound sentence* consists of two or more connected simple sentences. Each simple sentence that forms part of a compound sentence is an independent (or principal or main) clause.

Serious shortages exist in many drought-stricken areas, and the only permanent solution is the construction of more dams.

The coordinate conjunction *and* connects the two independent clauses, each of which could stand alone as a simple sentence.

This mark would be far short of the 51-foot crest of the mammoth July overflow, but businessmen in the three threatened industrial districts were taking no chances.

The coordinate conjunction *but* connects two independent clauses.

"I accept the appointment; I must finish the job my father began."

Here two related independent clauses form a compound sentence. A semicolon is used between the two parts of a compound sentence when they are not connected by a conjunction. Each clause could stand alone as a simple sentence.

Birds twittered in the trees; rabbits scampered through the brush; bass broke the surface of the stream; (and) bullfrogs plumped into the water at our approach.

Here semicolons punctuate four independent clauses which form a compound sentence. The coordinate conjunction *and* may be used before the fourth clause, but it is not necessary.

Remember that all the clauses in a compound sentence must be equal in rank. They must all be independent (principal) clauses. Such clauses may be called *coordinate*, because no one clause is subordinate to the other.

Journalists usually find less use for the compound sentence than for simple and complex sentences. However, the compound sentence does serve a specific purpose, and it can be used to lend variety to journalistic writing.

3. The *complex sentence* consists of two or more clauses which are not coordinate (of equal rank).

You have seen that the simple sentence is made up of one independent clause, and that the compound sentence is composed of two or more independent (principal or main) clauses which are said to be coordinate (equal in rank).

The complex sentence comprises two or more clauses that are not of equal rank or of equal importance. One of the clauses—and not more than one—is independent. At least one of the clauses in a complex sentence will be dependent upon the independent or principal clause. Such a clause is called a *subordinate* (dependent) *clause.*

Remember that the complex sentence may contain only one independent clause, but it may contain any number of dependent clauses.

As a journalist, you should soon discover that the complex sentence ranks next in importance to the simple sentence. Some journalists employ it more often than the simple sentence. Turn to the front page of any newspaper and check a few of the stories. You may find that more complex sentences have been used than any other kind. In writing for newspapers or magazines you often will wish to express at least two ideas in the same sentence, and you will realize that one of the two ideas is more important than the other. The best way to put the two ideas into the same sentence is to make one of them subordinate to the other in a complex sentence.

Study carefully the following examples of complex sentences:

Jaqueline Kennedy was the first to step from the plane and walk down the steps when the special Greek airliner landed at Andrivida.

Note that the main idea is expressed here in the independent clause *Jaqueline Kennedy was the first to step from the plane and walk down the steps.* The second idea, *when the special*

Greek airliner landed at Andrivida, is subordinate to the independent clause and depends upon the independent clause to give it meaning. Even if you reverse the order of the two clauses, you still have a complex sentence with the same idea subordinated to the other idea. Note that in either order the conjunctive adverb *when* joins the dependent clause to the independent clause. Conjunctive adverbs are discussed on pages 48–49.

The conference will get under way Tuesday, although Soviet Foreign Minister Andrei Gromyko may not arrive before Wednesday morning.

Or: Although Soviet Foreign Minister Andrei Gromyko may not arrive before Wednesday morning, the conference will get under way Tuesday.

Note that there is an independent clause, *the conference will get under way Tuesday,* and a dependent (subordinate) clause, *although Soviet Foreign Minister Andrei Gromyko may not arrive before Wednesday morning.* The subordinate conjunction *although* joins the two clauses. Subordinate conjunctions are discussed on pages 47–48.

President Johnson is the man who gave the order.

The dependent clause *who gave the order* is used adjectivally to modify the noun *man* in the independent clause. The relative pronoun *who* joins the clauses. The correct usage of *who* and *whom* is discussed later.

That an atomic war would be the end of the world was his prediction.

General Curtis E. LeMay told Keene that he and Broker had discussed the role of the Air Force until midnight.

In the first sentence, the noun clause *That an atomic war would be the end of the world* is used as the subject of the main verb *was.* This subordinate clause is the only subject that *was* can have. It answers the question "*What* was his prediction?" In the second sentence, the dependent (subordinate) clause *that he and Broker had discussed the Air Force until midnight* is used as the direct object of the verb *told* in the independent (principal) clause, *LeMay told Keene.* It answers the question: LeMay told Keene *what?* Noun clauses are discussed later.

As suggested earlier, look at several stories in a newspaper and note how often the complex sentence is used by reporters.

4. The *compound-complex sentence* is made up of a compound sentence (composed of at least two independent clauses) and one or more dependent (subordinate) clauses.

Curlee figured the values of several pieces of property which lie within the city limits, and he then wrote each property owner that the average cost of curbing would be about $30.60.

The sentence above contains two independent clauses joined by the coordinate conjunction *and.* The sentence has two dependent (subordinate) clauses. The relative clause *which lie within the city limits* is used adjectivally to modify the noun *property.* The noun clause *that the average cost of curbing would be about $30.60* is used as the direct object of the verb *wrote.* It answers the question "What did he write?"

Names of persons who are registered will be drawn each week, and several prizes will be awarded.

This compound-complex sentence contains only one dependent clause, but it has the necessary two independent clauses: *Names of persons will be drawn each week,* and *several prizes will be awarded.* The restrictive relative clause *who are registered* is an adjectival modifier of the noun *persons.*

Journalists, particularly newspaper reporters, use this type of sentence sparingly. It is likely to run too long and to become too involved. Good reporters always refrain from writing sentences in which the reader is likely to become entangled.

In studying and working with the remainder of the material

in this book, which deals largely with correct usage of the parts of speech and with spelling and punctuation, never lose sight of your main objective. You are reviewing grammar to make sure that, as a journalist, you will be able to write sentences which give your readers a maximum amount of information, which are easy to read and which are pleasing to the eye in their variety.

Quiz Answers

1. Substitute period for comma. 2. *Was* for *were*. 3. *Was* for *were*. 4. Substitute period for first comma; use comma after *therefore*, preferably. 5. Both owners finally relented . . . to the country, but since there was still no ordinance against livestock, Mrs. B. brought in the eleven pigs. Or, may start separate sentence with *But since* . . . 6. Semicolon for comma, or use two sentences. 7. *Has* for *have;* replace comma with semicolon; Use comma after *however*. Or, start new sentence with However, the police . . . Commas may be used to set off *as well as the two brothers* but are not necessary. 8. Replace second comma with semicolon. Convert fragmentary sentence into dependent clause: After all, Cavan . . . this year, although he appears. 9. *Have* for *has*. 10. *Was* for *were*.

3
Know the
Parts of Speech

Until he becomes adept in recognizing the parts of speech unerringly, the journalist cannot hope to write correct English consistently.

Test your ability to avoid making errors that result from your failure to recognize the eight parts of speech and their correct usage in the sentence. See how well you can do with the quiz that follows.

Quiz

In the first ten sentences you are to choose the correct word or phrase.

1. (*Who, Whom*) did the police come for?
2. The TV unit will (*try and, try to*) make a better film.
3. Coach Morgan looked over his three prize (*freshman, freshmen*) linemen.
4. He would like to talk with (*whomever, whoever*) drew the caricature.
5. The woman (*who, whom*) police believed took the jewels was cleared.

28

6. The monument inscription will read: "To (*he, him*) who gave his life—the soldier. To (*she, her*) who bore life and gave a son —the mother.

7. A gun held by Miss Ott discharged (*accidently, accidentally*) as the two scuffled.

8. Five hours (*is, are*) needed to finish the project.

9. The jury (*has, have*) failed to agree on a verdict.

10. The clerk felt (*bad, badly*) about making the mistake.

Correct whatever errors you find in the following five sentences.

11. The South Vietnamese show no signs of yielding on the question, nevertheless, the peace talks will continue.

12. There's five major bowl games on New Years Day.

13. He dived in the river and swam in the direction of the woman's cries whom he could not see.

14. "Lets you and I step aside and get ready for the next round," Crosby said to his partner.

15. Neither the sheriff or his deputies was able to catch the robber.

To see how you scored on the quiz, turn to the end of the chapter.

If you missed parts of the quiz, you need at least an overview of the *parts of speech* that are used in the construction of sentences. If you made a perfect score on the quiz, then you may wish to skip this chapter. Only a brief review of the eight parts of speech is presented here. Later chapters have more detailed discussion of the correct use of each part of speech.

All the words which make up the English language are classified into eight groups called *the parts of speech*. These eight parts of speech are: *verbs, nouns, pronouns, adjectives* (including *articles*), *adverbs, prepositions, conjunctions* and *interjections.*

VERBS

The verb is the most important word in the sentence. The word *verb* is derived from the Latin word *verbum* which means "word." The verb is the word which gives life and purpose to the sentence, and without a verb the group of words cannot be a complete sentence. Even a single word can be a sentence if it is a verb with an understood subject, as in the command: Halt! The subject *You* is understood: You halt!

In the preceding chapter you observed how a knowledge of verbs helps you to develop sentence-sense. You found that unless you can recognize verbs, you will find it difficult to determine whether certain groups of words are sentences or not, and you may continue to make sentence errors.

A verb is a word that denotes action, being or a state of being.

Most verbs are action verbs, but many verbs merely assert being or a state of being. Note the three types of verbs in the following sentences:

The heavyweight champion *rushed* from his corner.   (Action)
The handlers *were* in the champion's corner.   (Being)
The champion's wife *is* beautiful.   (State of being)

NOUNS

Nouns rank next in importance to verbs in building sentences. A sentence must have not only a predicate but also a subject, and the subject is a noun or a pronoun or an equivalent. Most subjects in journalistic writing are nouns.

Nouns are names of persons, animals, things, places, ideas, etc.

Any word used as a name is a noun. There are four kinds of nouns: common nouns, proper nouns, abstract nouns and collective nouns.

Common nouns are the ordinary names of common objects, human beings, animals, places, etc.

bed   man   cat   town

Proper nouns are the names of particular persons, places and things. Proper nouns are always capitalized.

Robert   Mr.   Dawson   Delaware   Bible   Wednesday   Lake Erie

Abstract nouns are the names of conditions and qualities.

sadness   beauty   speed   bravery   redness

Collective nouns are the names of collections or groups of persons, animals and things. The journalist must be able to recognize collective nouns if he is to avoid making errors in subject-verb agreement.

team   jury   flock   fleet
family   mob   herd   crew

The ability to recognize common nouns, proper nouns, abstract nouns and collective nouns will enable you to avoid many common errors in capitalization, in agreement of subject and predicate in number, and in agreement of pronouns with antecedents.

PRONOUNS

Pronouns are words that are used in place of nouns.

A pronoun designates a person, a place or a thing without naming it. The prefix *pro* means "for"; so *pronoun* means "for a noun."

There are six classes of pronouns: personal pronouns, demonstrative pronouns, indefinite pronouns, distributive pronouns, interrogative pronouns and relative pronouns.

PERSONAL PRONOUNS

A *personal pronoun* is one that shows by its form whether it denotes the speaker (first person), the person or thing spoken to (second person), or the person or thing spoken of (third person).

You must be able to recognize the personal pronouns and know when to use the nominative case (*I, he*) instead of the objective (*me, him*) if you are to be a good writer. You must also know that the pronoun *you* always takes a plural verb (*you are, you were*) and that the pronoun *he* must not be used with *don't,* the contraction of *do not.*

Review the following declensions of personal pronouns:

SINGULAR   PLURAL

First Person

Nominative	I	we
Possessive	my, mine	our, ours
Objective	me	us

Second Person

Nominative	you	you
Possessive	your, yours	your, yours
Objective	you	you

Third Person

	Masc.	Fem.	Neuter	
Nominative	he	she	it	they
Possessive	his	her, hers	its	their, theirs
Objective	him	her	it	them

The personal pronouns, unlike nouns, do not use the possessive sign—the apostrophe—to indicate possession.

The gun is *yours* (not your's).
That book is *hers* (not her's).
The dog scratched *its* back.

It's is a contraction of *it is.*

Compound personal pronouns are formed by adding *self*

and *selves* to some of the personal pronouns. There are no possessive compound personal pronouns.

myself	ourselves
yourself	yourselves
herself, himself, itself	themselves

Compound personal pronouns are used in two ways: (1) for emphasis; (2) as reflexives.

Eisenhower *himself* (or *He himself*) is given credit for the victory.

The compound personal pronoun in this sentence is in apposition with the noun (pronoun) to which it refers: *Eisenhower* (*He*). Such pronouns are sometimes called *intensive pronouns* because they add emphasis or force to the noun or pronoun. The intensive pronoun is usually placed next to the word to which it refers, but it may come elsewhere: *Eisenhower* did the job *himself*. Note that intensive pronouns are not set off by commas. Incorrect: Eisenhower, himself, did the job.

When a compound personal pronoun is used as a reflexive, the subject is indicated to be acting upon itself.

The *general* blamed *himself* for the defeat. (Reflexive pronoun)

DEMONSTRATIVE PRONOUNS

The *demonstrative pronouns* point out: *this* and *that* (singular); *these* and *those* (plural).

This is mine; *that* is yours; but *those* over there belong to Tom.

INDEFINITE PRONOUNS . .

The *indefinite pronouns* point out vaguely and indefinitely, and they cause grammatical trouble. The most common indefinite pronouns are:

SINGULAR		PLURAL		SINGULAR OR PLURAL
one	someone	both	many	all
anyone	everybody	few	several	none
everyone	another			some

DISTRIBUTIVE PRONOUNS

The *distributive pronouns* separate groups into individuals. There are only three distributive pronouns, and they are *always singular.*

each   either   neither

INTERROGATIVE PRONOUNS

Interrogative pronouns are used in asking questions, either direct or indirect.

Who was hurt in the accident?   (Direct question)
They do not know *who* was hurt.   (Indirect question)

The interrogative pronouns are *who, whose, whom, which* and *what,* and they are singular or plural according to the meaning of the sentence. The most common errors are made in using *who* and *whom* incorrectly and in confusing the possessive *whose* with *who's* (*who is*).

RELATIVE PRONOUNS

A *relative pronoun* connects (relates) a dependent clause to an antecedent (noun) in another clause.

Humphrey is the man who must run the race.
Nixon is the man whom we must nominate.

Who and *whom* both introduce a dependent clause and refer to the antecedent *man* in the independent clause. In the first sentence *who* is the subject of the verb *must run* in the dependent clause. In the second sentence *whom* is the direct object of the verb *must nominate* in the dependent clause.

The most common relative pronouns are: *who, whom, whose, which* and *that. Who* in its different forms is used to refer to persons. *Which* refers to things or animals, or to persons considered as a group. *That* may be used to refer to persons, places or things.

ADJECTIVES

Adjectives are words that modify nouns and pronouns.
Adjectives either describe or limit the meaning of the words they modify. The use of adjectives enables the writer to express conceptions that nouns alone do not convey.

The frail, 70-year-old Gerald Smathers died of malaria in the tropics. His two brothers died with him.

The descriptive adjectives *frail* and *70-year-old* give the reader a brief word-picture of the man. The use of the article *the* limits the two nouns *Gerald Smathers* and *tropics*. The use of the numeral adjective *two* limits the noun *brothers*.

You can see that it would be impossible to give adequate treatment to a news story, a feature story, an editorial, or an advertisement without the judicious use of adjectives. But don't overuse them in journalistic writing.

CLASSES OF ADJECTIVES

The two classes of adjectives are *descriptive adjectives* and *limiting adjectives.*

The *descriptive adjectives* describe the nouns they modify. They include such words as: *large, small, happy, sad, pretty, beautiful, clean, exhausted,* etc. Words like *American* and *Italian* are called *proper adjectives* and are capitalized.

The *gay little* pony trotted around the ring.
Several *American* soldiers were at the play.

Note that *American* can be a proper noun, also: That *American* speaks Greek.

Limiting adjectives limit the meaning of the words they modify.

It was *five* miles to *the* center of *the* town.

The definite article *the* and the indefinite articles *a* and *an* are sometimes classed as a separate part of speech, but most grammarians consider them limiting adjectives.

There are four *demonstrative adjectives*: *this* and *that* (singular); *these* and *those* (plural). They are limiting adjectives because they indicate which object or objects are referred to:

this hat   *these* hats
that book   *those* books

The *indefinite adjectives* are used to indicate indefinite numbers of persons and objects. Errors in agreement of subject and predicate sometimes result when indefinite adjectives are used. Note the following correct usages:

Each publisher has his own rules for correct writing.
Any newspaper likes to scoop its competitors.
Some reporters have their own by-lines.
Either number of the verb is correct there.

The *interrogative adjectives—whose, which, what—*are limiting adjectives used before nouns in questions.

Whose coat is that brown one?
Which story should I write next?
What method of typing do you use?

Relative adjectives can often be omitted if the journalist will learn to write shorter, better constructed sentences. Note the following:

Thirty-seven Air Force cadets were caught cheating on final examinations, for *which* reason they were expelled.
Thirty-seven Air Force cadets were expelled for cheating on final examinations.

Numeral adjectives refer either to number or to numerical order. They are classified as *cardinal numerals* or *ordinal adjectives,* according to their usage.

one	first	forty-five (dollars)
one hundred	hundredth	one hundred and twenty
five thousand	thousandth	twenty-fourth (man)
one million	millionth	six hundredth (man)

Three days after the *second* mishap they had a *third* accident.

COMPARISON OF ADJECTIVES

Many errors result from the writer's failure to use the correct degree of the adjective.

Adjectives have three degrees: positive, comparative and superlative.

The *positive degree* is used when no comparison is indicated.

He is *tall*. She is a *beautiful* girl. Harry is a *good* boy.

The *comparative degree* is used to compare two persons or things.

He is *taller* than Ted. She is *more beautiful* than Celeste. Harry is a *better* boy than Mike.

The *superlative degree* is used when more than two persons or things are compared.

He is the *tallest* of the three boys. She is the *most beautiful* of the three sisters. Harry is the *best* boy in the class.

ADJECTIVES MAY FOLLOW NOUNS

The adjective usually precedes the noun it modifies, but it may sometimes follow it.

When the adjectives follow the noun and are set off by commas, they are called *appositive adjectives*.

The old house, *drab* and *dilapidated,* was situated squarely in the center of the tract.

When the adjective follows the predicate, it is called a *predicate adjective*.

The new tennis champion is *handsome.*

If the adjective modifies the object of the sentence, it is called an *objective complement.*

The potato salad made the children *sick.*

ADVERBS

The journalist may find that he tends to use more adverbs than adjectives. This is to be encouraged, because the adverb is next to the verb and the noun in importance in the sentence.

Most adverbs are formed by adding the suffix *ly* to the adjective: easy—easily; careless—carelessly. Not all words that end in *ly* are adverbs, however, and not all adverbs end in *ly.* For example, *friendly* and *lovely* are adjectives, and *soon* and *once* are adverbs. To determine what part of speech a word is, always test it for its use in the sentence. If the word modifies a verb, an adjective or an adverb, it is an adverb.

ADVERBS CLASSIFIED AS TO USE

1. A word that modifies a verb, an adjective or an adverb is called a *simple adverb.*

Editor Holmes read the story *carefully.*   (Modifies the verb *read.*)
It was a *very* good story.   (Modifies the adjective *good.*)
The paper printed it *very* soon.   (Modifies the adverb *soon.*)

The simple adverb may modify a prepositional phrase.

The climbers were *nearly* at the top of the mountain.

The adverb *nearly* modifies the prepositional phrase *at the top.*
The simple adverb may modify a subordinate clause.

I'll help you *just* because you are my brother.

The adverb *just* modifies the subordinate clause *because you are my brother.*

2. Adverbs that ask questions are called *interrogative adverbs*.

Where is Jim Lehrer, the city editor? *When* do you expect him? He asked me *why* I was there.

3. *Parenthetical adverbs* are adverbs that do not change the meaning of the sentence, but which have merely a parenthetical use. They are often used at the beginning of the sentence. The most common are:

however	anyhow	namely
still	moreover	accordingly
indeed	furthermore	nevertheless
yet	likewise	consequently

These adverbs are also called *modal adverbs* because they indicate doubt or emphasize the certainty of the statement they introduce. They are usually set off by commas.

You can see, *moreover,* why this is true.
Still, I don't think you should go.
Fortunately, a doctor was immediately available.

Note that each adverb above modifies the entire sentence, not just one word or clause. Such adverbs are also called *sentence adverbs.* They can be omitted without changing the essential meaning of the sentence.

Some sentence adverbs, like *perhaps,* are considered essential to the meaning of a clause or a sentence and are not set off by a comma or commas.

Wallace is not regarded as a serious contender; *perhaps* he should be.

4. When the adverb *there* is used to introduce a sentence, it is called an *expletive*.

There is only one reporter here to cover the speech.
There are many menus to try this summer.

The word *There* merely "fills in" the sentence. Notice the difference in use of *there* in the sentence: Only two reporters were there. In this sentence *there* is an adverb of place modifying the verb *were*.

A test for expletives is to try leaving out *There* to see if the meaning of the sentence remains the same. If it does, *There* is an expletive. Take the sentence: *There* were three apples in the dish. If you leave out *There*, the sentence means: Three apples were in the dish. This proves that *There* in this sentence is an expletive.

5. *Flat adverbs* are adverbs that may be used correctly without the *ly* ending.

Drive *slow*.   Talk *loud*.   Hold it *tight*.

Of course, the *ly* form also is correct in these sentences: Drive *slowly*, etc.

6. *Conjunctive adverbs* are adverbs that are used like conjunctions, to connect clauses.

Schlenzer returned *before* the detectives expected him.

Such words are not true conjunctions, but because they are used like conjunctions, they are discussed in the section on that part of speech. (See pages 48–49.)

7. *Relative adverbs* are adverbs used to begin subordinate clauses.

This is the town *where* Bob Gibson was born.

8. Adverbs placed at the beginning of the sentence simply to introduce the sentence are called *introductory adverbs*. They are often followed by a comma. The sentence is complete in meaning if they are omitted.

Well, I believe we should interview Capote.
Now that is what I call a good suggestion.

Other introductory adverbs are *why, then,* and the like. Their chief use is conversational.

ADVERBS CLASSIFIED AS TO MEANING

1. Some adverbs refer to *time*.

The reporter, Darwin Payne, arrived *early* for the interview. Judy Garland was *late* for her appointment.

Other time adverbs are *soon, then, ago, once, first,* etc.

2. Some adverbs refer to *number*. Number adverbs are used preferably without the *ly* ending: *first* rather than *firstly*:

First, you should cover the plane accident; *second,* you should investigate the auto accident.

Always use *first* rather than *firstly* in such sentences as: Jones arrived *first*.

3. Some adverbs relate to *place*.

Correspondent Harsch arrived *there* by plane.
We expect to go *north* this summer.

Other place adverbs are *here, hither, where, aboard, east,* etc.

4. Some adverbs refer to *manner*.

Correspondent Richard L. Strout writes *well*.
They awaited *anxiously* the launching of Apollo 8.

Other manner adverbs are *badly, slowly, hastily, gracefully,* etc. Some manner adverbs that do not end in *ly* are *somehow, likewise, alike, wrong, fast, well*.

5. Some adverbs refer to *degree*. These include the comparative and superlative forms of the adverbs. (See comparison of adverbs on page 42 and in Chapter 10.)

Bernice paints *more* skillfully than her sister, Bertha.
They share the studio *equally*.
Jan Sych of Poland was *too* tired to continue the steeplechase.

Other degree adverbs are *very, somewhat, less, most, almost, rather, about, altogether, much.* Many of these words can be used as other parts of speech. For example, *most* may be either an adverb or a pronoun or it may be part of a degree adverb.

The director was *most* cordial.	(Adverb of degree modifying adjective *cordial*)
He received us *most* cordially.	(Adverb of degree modifying adverb *cordially*)
Most of the chaperones are young.	(Pronoun, subject of verb *are*)

6. Some adverbs refer to *result* and *reason*.

You have been late frequently; *therefore* your work has suffered. (Result)

Can you explain *why* you are late so often?   (Reason)

Note that *why* may be called an interrogative adverb in the second sentence, since it is used in a question. The answer to the question will supply a reason for the lateness. Other adverbs of result and reason are *hence, wherefore, consequently, accordingly.*

7. The adverb *yes* is an adverb of *affirmation.* The adverbs *no* and *not* are adverbs of *negation.* When *yes* or *no* begins a sentence, it must be followed by a comma.

Yes, Mr. Ball will resign his post as ambassador to the UN.

No, the board will *not* permit you to make a statement.

COMPARISON OF ADVERBS

Adverbs that end in *ly* are compared by using *more* and *most* or *less* and *least* before the positive form of the adverb.

slowly, more slowly, most slowly
likely, less likely, least likely

Some adverbs are compared irregularly.

much, more, most   much, less, least

The flat adverbs are compared like the adjectives they resemble.

slow, slower, slowest   loud, louder, loudest

NOUNS USED AS ADVERBS

Some nouns may be used as adverbs to refer to size, measurement, number, degree and place. They are then classed as adverbs, of course.

Ryun ran the *mile* in record time.
Nixon's speech will take only twenty *minutes*.
Senator Dirksen hurried *home*.

PREPOSITIONS

Prepositions are linking or connecting words. The preposition serves two purposes in a sentence: (1) it relates a noun or pronoun (the object) to another word in the clause or sentence; (2) it shows what relation exists between the two words.

That house *on* the hill is the home *of* the retired general.

The preposition *on* relates the noun *house* to the noun *hill*, the object of the preposition. The preposition *of* relates *home* to *general*.

Most prepositions are short words like *in, at, to* and *for;* but note such words as *between, toward, concerning*, etc.

CLASSES OF PREPOSITIONS

There are two classes of prepositions: simple and compound.

Simple prepositions are single words.

aboard	behind	down	over	toward
about	below	during	past	under
across	beneath	except	per	underneath
after	beside	excepting	regarding	until
against	besides	for	save	up
along	between	from	saving	upon
amid	beyond	in	since	via
among	but (except)	inside	through	with
around	by	into	throughout	within
at	concerning	outside	to	without
before	considering			

The *compound prepositions,* as the name implies, contain more than one word.

according to	in consequence of	in spite of
along with	in front of	on account of
because of	in reference to	with reference to
by means of	in regard to	with regard to
from among	in respect to	

PREPOSITIONAL PHRASES

The preposition and its object make a *prepositional phrase.*
The *object of the preposition* answers the question *what?* or *whom?* after the preposition.

The dog is *inside his kennel.*

Ask the question: inside what? The answer is *kennel;* so you know that *kennel* is the object of the preposition *inside.* The prepositional phrase is *inside his kennel.*

The letter is *from our old friend the mayor.*

The object of the preposition *from* is *friend.* The prepositional phrase is *from our old friend the mayor.*
   The preposition usually is the first word in the prepositional phrase, but it may follow the object, as in a question:

Whom did the police come *for?*

Whom is the object of the preposition *for.* Inverting the order of the words shows the construction: The police did come for whom? (*Whom,* not *who,* is correct, because the objective form is needed.)
   If the word has no object, it is not a preposition but an adverb.

The little boy fell *down* the hill.   (Preposition)
The little boy fell *down.*   (Adverb)

   A prepositional phrase that modifies a noun or a pronoun is used as an adjective and is called an *adjective prepositional phrase.* If the phrase modifies a verb, it is used as an adverb and is called an *adverb prepositional phrase.*

That picture *of the lake* is lovely.   (Used as adjective to modify *picture*)

Jackie's portrait hung *in the foyer.*   (Used as adverb to modify *hung*)

In news writing, prepositional phrases are used more often adverbially than adjectivally.

The prepositional phrase should always be placed where there can be no doubt as to what word it modifies. The journalist may obtain variety in his writing by beginning some of his sentences and even news leads with prepositional phrases, but the meaning must be clear.

CONJUNCTIONS

Conjunctions are words that connect (join) two words or two phrases or two clauses of equal rank, or that join a dependent (subordinate) clause to a word in the independent (principal) clause. Like prepositions, conjunctions are linking words.

The two broad classes of conjunctions are the *coordinate conjunctions* and the *subordinate conjunctions.*

COORDINATE CONJUNCTIONS

Coordinate conjunctions connect words or phrases or clauses of equal rank. Coordinate conjunctions are of two types: simple conjunctions and correlative conjunctions.

1. *Simple conjunctions* may denote addition or enumeration, contrast, choice or inference. Note the following:

ADDITION:

Mary *and* Ellen will come.	(Joins two nouns)
He sent flowers to Jane *and* to her mother.	(Joins two phrases)
John went to college *and* Jim joined the navy.	(Joins two phrases)

CONTRAST:

Schollander was tiring, *but* he held off the finishing drive of Australia's Mike Wenden to win.

The Ghanian tired rapidly, *yet* he kept on running.

CHOICE:

The men must swim *or* drown.

We must hurry *or* we'll be late.

INFERENCE:

He will not fail to be here, *for* he is always reliable.

The six coordinate conjunctions are easily remembered in rhyming form:

and, or, nor,
but, yet, for

For may also be a subordinate conjunction.

The connective adverbs are not true conjunctions, but they are often used as coordinate conjunctions. When one of these words begins the second of two independent clauses, it should be preceded by a semicolon and usually followed by a comma.

The connective adverbs that are used as simple conjunctions denote addition, contrast, choice and conclusion.

ADDITION: *also, likewise, moreover*

Estes will head the department *also,* he will serve as general coordinator of education.

CONTRAST: *however, nevertheless, still* (meaning *but*)

President Thieu shows no sign of yielding on the question; *nevertheless,* the Paris peace talks will continue.

CHOICE: *else, otherwise* (meaning *or*)

The Secretary of State must recover from his illness rapidly; *otherwise,* he will be unable to represent the United States at the conference.

CONCLUSION: *hence, therefore, accordingly, consequently*

Neither side will yield an inch; *therefore,* the conference apparently will end in failure.

2. The *correlative conjunctions* are used in pairs or series. They often connect clauses so closely related that neither clause makes complete sense without the other. The most commonly used correlative conjunctions are:

both—and   neither—nor
either—or   not only—but also

Both Bess Ann *and* Margaret will attend the summer session.
Either he must appear before the committee *or* he must give a satisfactory excuse for his absence.
Neither the sheriff *nor* his deputies have arrived.
Baker is guilty *not only* of hitting the child *but also* of leaving the scene of the accident.

Other correlative conjunctions that are not used so frequently are:

although—yet   now—now   though—yet
as—as   now—then   whereas—therefore
as—so   so—as   whether—so
if—then

SUBORDINATE CONJUNCTIONS

Subordinate conjunctions introduce dependent (subordinate) clauses and join the subordinate clause to the independent clause in the sentence.

Subordinate conjunctions denote cause or reason, comparison, concession, condition and supposition, purpose and result. Study the following:

CAUSE OR REASON: *as, because, for, since*

The secretary cannot attend the conference *because* he is ill.
Since the secretary is ill, he will be unable to attend the meeting.

COMPARISON: *than*

Cokes is taller *than* his opponent (is tall).

CONCESSION: *although, though, even if*

Even if he is guilty, he should be given a fair trial.

CONDITION: *if, unless* (referring to negative condition)

If it rains soon, most crops can be saved.
Unless athletes have an average of C, they are not allowed to compete in intercollegiate contests.

PURPOSE: *that, in order that, so that*

He went by air *so that* he would be there on time.

RESULT: *so that, such that*

A deadly crossfire caught the platoon, *so that* not a man escaped.

When the subordinate conjunction introduces a clause that is used as a noun (a substantive), it is said to have a substantive use.

Whether (or not) U Thant will attend the meeting will be decided by his physician.

The clause *Whether (or not) U Thant will attend the meeting* is the subject of the verb *will be decided.*

The doctor will decide *whether* (or not) U Thant may attend.

The clause *whether U Thant may attend* is the direct object of the verb *will decide.*

Although *conjunctive adverbs* are not true conjunctions, they are sometimes used as subordinate conjunctions. They denote manner, place and time, and they may introduce clauses that are used as nouns.

MANNER: *as, as if*

The one-time millionaire now worked again from dawn to dusk, *as* he had done in the days of his youth.

PLACE: *where, whence, whither*

The soldier accidentally dropped his gun *where* the water was
deepest.

TIME: *after, as, before, ere, since, till, until, when, while*

Until Lodge arrives in South Viet Nam, nothing can be decided.
O. J. Simpson was running wild with the football *before* he injured
his ankle against Northwestern.

When the adverbs *how* and *why* introduce clauses that are
used as nouns, they have a substantive use.

Why Bunker is going to West Germany is a mystery.

The clause *Why Bunker is going to West Germany* is the subject of the verb *is.*

We do not see *how* we can possibly get there.

The clause *how we can possibly get there* is the direct object of
the verb *do see.*

You will note that the conjunctive adverbs in these examples
appear to modify the verbs in the clauses they introduce,
whereas subordinate conjunctions merely introduce dependent
clauses. Since the primary use of the conjunctive adverbs is to
connect the clauses, it seems practical to consider them as conjunctions. It is important for the writer to be able to recognize
them so that he will use the correct punctuation in his sentences.

INTERJECTIONS

Interjections are words or phrases used to express strong or
sudden feeling or emotion or to attract attention. The interjection has no grammatical relation to the other words in the sentence; it is an independent construction.

Various parts of speech may be used as interjections. Note
the following:

O *or* Oh!   Good gracious!   Whew!   Hurrah!
Alas!   Great Ceasar!   Pshaw!   Eureka!

Some grammarians call such interjections as *Sorry!* an adjective in exclamation, and call *Halt!* a verb in exclamation. It does not matter how you classify such words as long as you know how to punctuate them correctly when you use them as interjections.

The interjection is usually followed by an exclamation mark, and the next word is capitalized.

Hurrah! We have won the game.
Good gracious! I didn't think you could make it.

If the interjection is used in close connection with what follows, however, it may be followed by a comma, and the exclamation mark may be placed at the end of the sentence.

Oh, don't bother me now!

An order or a command may be given in the form of an interjection, in which case it is followed by an exclamation mark. Note these imperative sentences:

Forward march!   Don't touch that wire!   Come quickly!

There is a distinction between *O* and *Oh*. *O* is usually used with a noun or a pronoun in direct address, and it must always be capitalized. *Oh* is used to express pain, surprise, sorrow, hope, and so on.

O my lover, come back to me!
Oh, how my head hurts!
We were afraid, and *oh,* how we trembled!

Quiz Answers

1. Whom. 2. try to. 3. freshman. 4. whoever. 5. who. 6. him, her. 7. accidentally. 8. is. 9. have. 10. bad. 11. Substitute semicolon for comma. Also, a comma is preferred, but is not necessary, after *nevertheless.* 12. Change *there's* to *there are;* use apostrophe in

year's. 13. He dived *into* (not *in*) the river and swam in the direction of the cries of the woman whom he could not see. 14. *Let's* you and *me* (not I) step aside and . . . Use objective form after Let's. Test by asking if you would write: Let's *we* instead of let's *us.* However, use of *I* colloquially, as in the Crosby quote, would be accepted in electronic journalism and by some newspaper editors. 15. Neither the sheriff *nor* (not *or*) *were* (not *was*) able to catch the robber. (The verb agrees with subject nearest to it.)

4

The Framework
of the Sentence

Head bone connected to the backbone,
Backbone connected to the hip bone,
Hip bone connected to the thigh bone . . .

You might keep the words of the Negro spiritual in mind
as you study this chapter. Up to this point you have observed
that the subject and the predicate are essential in constructing
a sentence. In other words, the subject and the predicate are
the two main parts of the skeleton—the framework—on which
the sentence is built. They may be compared to the head bone
and the backbone in the human skeleton.

A simple subject and a simple predicate may be a whole sentence: Smathers died. A sentence may even be a single word, a
verb with an understood subject: Halt! However, most simple
sentences have a third part also. So do many clauses within the
other kinds of sentences. This third part may be either a direct
object of the verb or a predicate nominative. Wherever this
third part is used in a clause or in a simple sentence, it will be
an important part of the skeleton—the framework—of the
clause or sentence, because it is essential in giving the clause or
sentence real meaning.

The *direct object* of the verb and the *predicate nominative,* then, may be compared to the *legs* and the *arms* of the human skeleton.

Until you can identify these parts of the sentence without hesitation, and until you can recognize the three kinds of verbs —transitive, intransitive and linking—you will find yourself making errors that a journalist simply should not make.

You may ask, "Why do I need a review of transitive, intransitive and linking verbs?" This is a fair question, one that you can best answer for yourself by testing your knowledge.

In each of the following 15 sentences, ask yourself which of the words in parentheses is the correct one to use—and why.

Quiz

1. Humphrey said he really did not feel too (*badly, bad*).
2. The skunk smelled (*bad, badly*).
3. The UN delegates arrived (*safe, safely*).
4. One out of ten (*lays, lies*) dead on the beach. (TV broadcast)
5. Randall (*laid, lay*) flat on his back on the Sugar Bowl turf.
6. He would never let the baby (*lay, lie*) still.
7. A foul flag was thrown at the prone figures of two Packers (*lying, laying*) in the end zone.
8. The grandmother tried to (*set, sit*) the cups on the shelf.
9. The desk (*set, sat*) in the far corner of the room.
10. The wounded Marine had (*laid, lain*) on the battlefield for seven hours.
11. Hanratty (*lay, laid*) the ball squarely into Allan's outstretched hands.
12. It was (*he, him*) who made the error.
13. The prime minister (*sat, set*) (*erect, erectly*) across the room.
14. (*Who, Whom*) do you think the judges will select as Miss Teen-Ager?
15. It is (*he, him*) (*who, whom*) must deliver the keynote speech.

If in the first sentence you selected the word *badly,* you need not feel too *bad,* because you committed one of the most common errors in English grammar. *Bad* is correct because it is a predicate adjective following a linking verb and refers back to the subject, which it modifies. Use of the adverb *badly* would give the sentence an entirely diffrent meaning, implying that Humphrey's sense of touch is impaired. Unless you can recognize *feels* as a linking verb, rather than as a transitive or intransitive verb, you will make this error—and others like it. In sentence 2 you should be able to recognize that *bad* is a predicate adjective following the linking verb *smelled,* and that use of the adverb *badly* would imply that the skunk's sense of smell is not up to par. In sentence 3 the same rule applies: The correct word is the predicate adjective *safe,* which follows the linking verb *arrived* and refers back to the subject delegates.

In sentences 4, 5, 6, 7, 8, 9, 10, 11, 12 and 13, the correct words, respectively, are: *lies, lay, lie, lying, set, sat, lain, laid, he, sat, erect.* If you missed a single one of these, you need to review transitive and intransitive verbs. Even if you got all the words correct but could not tell *why* you selected these words, you need a review of transitive and intransitive verbs to make sure that you can select correct words unerringly. A journalist should not have to guess why *bad* instead of *badly* or *lying* instead of *laying* is correct in a certain sentence. He should know why it is correct, and be able to prove it.

(In sentence 14 in the quiz, *Whom* is correct, and in sentence 15 *he* and *who* are correct.)

THREE KINDS OF VERBS

Now to continue with a review of the important points.

Verbs are classified, according to their use, as transitive verbs, intransitive verbs and linking verbs.

TRANSITIVE VERBS

1. A *transitive verb* is a verb that takes a direct object to complete its meaning.

The mother *laid* the baby on the bed.

Ask: The mother laid what? The answer is *baby;* so you know that *baby* is the direct object of the verb *laid,* and that use of the intransitive verb *lay* would be incorrect.

Not a word *could* they *wring* from the prisoner.

Ask: They could wring what? The answer is *word,* the direct object of *could wring.*

When a transitive verb is used in the passive form, there is no direct object, but the subject receives the action of the verb. The transitive passive verb is always a verb phrase made up of some form of the verb *be* plus the past participle of the transitive verb.

The game *was cancelled* because of rain.

A transitive verb, then, is in the active voice if its subject performs the action. It is in the passive voice if its subject is the receiver of the action. Use the active voice in preference to the passive in your writing.

INTRANSITIVE VERBS

2. *Intransitive verbs* do not take direct objects. In other words, an intrasitive verb is one in which the action ends; the action is not carried across to some person or object.

The gunman *turned* quickly.
The policeman *sat* on his prisoner.

The adverb *quickly* modifies the verb *turned.* The prepositional phrase *on his prisoner* modifies the verb *sat.* Neither verb has a direct object.

You will not make errors in the use of intransitive and transitive verbs if you remember to ask Who? or What? after the verb. You can see that *set* would be incorrect in the second sentence because *set* would need an object to complete its meaning: Set what?

Remember, then, that three parts—the subject plus the predicate plus a direct object or a predicate nominative—make up the essential framework of a majority of the simple sentences and of many clauses within the other kinds of sentences which the journalist will write. All other words are simply modifiers of these three parts, added to make the meaning clearer. Note these sentences, in which the essential words are italicized:

1. The *explosion shattered* the *cafe.*
2. An *explosion shattered* a crowded *cafe* in this southeastern Utah uranium mining town last night, killing 15 and injuring about 50 diners.
3. *Jerry Rodgers is manager* of the cafe.
4. The *explosion was terrific,* according to Fire Chief Robert F. Bryan, *who will begin* an *investigation* today to determine the cause.

In the first two sentences, *cafe* is the direct object of the verb (predicate) *shattered.* This direct object is necessary to complete the meaning of the sentence.

In the third sentence, *manager* is a predicate nominative. It follows the verb *is* and refers back to the subject, *Jerry Rodgers.* It means the same thing as the subject.

The predicate nominative may be a noun, a pronoun or an adjective. Here's an example of a predicate pronoun: The manager is *he.*

In the fourth sentence *terrific* is a predicate adjective, and predicate adjectives may be classed as predicate nominatives. Like a predicate noun or pronoun, the predicate adjective follows the verb and refers back to the subject. However, instead of meaning the same thing as the subject, the predicate adjective modifies (describes) the subject. Here *terrific* refers back to *explosion.*

In the four sentences you will find that all words and phrases which are not italicized are modifiers of one or more of the essential three parts. The second half of the fourth sentence—*who will begin an investigation today to determine the cause*—is a subordinate clause used as a modifier. It is a relative clause used adjectivally to modify *Fire Chief Robert F. Bryan.*

Remember that some nouns can be used as adverbs when they refer to size, measurement, number, degree and place. Don't let these nouns fool you into thinking that they are direct objects. Example: The wounded soldier had been *lying* (or *laying*) there an *hour. Hour* is a noun used adverbially. It modifies the verb and answers the question: How long? It cannot possibly be a direct object; therefore the intransitive verb *lying* is correct.

LINKING VERBS

3. A *linking* or *copulative verb* is one that links or couples the subject to an equivalent word in the sentence. The equivalent word may be a noun or pronoun or an adjective, and it is called a predicate noun or predicate pronoun or a predicate adjective. It answers who? or what? following the verb and refers back to the subject.

There are two kinds of linking verbs. The forms of the verb *be,* such as *is, are, was, were,* may be used as linking verbs. The other kind of linking verb, often called a copulative verb, is really an intransitive verb used in a weakened sense, such as *seem, smell, appear, feel* and *look.* When these verbs are followed by predicate nominatives, they are copulative or linking verbs.

The main point to remember in identifying linking verbs is that the predicate noun or predicate pronoun must mean the same thing as the subject. The predicate noun or predicate pronoun simply completes the predicate and refers back to the subject, meaning the same as the subject. The predicate adjective also completes the predicate and refers back to the subject, but it does not mean the same thing as the subject; it simply modifies (describes) the subject.

Remember that the predicate nominative must always be in the nominative case; otherwise, you are likely to use incorrect forms of the pronoun, such as: It is *me* who must do it. *I* is correct.

The captain of the team is her *brother*.	(Predicate noun)
The victim of the robbery was *he* (not *him*).	(Predicate pronoun)
That yellow rose smells *sweet*.	(Predicate adjective)

Test the first example above: *captain* (subject) is (verb) *what* or *whom?* *Brother* answers the question *what*. It refers back to the subject and means the same thing as the subject. Therefore, *brother* is a predicate noun following the linking verb *is*.

The second and third examples illustrate why you need to recognize linking verbs if you are to avoid making common errors. In the second sentence the pronoun follows the linking verb *was* and is identical with the subject, the noun *victim*. *He* (not *him*) is correct since predicate nominatives must always be in the nominative case. In the third example the adjective *sweet*, not the adverb *sweetly*, is correct, because it is a predicate adjective referring back to—and modifying (describing) —the subject *rose*.

The verbs *lie* and *sit* sometimes function as linking verbs. Most errors occur in using the past tense of *lie*, which is *lay*. The transitive verb *lay* has the past tense *laid*.

The beautiful blonde actress *lay* motionless on the bed.
Her mother *sat* erect in a chair near the door.

Do not use the adverbs *motionlessly* and *erectly* in these sentences. *Motionless* in the first sentence is a predicate adjective that refers back to the subject *actress*. *Erect* in the second sentence is a predicate adjective modifying *mother*.

In the following sentence the adjective *bad* (not the adverb *badly*) is correct. Here *look* is a linking verb, linking the subject *woman* to the predicate adjective *bad*, which describes the subject.

The woman looks *bad*.

Bad is a predicate adjective modifying the subject *woman*. If you said, "The woman looks *badly*," you would be referring to her eyesight, not to her general appearance.

Humphrey said he did not feel *bad* about losing to Nixon.

Some authorities would accept the adverb *badly* in this sentence, particularly since it is used colloquially here. However, most editors will not approve use of *badly* after the verb *feel* except when *badly* actually modifies the verb, not the subject, as in the following sentence.

The citizens feel *badly* the need for a youth center.

The most common linking verbs are *be, appear, become, feel, get, grow, lie, sit, look, prove, remain, seem, smell, sound, taste* and *turn*.

Remember that many verbs, such as *turn*, may be transitive, intransitive or linking according to use in a sentence.

The milk *turned* sour.   (Linking)
He *turned* the pages quickly.   (Transitive)
The gunman *turned* quickly.   (Intransitive)

SUBJECT OF THE SENTENCE

Next to the verb, the subject is the most important part of the sentence. A simple subject and a simple predicate can make a complete sentence: Smathers died.

The subject of the sentence answers the question *What?* or

Who? placed before the verb. The simple subject may be any one of the following:

1. A noun: The *lake* was calm.
2. A pronoun: *He* limped painfully along the road.
3. An infinitive: *To play* bridge well requires concentration.
4. A gerund: *Making* a lot of money is not his aim in life.
5. A noun clause: *That the bond issue would be approved* was evident.

OBECT OF THE VERB

The *direct object* of the verb is the word that receives the action of the verb. The simple object is found by asking *What?* or *Whom?* after the verb. Only transitive verbs take direct objects.

The hunters shot ten *geese* in all.
The editor advised *them* carefully.

The direct object of the verb may be any one of the following:

1. A noun: The hunters killed five wild *geese.*
2. A pronoun: Johnston interviewed *him* yesterday.
3. An infinitive: Do you want *to play?*
4. A gerund: He abhors *dancing.*
5. A noun clause: The mayor thinks *that the bond issue will be approved.*

PREDICATE NOMINATIVES

A *predicate nominative,* remember, is a word or group of words that means the same thing as the subject or that modifies the subject. Predicate nominatives are used after linking verbs. They may be predicate nouns, predicate pronouns, or predicate adjectives. Since they refer to the subject, predicate nouns and pronouns are always in the nominative case.

The following may be used as predicate nominatives:

1. A noun: Milton Eisenhower is Ike's *brother*.
2. A pronoun: It was *he* who made the error.
3. An infinitive: The secretary's job is *to collect* the fees.
4. A gerund: His only recreation is *swimming*.
5. A noun clause: The mayor's hope is *that the bond issue will be approved.*

POSITION OF PARTS IN THE SENTENCE

The regular order of the essential parts of the sentence is subject—predicate—direct object or predicate nominative. In interrogative sentences, however, the object often comes first:

Whom do you think the judges will select?

Whom is the object of *will select*.

Study the following methods of obtaining variety.

1. Begin some sentences with the expletive *it* or *there*.

It was his aim to delay the meeting.

The normal order would be: His aim was to delay the meeting.

There are two letters missing from the file.

Journalists should use expletives sparingly in their sentences.

2. Begin some sentences with an adverb.

Occasionally a coyote's plaintive wail disturbed the campers.

3. Begin some sentences with a prepositional phrase.

In the seventh inning the Giants evened the score.

4. You can even begin some sentences with the object of the verb.

Not a *sound* could they hear.
Whom I love, I cherish.

5
More About Verbs

About half the grammatical errors made in writing are mistakes in the use of verbs. The purpose of this chapter, then, is to give you a review of that most powerful but also most troublesome part of speech—the verb.

You need, then, to test yourself on use of the verb. This is the most comprehensive quiz you will have in any of the chapters.

Quiz

1. Sophomore quarterback Scott Hunter led his receiver and (*laid, lay*) the ball into the hands of George Granger for a go-ahead touchdown.
2. The man paused in his work, (*lay, laid*) down the heavy shovel and wiped away the perspiration.
3. The Marines just (*lay, laid*) there in their hastily dug foxholes.
4. Part of the marijuana was (*lying, laying*) on the kitchen table.
5. As the Viet Cong approached, we just (*set, sat*) there.
6. He carefully (*set, sat*) the rifle on the floor.
7. He had (*laid, lain*) there for three hours.

8. The child saw him (*set, sit*) the bottle on the shelf.

9. The river was slowly (*rising, raising*).

10. The little girl was trying to (*sit, set*) her baby sister on the stool.

11. Her hat (*set, sat*) jauntily upon her head.

12. Grandma (*sat, set*) the table before we arrived.

13. The mob (*dragged, drug*) the screaming man from his cell and (*hung, hanged*) him from an oak tree in the town square. His body (*hanged, hung*) there for almost an hour before it was removed.

14. Schmidt (*swam, swum*) out, (*dove, dived*) to the bottom and (*drug, dragged*) the (*drowned, drownded*) child from the creek.

15. Coach Fry's selection of Chuck Hixon as his starting quarterback (*paid, payed*) big dividends, since Hixson (*lead, led*) the nation in passing for the 1968 season.

Do you find anything wrong with the following sentences?

16. Grasp the ball firmly; then it is released with a quick twist of the wrist.

17. Halfback Ron Johnson, who last season broke the great Tom Harmon's rushing records at Michigan, had galloped 53 yards and shook off three or four Duke players to score standing up.

18. If I was in his place, I would ask for a conference.

19. If Haywood were involved in the swindle, he probably has left Syracuse by now.

20. The 42-year-old housewife was beaten severely about the face, and all four of her abductors raped her.

To see how well you did on this test, see the end of the chapter.

REGULAR AND IRREGULAR VERBS

Verbs are classified according to use as transitive verbs; intransitive verbs and linking or copulative verbs.

Verbs are classified according to form as regular verbs and irregular verbs.

A *regular verb* is one that forms its principal parts by adding *d* or *ed* to the present tense to form the past tense and the past participle.

walk, walked, walked   prove, proved, proved

An *irregular verb* is one that forms its past tense and past participle by changing the form of the present tense.

grow, grew, grown   swim, swam, swum

TENSE

The word *tense* means "time." The tense of a verb shows the time of the action or being of the verb.

1. The *present tense* denotes present time.

I *am* late.   I *see* him.

2. The *past tense* denotes past time.

I *was* late Friday.   I *saw* him yesterday.

3. The *future tense* denotes future time:

I probably *shall be* late.   I *shall see* him tomorrow.

4. The *present perfect tense* is used to show that the action expressed by the verb is perfected, that is, completed, but that the action is still important at the present time. It is formed by using *has* or *have* with the past participle.

I *have been* late three times this week.
I *have seen* him only once today.
Mary *has lost* her purse.

5. The *past perfect tense* is used to show that the action expressed by the verb occurred in the past and that the action was important at some time in the more recent past. It is formed by using *had* with the past participle.

I *had been* late several times before that.
I *had seen* the editor before you arrived.
Mary *had lost* her purse before she met me.

6. The *future perfect tense* is used to show that the action of the verb will be perfected, or completed, at some time in the future. It is formed by using *shall* or *will* plus *have* and the past participle.

We *shall have seen* him before you arrive.
He *will have been* traveling four days.

Most tense errors result from using wrong forms of the irregular verbs. If you learn the principal parts of the verbs given in this chapter, you should not make mistakes.

There are also *progressive forms* of the verb, but the journalist will have little trouble with these if he knows the tenses discussed above and learns the principal parts of verbs.

I *am living* well now.
I *was living* well two years ago.
I *shall be living* well by next year.
She *was lying* (not *laying*) down.

You should keep in mind that the present tense form is the first one of the principal parts, and that it is used also with certain *auxiliary verbs* to form verb phrases:

General Wheeler said he *could go* next week.
Jackie's children *may swim* in the Mediterranean today.

AUXILIARIES

Some verbs are called *auxiliary verbs* because they are helping verbs.

1. Forms of *be* help make the passive and progressive forms of other verbs.

The rewriting *was done* in a hurry.
I *am helping* with the review.

2. Forms of *do* help to ask questions, help to emphasize and help to make negative statements.

Do you *expect* to meet him at the airport?
I *do* not *like* the way he said that.

3. *Have, has* and *had* and *shall* and *will* help to make the tenses.

The reporter *has had* a hard day.
Where *shall* we *go* for our vacation?

4. *Can, could, may, might, should* and *would* help express mood.

You *may see* the story tomorrow after class.
That *would be* useful to the writer.

An auxiliary verb used with a main verb makes a *verb phrase:* shall go, was done, am helping, may see. If the predicate is a one-word verb, it is not an auxiliary verb. Always look to see if one of the verbs listed above is used with another verb.

To avoid many errors made in use of tense, you should be sure never to use *past tense* forms in verb phrases. The past tense is *never* used with auxiliary verbs. Example: I *had swam* past him.

The *past participle* is always used with an auxiliary verb to form a verb phrase. Examples: I *have swum* the river. I *had swum* the river before.

Never use the past participle alone as a verb. Examples: I *swum* the river yesterday. The teacher *rung* the bell.

PRINCIPAL PARTS OF VERBS

To use the tense forms correctly, you must know the *principal parts* of verbs. These are the present tense form, the past tense form and the past participle of the verb.

The *present tense* form is the root form of the verb. It is the same as the *present infinitive* form: to break, to shave.

The *past tense* form is made by adding *d* or *ed* to the present tense form if the verb is regular. It has a different form from the present tense form in the irregular verbs.

The *past participle* is the same as the past tense form in many regular verbs, but it has a different form in most irregular verbs. This form is used with *have, has* and *had:* have *eaten,* had *drunk.*

The following list contains most of the verbs with which you may have trouble at times. As you study the list, a useful mental exercise will be to use each part in a sentence in which an adverb is included to indicate the time, or tense. For example: *Every day* I swim here. *Yesterday* I swam here. *Many times* I have (had) swum here. Another good mental exercise is to identify the tense which you have used in the sentence. Verbs that most often give students difficulty are marked with an asterisk (*).

PRINCIPLE PARTS OF VERBS

PRESENT	PAST	PAST PARTICIPLE
awake	awoke *or* awaked	awaked
be—am, is, are	was, were	been
beat	beat	beaten
bid	bade *or* bid	bidden *or* bid
bite	bit	bitten
blow	blew	blown
break	broke	broken
burst	burst	burst
choose	chose	chosen
come	came	come
dive	*dived[1]	dived
do	did	done
*drag	dragged	dragged
draw	drew	drawn
drink	drank	drunk
drive	drove	driven
drown	drowned (*not* drownded)	drowned
eat	ate	eaten

[1] Colloquial: *dove.*

PRESENT	PAST	PAST PARTICIPLE
fall	fell	fallen
flee	fled	fled
flow	flowed	flowed
fly	flew	flown
forbid	forbade	forbidden *or* forbid
forget	forgot	forgotten *or* forgot
freeze	froze	frozen
get	got	got *or* gotten[2]
give	gave	given
go	went	gone
grow	grew	grown
*hang (to suspend something)	hung	hung
*hang (to put to death)	hanged	hanged
hide	hid	hidden *or* hid
hurt	hurt	hurt
know	knew	known
*lay	laid	laid
*lead	led (*not* lead)	led
lend	lent	lent
loan	loaned	loaned
*lie	lay	lain
light	lighted *or* lit	lighted *or* lit
*loose (to free)	loosed	loosed
*lose (to part with)	lost	lost
mow	mowed	mowed *or* mown
pay	paid (*not* payed)	paid
prove	proved	proved (*not* proven)
*raise	raised	raised
rid	rid	rid
ride	rode	ridden
ring	rang	rung
*rise (*intransitive*)	rose	risen

[2] *Got* is preferred, but *gotten* is still popular in the United States.

PRESENT	PAST	PAST PARTICIPLE
run	ran	run
saw (to cut)	sawed	sawed *or* sawn
see	saw	seen
*set	set	set
sew	sewed	sewed *or* sewn
shake	shook	shaken
shave	shaved	shaved *or* shaven
shed	shed	shed
shine (to emit light)	shone	shone
shine (to polish)	shined	shined
show	showed	shown *or* showed
shrink	shrank	shrunk
sing	sang *or* sung[3]	sung
sink	sank *or* sunk	sunk
*sit	sat	sat
slay	slew	slain
sow (to plant)	sowed	sown *or* sowed
speak	spoke	spoken
speed	sped	sped
spring	sprang *or* sprung	sprung
steal	stole	stolen
sting	stung	stung
stink	stank *or* stunk	stunk
strew	strewed	strewed *or* strewn
string	strung	strung
strive	strove	striven *or* strived
swell	swelled	swelled *or* swollen
swim	swam	swum
take	took	taken
tear	tore	torn
tread	trod	trod *or* trodden
use	used (*not* use to live)	used
wring	wrung	wrung
write	wrote	written

[3] Recent usage strongly favors *sang*.

SOME TROUBLESOME VERBS

The following pairs of verbs often give trouble. To avoid using the wrong verb, you need to do only two things. (1) Learn the principal parts of these verbs. (2) Learn to identify the verbs as being either transitive or intransitive. Before using one of these verbs in a sentence, first check to see whether it does or does not take an object. It's as simple as that! Carefully study the following sections.

1. The verbs *lie* and *lay* are sometimes confused.

Lie—lay—lain is intransitive. It may be modified by an adverb or a prepositional phrase, but it never takes an object. Do not confuse the past *lay* with the present tense of the verb *lay*.

Mother *is lying* down.	We *had lain* in the sun.
I like *to lie* in the sun.	The book *lay* on the table.
Your book *lies* on the table.	She *lay* down.

Lay—laid—laid is transitive. It takes an object.

John *is laying* the book on the table.
Lay the book on the table. (The object is *book*.)
John *laid* the book on the table.

2. The verbs *sit* and *set* are often confused.

Sit—sat—sat is intransitive. It does not take an object.

He *was sitting* in the living room.
Mary always *sits* here.
She *sat* up front at the concert.
Have you ever *sat* here before?
Sit down, Bowser.

Set—set—set is transitive. It takes an object.

He *is setting* fire to the barn.
The errand boy *set* the package on the floor.
Where *have* you *set* the radio?

But note two exceptions in which *set* is intransitive.

The sun *sets* in the west.
The hens *are setting* (on the eggs).

3. The verbs *rise* and *raise* have different meanings.
Rise—rose—risen is intransitive. It does not have an object.

Please *rise* when the judge enters.
Prices *were rising* dangerously.
James *rose* to the occasion.
The plane *had risen* from the ground safely.

Raise—raised—raised is transitive. It takes an object.

Charles Mayhew *raises* Hereford cattle.
The landlord *was raising* rents.
Can you *raise* that window for me?
The man slowly *raised* himself from the bed.   (Reflexive object)

The safe *has been raised* to the fifth-   (Subject is acted
story window.   upon)

4. The verbs *drag* and *drug* should not be confused.
Drag—dragged—dragged is transitive and takes an object,
the thing or person that is pulled along by force.

The men *dragged* (not *drug*) the lifeless body into the camp house.

The verb *drug—drugged—drugged* means "to administer
drugs to."

Police said the woman *had drugged* the kidnapped boy.

5. The verb *hang* has two forms, according to whether it
refers to an act performed on a person or on an object.
Hang—hung—hung refers to objects.

He *hung* the mirror over the sideboard.
We *will hang* the curtains tomorrow.
Your picture *was hung* in the living room.

Hang—hanged—hanged refers to the act of suspending a person by his neck until dead.

They *hanged* the murderer at dawn.
Criminals convicted of murder or rape are *hanged* in Oklahoma.

VOICE OF THE VERB

Voice is the form of transitive verbs that shows whether the subject acts or is acted upon.

A verb is in the *active voice* when it shows that the subject acts or does something.

Sheriff Decker *shot* the robber.

The subject *Sheriff Decker* performs the action of the verb *shot*. The direct object is *robber;* it is acted upon.

A verb is in the *passive voice* when the subject of the verb is acted upon.

The robber *was shot* by Sheriff Decker.

The passive voice is formed by using some form of the verb *be* with the past participle of the action verb: *is shot, was shot has been shot, had been shot, may be shot, will be shot.* The passive voice is regarded by journalists as the weaker voice, and they use whenever possible the more direct and more vigorous active voice. However, the passive voice is often used by copy editors in writing headlines, and reporters should use it in sentences in which the person or thing receiving the action is more important than the person who is doing the acting. For example, the passive voice is right in the following lead:

Herbert Noble, "The Cat," was blown to bits by unidentified gangsters Friday.

The fact that Noble, who had escaped so many attempts on his life, was finally killed was more important than who killed him.

On the other hand, consider this example:

Governor Ferguson shot and wounded a burglar who entered the governor's mansion Friday.

The active voice is needed here because the readers are more interested in the governor and what he did than they are in the unidentified burglar.

Be especially careful to avoid using the passive voice when it would make the sentence sound awkward or affected, as in the following:

Casper's eyes twinkled as he declared, "That lesson was learned early in life by me."

Perhaps Caspar's modesty led him to avoid using the pronoun *I*, but the sentence would sound better if it read: I learned that lesson early in life.

Avoid shifting from one voice to the other, and especially shifting from the active to the passive. Notice this error in the following:

Frances McCartney, who will portray Gigi's mother Andree, *majored* in music at SMU, *acted* for Arden Club and *was employed by WFAA–TV.*

After using the two active verbs *majored* and *acted,* the writer should have written: and *worked* for WFAA-TV. This keeps all three verbs in the active voice.

MOOD OF THE VERB

The *mood* of the verb refers to the manner in which the action or the being or the state of being of the verb is stated.

In English there are three moods: the indicative, the imperative and the subjunctive.

1. The *indicative mood* states a fact or asks a question.

The dog *is* not dead.   *Is* that plant alive?
His master *died* yesterday.   Plants *live* on soil and water.

2. The *imperative mood* expresses a command or makes a request or an entreaty. The subject of a verb in the imperative mood is always *You* and is usually omitted. *You* is then said to be an understood subject.

Close the door!
Please *close* the door when you go out.

Note that the exclamation mark is used after a command if it is given as an exclamation.

3. The *subjunctive mood* expresses a supposition contrary to fact, a supposition with indefinite time, a condition contrary to fact, a future contingency, a doubt, a wish or a desire. In other words, the subjunctive mood deals largely with statements that are contrary to fact or about which there is some doubt.

He acts as if he *were* afraid.	(Doubt)
I wish I *were* old enough to enlist.	(Wish)
If he *were* my brother, I might be able to take him.	(Contrary to fact)

Do not use *was* in such statements.

The uses of the subjunctive with which the journalist ordinarily will be most concerned are to express a wish or a desire, the fulfillment of which is doubtful, and to express a condition contrary to fact.

The subjunctive forms are introduced by conjunctions of concession, condition, contingency, possibility, etc. The most common ones are *if, as if* and *as though*. Note, however, that these conjunctions are often used with the indicative forms. It is now considered better to say: If he *is* not here by Thursday, . . . than to say: If he *be* . . . In stating conditions contrary to fact, the subjunctive is the correct form: If the reporter *were* a good writer, he would not be fired. Use the indicative in stating merely a condition, as in this sentence: If he *was* involved in the affair, he probably has left the city.

Note that the auxiliary verbs *may, can, must, might, could, would* and *should* are used to express a possibility, a wish, a desire, a necessity, an entreaty, etc. The conjunctions *if, unless* and *though* often introduce the subordinate clauses.

If I *could see* him tomorrow I *would go* into town with you.
He *may arrive* early, though it *must be* an effort for him to come.

4. The *infinitive* is sometimes classed as a mood. It is used to express an action or condition without regard to person or number.

The sophomores challenged the juniors *to fight.*
To fight at that time was foolish.
Her only ambition was *to be* glamorous.

The infinitive is also classed as a *verbal.*

PERSON AND NUMBER OF VERBS

The verb must always agree with its subject in *person* and *number.* The only special form occurs in the third person singular of the present tense. The verb adds an *s* after *he* or *she* or *it* in the present tense.

He *rides.* She *walks.* It *falls.*

The exceptions are a few irregular verbs: I *have,* he *has;* I *am,* she *is,* etc.

A compound subject composed of two nouns and/or pronouns connected by *and* is plural, and it takes a plural verb. A compound subject consisting of nouns and/or pronouns connected by *or* is either singular or plural, depending on whether the nouns and/or pronouns are singular or plural. If the nouns and/or pronouns joined by *or* differ in number, the verb agrees in number *with the noun or pronoun nearest the verb.*

The father and the mother *are* meeting him tomorrow.
You and I *are* meeting him tomorrow.
Either the mother or the two sisters *are* coming.
Either the two sisters or the mother *is* to be there.

Either you or he *is* supposed to cover the speech.
Either Hunter or you *are* supposed to cover the speech.

THE VERBALS

Three special forms of the verb are called the *verbals*. They are the infinitive, the participle and the gerund. They have certain characteristics of the verb, but they are not used alone as verbs. Some grammarians call them verbal phrases, also.

1. The *infinitive* is the simple form of the verb preceded by *to* either expressed or understood. *To* is usually omitted if it would make the sentence awkward or stilted: Bid him *go*.

The infinitive is usually used as a noun, an adjective or an adverb.

As a noun:

To fight was foolish.	(Subject of verb *was*)
He plans *to fight* if necessary.	(Object of verb *plans*)
His plan is *to fight*.	(Predicate nominative)

As an adjective:

This is the way *to fight* him.　(Modifies noun *way*)

As an adverb:

He is ready *to fight*.　(Modifies the adjective *ready*)

2. The participles of a verb may be used as adjectives and as parts of phrases used as adjectives.

The *present participle* is formed by adding *ing* to the simple form of the verb: falling; writing; raising. The *past participle* is the third principal part of the verb: been; fallen; raised.

Used as an adjective:

The children watched the *escaping* water.	(Modifies noun *water*)
The *fallen* tree was removed from the road.	(Modifies noun *tree*)

Used in an adjectival phrase:

Raising his hand, the man asked to speak.	(Modifies noun *man*)
Depressed in spirit, I went home.	(Modifies pronoun *I*)
The tree, *fallen across the road,* was removed.	(Modifies noun *tree*)

Always be careful not to have a participle "dangle." For example, someone might say: Climbing through the barbed-wire fence, his coat was torn. Surely it was a person, not his coat, that climbed through the fence. Correct: Climbing through the fence, the hunter tore his coat.

Quiz Answers

1. laid. 2. laid. 3. lay. 4. lying. 5. sat. 6. set. 7. lain. 8. set. 9. rising. 10. set. 11. sat. 12. set. 13. dragged, hanged, hung. 14. swam, dived, dragged, drowned. 15. paid, led.

Sentences 16–20 should read as follows: 16. Grasp the ball firmly; then release it with. . . 17. Halfback Ron Jackson who. . . had galloped 53 yards and had shaken off three or four. . . 18. If I were in his place. . . 19. If Haywood was involved. . . 20. The 42-year-old housewife was beaten severely about the face and was raped by all four of her abductors.

6
Properties of
Nouns and Pronouns

In most of the remaining chapters you will find yourself concerned with proper usage of the parts of speech in writing correct sentences. In the preceding chapter you reviewed verbs and predicates. Before proceeding, then, to a study of errors commonly made in the use of the subject and the predicate together, it is logical that you first have further review of *nouns* and words and constructions used as nouns—and of *pronouns*.

Test your knowledge of nouns and pronouns—and their correct use—by taking the following quiz. If you have difficulty with the quiz, you need further study of the properties of nouns and pronouns, particularly of *case* and *number*.

Quiz

Correct any errors in the following:

1. The dog is lying on it's back, but I cant tell whether its dead or not.
2. The dean objected strenuously to us breaking the rule.
3. Prospects of them being written into labor law were dim.

4. The two Negro's faces looked familiar.
5. Her lady's hats are famous throughout the nation.
6. This pencil is Charles's, not Mary's.
7. The garage's roof sloped sharply.

Select the correct word in the following:

8. They asked for Reese and (I, me).
9. If I were (he, him), I would resign.
10. (Who, Whom) will be nominated in 1972?
11. Between you and (I, me), I think she is guilty.
12. Most of these people, like (us, we) Americans, have the free ballot.
13. (Whom, who) do the experts think will win the Orange Bowl game?
14. Could it have been (him, he) (who, whom) was injured?
15. Do you recall (him, his) mentioning the matter?
16. Do you remember (who, whom) it was (who, whom, that) **we** invited first?
17. (Who, Whom) do the police suspect?
18. "Let's you and (I, me) step aside and get ready for the next round," said Crosby.
19. It looks as if no one except (myself, me, I) can be there early.
20. The captain ordered John and (I, me) to clean our rifles.

See the end of the chapter to see how many errors you missed.

Briefly review the discussion of nouns and pronouns in Chapter 3. Recall that nouns are words used to name persons and things, and that there are four kinds of nouns: common, proper, abstract and collective. And, recall that a pronoun is a word used in place of a noun.

Nouns and pronouns have four properties: gender, number, person and case.

GERUNDS ARE NOUNS

The present participle form of the verb, ending in *ing,* is called a gerund when it is used as a noun. It is also called a verb-noun. Unlike a noun, however, a gerund retains some of the characteristics of a verb and may take an object. It requires the possessive case of any noun or pronoun used with it. Note the following examples of gerunds:

The constant *pounding of the*
waves weakened the rocks.   (Subject of verb *weakened*)
Complaining about it will not help
you.   (Subject of verb *will help*)
I don't like your *going* to that meet-
ing.   (Object of verb *like*)

Note the possessive *your* with the gerund *going* in the last sentence.

GENDER OF NOUNS AND PRONOUNS

Nouns and pronouns indicate sex by their *gender.* There are four genders: feminine gender, masculine gender, neuter gender and common gender.

Feminine gender: girl, woman, actress, queen, cow
Masculine gender: boy, man, actor, king, bull
Neuter gender: house, flower, automobile, television
Common gender: child, dog, cat, bird, person, pupil

Neuter gender implies no sex, although such things as flowers are said to be female and male. *Common gender* implies that the person or animal may be masculine or feminine, but the gender is not stated.

NUMBER OF NOUNS AND PRONOUNS

The *number* of a noun or a pronoun indicates whether it is *singular,* indicating a single person or thing, or *plural,* indicating more than one person or thing. A few exceptions are nouns which may be either singular or plural: fish, deer.

Journalism students must know the following rules for forming the plurals of nouns if they are to write correct sentences in which the verb and its subject agree in number. Also, remember that it is necessary to know plural forms in order to use the possessive case correctly. Study these rules:

1. Most nouns form their plural by adding *s* to the singular.

boy, boys   hat, hats   relation, relations

2. If a noun ends in a sibilant—as *s* sound (*s, x, sh, z*)—it forms its plural by adding *es* to the singular.

dish,   dishes   box, boxes   bush, bushes   buzz, buzzes

3. Some nouns change the stem root vowel to form the plural.

woman, women   man, men   mouse, mice   foot, feet

4. Some nouns add *en* to form the plural.

ox, oxen   child, children

5. Some nouns have the same form for singular and plural.

deer, deer   fish, fish[1]   sheep, sheep

6. Most nouns ending in *f* or *fe* form the plural by adding *s,* but some nouns change the *f* to *v* before adding *s* or *es.*

chief, chiefs   leaf, leaves
belief, beliefs   wife, wives

[1] Note that the dictionary gives the plural *fishes* as also correct.

7. Nouns that end in *y* preceded by a vowel add *s* to form the plural. If the *y* is preceded by a consonant, the *y* is changed to *i* before *es* is added. Watch this type of noun!

boy, boys   lady, ladies   sky, skies
relay, relays   city, cities   party, parties

8. Proper names that end in *y* do not change the *y* to *i* before adding s or *es* to form the plural.

Mary   the two Marys

9. *The* usually precedes the plural of a proper name: the Astors, the Thomases (referring usually to families). Be particularly careful in forming the plural of proper names ending in *s*.

the Thomases   the Holmeses   the Joneses

10. Most nouns ending in *o* add *s* to form the plural.

alto, altos   Eskimo, Eskimos   folio, folios
cello, cellos   cameo, cameos   radio, radios
piano, pianos   curio, curios

Some nouns that end in *o* preceded by a consonant add *es* to form the plural, however.

cargo, cargoes   Negro, Negroes   tomato, tomatoes
echo, echoes   potato, potatoes   hero, heroes

Some nouns ending in *o* may add either *s* or *es* to form the plural. The dictionary will show which form is preferred.

halo, halos *or* haloes   mosquito, mosquitos, *or* mosquitoes
motto, mottos *or* mottoes   tornado, tornados *or* tornadoes
zero, zeros, *or* zeroes   volcano, volcanos *or* volcanoes

11. Most nouns ending in *i* form the plural by adding *s*.

alibi, alibis   rabbi, rabbis

12. Some foreign nouns retain the foreign plural.

alumnus, alumni   crisis, crises   thesis, theses
addendum, addenda   datum, data   radius, radii

Many foreign words are now used correctly in either the foreign plural or the English plural. Consult the dictionary when in doubt.

antenna, antennae *or* antennas
appendix, appendices *or* appendixes
tableau, tableaux *or* tableaus
curriculum, curricula *or* curriculums
formula, formulae *or* formulas
index, indices *or* indexes
medium, media *or* mediums
stratum, strata *or* stratums
phenomenon, phenomena *or* phenomenons
beau, beaux *or* beaus
memorandum, memoranda *or* memorandums

13. Some words, like *day, foot, head, hour, mile, dozen, score,* etc., may be used as plurals without pluralizing them in form. This may be done only when the word is used together with a numerical adjective, especially to form a hyphenated adjective which modifies a noun that follows, as: There was a *three-hour* delay.

a three-day session   three score and ten
a 24-foot jump   75 head of cattle
a two-mile race   four dozen cookies

14. Some nouns that are plural in form are singular in meaning and use. They require singular predicates.

Mathematics is a difficult course for the student.
Your *news is* most interesting.
Measles is a painful disease of childhood.

Other nouns in this category include the following. Always consult the dictionary to find how to use a word correctly if you are in doubt.

acoustics	dynamics	optics
aeronautics	economics	phonetics
ballistics	measles	physics
checkers	molasses	tactics
dominoes	mumps	whereabouts

Some of these nouns have a singular or a plural meaning according to the use made of them. For example, *checkers* and *dominoes* are regarded as singular nouns when they refer to a game. *Statistics* is singular when you refer to a body of facts, but it is plural when you designate separate facts that are grouped together. Similarly, *athletics* is singular to refer to a system of physical training; it is plural when it refers to two or more sports. For example: Athletics has transformed him from a weakling into an Olympic star; but: Intercollegiate athletics have been abandoned by the college.

15. Most compound words make the last word plural in forming the plural of the noun. Nouns that are called *solid compounds*—those that do not have a hyphen—usually follow the regular rules for plurals. Note carefully the solid compounds ending in *-ful*.

airship, airships	cupful, cupfuls
bookkeeper, bookkeepers	handful, handfuls
textbook, textbooks	spoonful, spoonfuls

Compound nouns that are hyphenated form the plural by adding *s* to the main word in the compound.

by-line, by-lines	father-in-law, fathers-in-law
passer-by, passers-by	great-grandmother, great-grandmothers
hanger-on, hangers-on	maid-of-honor, maids-of-honor

Compound words that consist of two words used without a hyphen make both words plural in some cases, and make only the main word plural in other cases.

chargé d'affaires, chargés d'affaires
attorney general, attorneys general

notary public, notaries public

16. The plural of letters, figures and symbols, and of specifically designated words and phrases is usually formed by adding an apostrophe and *s* (*'s*).

two i's and three s's   too many and's
6's and 7's   the ABC's

There is a trend to omit the apostrophe when the words are used with a special meaning: pros and cons, the whys and the wherefores, 14 noes, etc.

PERSON OF NOUNS AND PRONOUNS

Nouns and pronouns have three persons. The *first person* indicates the person speaking. The *second person* indicates the person spoken to. The *third person* indicates the person or thing spoken about.

First person: *I* am going to the game today.
Second person: Are *you* coming with me?
Third person: We can meet *them* at the gate.

The journalist who aspires to top rank as a writer must learn to use original and appropriate figures of speech. Figures of speech are an essential element of writing style—along with words, sentences and paragraphs. *Personification* is a figure of speech in which inanimate things, animals and abstract ideas are spoken of as though they were persons. Note the following:

Nature bedecked herself in spring finery.
Actions always speak louder than words.
The cottonwoods murmured among themselves.
Fields of young corn nodded promises to their farmer.
Windshield wipers, eternally bowing gracefully to each other. . .
Megaphones of daffodils shouting to the world.

CASE OF NOUNS AND PRONOUNS

One of the most common faults of writers is the incorrect use of case.

Case indicates the relationship of a noun or a pronoun to other words in the sentence. There are three cases: nominative, objective and possessive.

Remember that the case of a noun or pronoun is always determined by its use in the sentence or clause.

NOMINATIVE CASE

A noun or pronoun is in the nominative case when it is used in one of the following ways.

1. The *subject* of the verb is in the nominative case.

Sheriff Bill Decker shot the robber.
John Tower is the man *who* has the chairmanship of the Senate Republican Campaign Committee "locked up."

2. A noun or pronoun used as a *predicate nominative* is always in the nominative case.

Bill Decker is *sheriff*.
It is *he* (not *him*) who shot the robber.

3. A noun or pronoun used in addressing a person is called a *nominative of address*. If it is used in an exclamatory sense, it is sometimes called a *nominative by exclamation*.

Judge Atwell, I object to his question.
Poor Mary! She has lost her report.
You there! You are not listening to me.

But note that you would use *Poor me!* in preference to *Poor I!*

4. A noun or a pronoun used independently in an absolute construction or with a participle is called a *nominative absolute*.

The bow having been rammed, the ship began to sink.
He being badly injured, they called for an ambulance.

In any nominative absolute construction there must be a noun (*bow*) or a pronoun (*He*) modified by a participle, and this whole construction is grammatically independent of the rest of the sentence.

5. A noun or pronoun used in a phrase that is parallel to and explains another noun is called an *appositive*. When the noun to which it refers is in the nominative case, the appositive is in the nominative case. In other words, an appositive agrees in case with the word which it explains.

Appositives are inserted loosely into the sentence and are usually set off by commas or dashes. The exceptions are single-word appositives: his brother *John*. Such appositives are called *restrictive appositives* because they are essential to the meaning of the sentence.

They live east of the city on a 550-acre ranch, *Rancho Rio*.
Felix McKnight, *the editor*, called us into his office.
That is Felix McKnight, *the editor*.
Police told him that his brother *John* was injured.

The appositive usually is placed immediately after the word with which it is in apposition, but it can have other positions, thus:

There is one course I never liked—*mathematics*.

Mathematics is in apposition with the noun *course*.

OBJECTIVE CASE

The objective case is used in the following ways:

1. The *direct object* of the verb is in the objective case.

Shuford blocked *Tucker* and *him* on the two-yard line.
The committee will send *Black, Jones* and *me* to Mexico.

2. The *object of the preposition* is in the objective case.

The choice is between *Sharp* and *me*.
For *him* there is no other choice.
Take it to the person for *whom* it was bought.

3. The *indirect object* of a verb is in the objective case.

Street handed *Gilbert* the ball.

Note that you can find the indirect object by inserting *to;*
handed the ball *to Gilbert;* told the story *to him and me*.

4. Also in the objective case is the object of a passive verb.
Some grammarians call this a *retained object*, although it is actually a direct object.

Coach Bear Bryant was given an *auto*.

The verb *was given* is passive because the subject, *Coach Bry-
ant*, receives the action of the verb. *Auto* answers the question:
Was given what? The active form of the sentence would be:
The fans gave Coach Bryant an auto. In this sentence *Coach
Bryant* is the indirect object of the verb *gave*.

5. A noun or pronoun that follows a direct object and explains it or means the same thing as the object is called an *objective complement*. Objective complements usually come after
such verbs as *elect, appoint, name, declare*, etc.

They elected Bill *secretary*.
The committee appointed him *chairman*.
Henry declared the book *his*.
What did they name the baby?

6. The *subject of the infinitive* is always in the objective
case.

They urged *me* to go.
The reporter asked *them* to answer some questions.
They urged *Mason, Johnson* and *me* (not *I*) to go.

7. A noun that is used as an adverb to modify a verb, an adjective, or an adverb is called an *adverbial objective*. An

adverbial objective answers such questions as: Where? When? How much? How far? How long?

John went *home* early.   (Modifies verb *went*)
It came this *afternoon*.   (Modifies verb *came*)
He ran a *mile*.   (Modifies verb *ran*)

Also note the following:

John arrived an *hour early*.   (Modifies adverb *early*)
The fishing rod is worth ten *dollars*. (Modifies predicate adjective *worth*)

Possessive Case

The *possessive case* indicates the person or thing that possesses something. Most errors are made in placing the apostrophe. Make sure that you know how to indicate singular and plural possessives of nouns.

Nouns indicate possessive case in three ways:
1. By use of the *apostrophe*

Have you seen *Marie's* new hair-do?
The *children's* toys must be put away.
Five *boys'* hats are in the hall.

2. By use of the preposition *of*, making a prepositional phrase

The point *of the pen* is broken.
The man is a pal *of that hoodlum*.

3. By use of both the apostrophe and the preposition *of*

Are you a friend *of John's?*

Pronouns indicate possession in two ways:
1. By *inflection*

She left *her* coat.   That copy is *mine*.
That coat is *hers*.   The dog lost *its* collar.
Which hat is *his?*   They launched *their* boat today.

The possessive pronouns do not require an apostrophe to show possession. Note *hers* and *its* in the examples above.

2. By use of the preposition *of* with the possessive pronoun forms

The Temple fans were thrilled by that run *of his.*
He is a special friend *of mine.*

FORMING POSSESSIVES OF NOUNS

The author is convinced that journalism students would have no difficulty with possessives of nouns if they would learn the correct plurals of nouns. If you are not sure of the plurals of nouns, you should turn back to p. 81 before proceeding with this section.

Singular Possessives

You will not make errors if you follow these two steps in forming the singular possessives of nouns:

1. Make sure that you have written the whole *singular* word.

2. Add *'s* to the word unless it comes under one of the exceptions listed below.

a) Singular nouns add *'s* to form the possessive.

John's hat   a princess's tiara
the man's hat   Charles's auto

There are a few exceptions to this rule. If a noun ends in *s,* and *'s* makes the word disagreeable to the ear or difficult to say, the apostrophe alone may be used. Most newspapers now add only the apostrophe in such cases.

Burns' poems   princess' tiara
Dickens' novels   Frances' desk

But many magazine editors require the use of *'s* for proper nouns of one syllable.

Burns's poems   Charles's auto

b) Only the apostrophe is used in possessives before the word *sake*, and in phrases that would be difficult to pronounce if an *s* were added.

for goodness' sake   Moses' commandments

Plural Possessives

Follow these three steps in forming the plural possessives of nouns:
1. Write the correct plural of the word.
2. If the plural ends in *s*, add only the apostrophe.
3. If the plural does not end in *s*, add *'s*.

A plural noun that ends in *s* forms the possessive by adding only an apostrophe.

the Joneses' house   those reporters' cards

A plural noun that does not end in *s* forms the possessive by adding *'s*.

the men's suits   the children's toys

Miscellaneous Uses of the Possessive

Study these further rules for correct form of the possessive.
1. If joint ownership is to be shown, use the *'s* with the last name only.

Cullum and Boren's store   Jane and Betty's sister

2. If separate ownership is to be shown, use *'s* with each name.

Fathers' and Sons' banquet
Warren's and Blake's clothes

3. Most compound nouns form the singular possessive by adding *'s*. The possessive of plural compound nouns is best indicated by using an *of* phrase.

her son-in-law's home   the homes of her sons-in-law
the passer-by's comment   the comments of the passers-by

4. Possession by an inanimate object is best indicated by use of an *of* phrase.

the roof of the barn   the noise of the whistles
the wheels of the cars   the sigh of the wind

Exceptions are certain phrases which are considered correct.

a minute's time   the sun's course   the ship's side

5. The apostrophe usually is omitted in the names of many institutions, organizations and geographic locations.

Sam Houston Teachers College   Loyola Mothers Club
Idaho State Teachers Association   Pikes Peak

CORRECT USE OF NOMINATIVE CASE

A thorough study of the rules that follow will enable you to avoid making the most common errors in use of the nominative case.

1. Always remember that the subject and the predicate nominative of a clause or a sentence must be in the nominative case. Watch *inverted sentences* particularly, where the subject follows the predicate, as it often does in interrogative sentences.

Who (not *whom*) was elected? (*Who* is the subject.)
Who (not *whom*) shall it be? (*Who* is the predicate nominative: It shall be *who*.)

2. Watch closely any clauses and sentences in which the subject precedes the predicate but in which several words or phrases or a thrown-in clause comes between them.

Who do you think will be elected?

Who is the subject of the verb *will be elected.*

3. Be careful to use the relative pronoun *who—whom* correctly. A relative pronoun used as the subject of a dependent clause must be in the nominative case. It is also in the nominative case if it is used as a predicate pronoun.

Do they know *who* he is?

The pronoun *who* is a predicate nominative in the clause *who he is.* (He is *who.*)

The man *who* was to come today is ill.

The pronoun *who* is the subject of the verb *was* in the dependent clause, *who was to come today.*

Senator Kerr, *who* they predicted would lose, won the election.

The clause *who would lose* is the object of the verb *predicted.* In this clause, *who* is the subject of the verb *would lose.*

To the question of *who* would run, the senator named two men.

Although *who* follows the preposition *of* in this sentence, it is not the object of the preposition. The entire clause *who would run* is the object of the preposition *of,* and *who* is the subject of the verb *would run.*

They asked him *whom* he would name.

In this sentence, *whom* is the object of the verb *would name.*

Always determine how the pronoun is used in the sentence to know which word, *who* or *whom,* is correct.

4. After the conjunction *than,* the pronoun must be in the nominative case if the pronoun is the subject in that clause, even though the rest of the clause is not expressed.

Henry is older than *I* (am old).

When the pronoun is the object in the dependent clause, it must be in the objective case.

He likes him better than (he likes) *me.*

Always complete the clause mentally to determine the case of the pronoun.

5. Nouns and pronouns that are connected by a form of the verb *be* are usually in the same case.

It *is I.*

The subject *It* and the predicate pronoun *I* are both in the nominative case.

This rule is considered controversial by some editors. They accept "It is me" as correct, especially in quoting a person, but the use of *me* in this case is colloquial and should not occur in formal writing.

CORRECT USE OF OBJECTIVE CASE

Nouns and pronouns used as objects of verbs, of prepositions or of participles, gerunds or infinitives, or as subjects of infinitives, are in the objective case.

Here again remember that the use of the word determines its case.

1. The relative pronoun *who—whom* often gives trouble. Its case is determined by its use in the sentence.

It was O. J. Simpson *whom* the coach praised so highly.

Whom is the object of the verb *praised* in the subordinate clause.

Whom are you going with?

Whom is the object of the preposition *with.* You will see the construction if you turn the sentence around: With whom are you going? *or* You are going with whom?

If there is an extra clause in an interrogative sentence, you must check the construction carefully to know whether *who* or *whom* is correct.

Who do you suppose will be our next President?

Do you suppose is a parenthetical clause that is inserted between the subject and the predicate. If you leave out *do you suppose,* you see at once that *who* is the subject of the verb *will be.*

2. Pronouns used as objects of verbs and prepositions must be in the objective case. The chief errors are made when the object is compound.

Between *you* and *me,* I think the award should go to Mary and *her.*

You and *me* are objects of the preposition *between; her* is part of the compound object of the preposition *to.*

The policeman arrested both *him* and *me.*

Him and me is the compound object of the verb *arrested.*

3. A pronoun used as an appositive agrees in case with the word with which it is in apposition.

The chairman selected two men, *you* and *me.*

You and *me* are in the objective case; they are in apposition with *men,* object of the verb *selected.*

The chairman called on three men—Goodman, Todd and *me.*

The antecedent of the appositive is *men,* object of the preposition *on.*

Mrs. Art Goering had a card party for *us* girls.

Us, a restrictive pronoun appositive, must be in the same case as the noun which it explains, *girls,* which is the object of the preposition *for.* Compare with the following sentence, which shows the correct use of the nominative form, *we.*

We girls—Amelia, Catherine, Natalie and I—were asked to serve.

4. The subject of an infinitive is always in the objective case.

The captain ordered John and *me* to hurry.

The compound subject of the infinitive is *John and me*.

They found the winners to be John and *me*.

Me is correct because *John and me* refers to *winners*, which as the subject of the infinitive is in the objective case.

They found John and *me* to be the winners.

Me is correct. The compound subject of the infinitive *to be* is *John and me*. Of course the object of an infinitive is always in the objective case, but errors often are made in writing a question, such as:

Whom (not *Who*) do you wish to appoint? (You do wish to appoint *whom?*)

CORRECT USE OF THE POSSESSIVE CASE

1. A common error on the part of journalists is the failure to use the possessive case of the noun or pronoun with the gerund.

I don't mind *your* (not *you*) asking.
The audience did not approve of the *man's* speaking first.

Note that a different meaning is given in the sentence: I did not approve of the man speaking first. Here the approval relates to the man, not to the speaking.

2. Pronouns in the possessive case do not require an apostrophe. The most common errors are in the use of *its* and *it's.* *Its* is the possessive pronoun. *It's* is the contraction of *it is.*

The cat licked *its* paws.
It's time to start for the office.

3. Take care not to confuse the possessive pronoun *whose* with the contraction *who's*, which means *who is.*

Whose car it that out front?
She's a girl *who's* always willing to help.

4. Be careful not to confuse the possessive pronoun *your* with the contraction *you're,* which means *you are.*

When *your* car arrives, we'll be ready.
If *you're* going downtown, I'll go along with you.

5. Avoid the use of possessive nouns in appositive expressions. It is better to use a prepositional phrase with *of.*

AWKWARD: The Mustang coach Hayden Fry's car was wrecked.
BETTER: The car of the Mustang coach, Hayden Fry, was wrecked.

6. Avoid such awkward expressions as the first sentence following:

AWKWARD: President Chapman's son's car was wrecked.
CORRECT: The car of President Chapman's son was wrecked.

USING REFLEXIVE AND INTENSIVE PRONOUNS

Reflexive pronouns should not be used as part of a compound subject or compound object of a verb or preposition.

WRONG: Dick and myself are going to drive home.
CORRECT: Dick and *I* are going to drive home.
WRONG: He praised Dick and myself for our work.
CORRECT: He praised Dick and *me* for our work.

When reflexive pronouns are used as appositives of subjects, they are called *intensive pronouns* and may be used correctly to give emphasis.

I *myself* will see that it is done.
He decided to do the work *himself.*

The last sentence can also be worded: He himself decided to do the work.

Of course you know that there are no such words as "hisself," "theirself," and "theirselves."

Quiz Answers

Sentences 1–7 should read as follows: 1. The dog is lying on its back, but I can't tell whether it's dead or not. 2. The dean objected strenuously to our breaking the rule. 3. Prospects of their being written into. . . 4. The two Negroes' faces looked familiar. 5. Her ladies' hats are. . . 6. This pencil is Charles' (or Charles's), not Mary's. (Newspaper and wire service stylebooks call for Charles'.) 7. The roof of the garage sloped sharply.

Correct words in sentences 8–20 are: 8. me. 9. he. 10. Who. 11. me. 12. us. 13. Who. 14. he, who. 15. his. 16. who; whom or that. 17. Whom. 18. me. 19. me. 20. me.

7
Agreement of Subjects and Predicates

Failure to recognize the grammatical principle of *agreement* results in far too many errors made by journalists. Journalism students commit this type of error almost as often as all other errors in grammar, and the error is found repeatedly in newspapers.

This chapter reviews the agreement of subject and predicate.

A verb must agree with its subject in number and person. Certain types of construction may give writers difficulty in following this rule.

Before we take a look at the most common errors in agreement of subjects and predicates, suppose you test yourself on this most important subject by taking the following quiz.

Quiz

Select the correct word in each sentence.

1. There (are, is) only one minute and twenty seconds left to play, the sportscaster reported.

2. Intramural athletics (is, are) stressed at Duquesne.

3. A number of political bigwigs (was, were) gathering at the courthouse.

4. Dr. Hal Dewlitt, city health director, stated that measles in adults (are, is) dangerous.

5. Not only the Cubs' manager but also the players (were, was) blamed for the slump.

6. The store with all its contents (were, was) damaged.

7. Among the dead (was, were) Herbert Asbell of Brooklyn, John Mooney of Toledo and Horace Apfelbaum of Dallas.

8. Where (is, are) the data you gathered?

9. About 600 Eskimos (was, were) examined.

10. Fire Marshal Lawrence said there (has, have) been three losses, none of which (have, has) exceeded $50.

11. The mayor, as well as half the councilmen, (were, was) late for the meeting.

12. Neither the twins nor Mr. Howard (intend, intends) to do a complete "fade-out."

13. The couple (was, were) arrested last night in a Milwaukee cafe.

14. This season there (is, are) Southern Cal's O. J. Simpson, Alabama's sophomore quarterback, Scott Hunter, and Purdue's fabulous Leroy Keyes who are setting a fast pace.

15. Neither the Green Wave coach nor the players (were, was) downcast.

16. There (was, were) one Dalmatian, four Toy Bostons and eight Poodles in the dog show.

17. Many a boy and girl in American universities (is, are) in need of financial assistance.

18. A constant stream of refugees (were, was) seen passing over the bridge.

19. This brand of bluejeans (are, is) in most demand today.

20. Every one of the players we have named (enjoy, enjoys) football for what it is—a great sport.

21. The depth of the drainage ditches (vary, varies) no more than a foot.

22. The heart of the newspaper (is, are) the editorials.

23. The emcee asked, "Now, (what's, what are) their names?"

24. None of the advertising agency's clients (were, was) lost.

25. None of the teachers (was, were) willing to sign contracts.

To see how well you did on this most important quiz, see the end of the chapter.

1. The *compound subject* made up of two or more parts connected by *and* requires a plural verb.

Mrs. Shelton and her son Bob *have gone* fishing.
The fishing and hunting *were* good that year.

The compound subject made up of more than two parts joined by *and* sometimes leads to an error. Also watch the agreement carefully in inverted sentences in which the subject follows the verb.

Rain, hail and wind *have caused* an estimated $22,000,000 damage to crops and livestock.
Among the injured *were* Harold Bell of Brooklyn and John Boone of Toledo and his son.

The error of using *has caused* and *was* in these two sentences might be overlooked in conversational English, but the good reporter will not use them in his writing.

When a sentence starts with the expletive *there,* remember that the expletive is *not* the subject of the verb. The subject follows the verb, and the verb must agree with the subject in number.

There *are* some neat *performers* on the squad—Alabama's Scott Hunter, Florida's fullback, Larry Smith, and South Carolina's Tommy Suggs.

The subject is *performers;* the plural verb is correct.
The following sentence is also grammatically correct.

There *are* (not *is*) Alabama's Scott Hunter, Florida's Larry Smith and South Carolina's Tommy Suggs—all neat performers.

In this sentence the names of the players are the compound subject.

When the subject that follows the verb consists of two or more nouns that are mixed in number, however, the singular verb may be used if the first subject—the noun nearest the verb—is singular.

There *was* one Dalmatian, four Toy Bostons and eight Poodles entered at the dog show.

Consult your editor or your publication's style book in regard to this usage.

There are three *exceptions* to this rule:

a) It is correct to use a singular verb with certain compound expressions that have come to be thought of as a unit.

This ice cream and cake *is* good.
Ham and eggs *is* a good breakfast.
Bread and butter *makes* a tasty snack.

b) It is correct to use a singular verb when the two nouns in the compound subject refer to the same person or thing. If two persons are meant, the verb must be plural and the article *the* should be inserted.

The secretary and treasurer *is* absent.   (One person)
The secretary and the treasurer *are* both away.   (Two persons)

c) Compound subjects modified by *each, every* and *many a* require a singular verb.

Every boy and every girl in this room *is* entitled to a copy.

The meaning is: Every boy is entitled and every girl is entitled.

Many a man and woman in this community *finds* himself in need.

Without knowing the rule, you might make two errors in this sentence by writing: Many a man and woman . . . *find them-*

selves. . . . The verb should be the singular *finds* and the reflexive pronoun should be the singular *himself.*

2. When the parts of a compound subject are joined by *or,
nor, either . . . or* or *neither . . . nor, not only . . . but also,*
the verb must agree with the subject nearest to the verb. This
is a foolproof rule to follow.

Neither the Kansas players nor the coach *was* overconfident.
Neither the Kansas coach nor the players *were* confident of victory.

3. When an affirmative expression and a negative expression
are joined to make a compound subject, the verb agrees with
the *affirmative* subject.

The *teacher,* not the students, *was* wrong.
The *students,* not the teacher, *were* wrong.

4. Collective nouns, which often give journalists "agreement
trouble," are used correctly as follows:

a) If the action of the collective noun is performed by the
group as a whole, acting as a unit, the verb is singular.

The anti-crime committee *makes* its report tomorrow.
Stewart, Burgess, Morris & George (a law firm) *has announced* a
new policy.

b) If the members of the group are reported as acting separately, the collective noun subject takes a plural verb.

The committee *have returned* to their homes.

Since the plural verb in sentences like this may sound awkward, it is often best to make the sentence read: The committee members (*or* members of the committee) have returned.

c) If the collective noun names a group of persons among
whom there has been a difference of opinion or action, the
noun requires a plural verb. This is merely another application
of rule *b* above, since the members of the group are regarded
as acting separately instead of in unison.

The jury *have failed* to agree on a verdict.

Here again it may be better to say: The members of the jury have failed.

To decide whether to use a singular verb or a plural verb in such sentences, test your subject and decide what idea it conveys. If the subject refers definitely to a number of individuals acting as a single unit, a singular verb is required. If the persons who make up the group named in the subject are acting individually, the plural verb is the correct one to use.

5. If the subject is modified by a phrase which begins with such an expression as *along with, as well as, in addition to, together with,* the verb must agree with the *simple subject,* which is not changed by the expression.

The *father* as well as his sons *is* going to enroll.
Bill, together with his sisters, *was* hurt in the accident.
The *truck* along with all its contents *was* destroyed.
The *barn,* in addition to the house, *was* burned.

Note that it is often better to set off the phrase with commas.

6. Nouns that designate an amount of money, a period of time, a unit of measure, and the like, although plural in form, are regarded as referring to a unit and take a singular verb. This is an important rule for the journalist to remember.

The treasurer thought that sixty-five dollars ($65) *was* not too much to ask.
Six months *is* too short a time, General Westmoreland warned.
Three miles *was* too long a distance for Freedman to run.
Five hours *is* needed to complete the outline.

The meaning in the last sentence is: Five hours is the time needed.

7. The verb agrees with the *true* subject, be sure to remember—not with a noun which comes between the subject and the predicate, such as a noun that is the object of a prepositional phrase which modifies the subject. Watch this construction especially in the case of *compound* subjects modified by an *of* phrase.

A *committee* of five men and three women *is* to consider the matter.
The series of three games *was* completed quickly.
The increasing rate of births in India *is* viewed with alarm.

However, when the complete subject—including a modifying *of* phrase—strongly conveys the idea of *individuals,* a plural verb should be used, even though the simple subject is singular. Study the following sentences:

An *average* of twenty-five persons *apply* each month.
An *average* of twenty-five applications a month *is* not unusual.
A *majority* of the town's younger men *are* moving to the city.
A *majority* of three votes to one *was* recorded.

8. A verb must agree in number with its subject, not with any predicate nominative used in the sentence.

The strongest unit in the Panther team *was* the tackles.

The subject is *unit,* a singular noun. The verb agrees with *unit,* not with the predicate noun *tackles.*

Long study and constant practice are the secret of Maria Callas' success as a singer.
The bellows of the bull *were* the only sound that reached his ears.

To avoid awkwardness in such sentences it is sometimes better to change the construction of the sentences, thus:

The Panther team *is* strongest at the tackle positions.

9. Certain nouns that are plural in form but singular in meaning take singular verbs.

All the *news* on the front page today *is* bad.
Mumps is contagious.
What *is* Nixon's *politics?*

Some nouns, however, may take either a singular or a plural verb, depending on the exact meaning of the word in the sentence.

Athletics (a system of training) *has transformed* him from a weakling into a star.

Intercollegiate *athletics* (all intercollegiate sports) *have been* discontinued at that university.

10. Titles of books, poems, movies and so on require a singular verb, even if the title has a plural form.

Twice Told Tales is a good book for children.

11. Such nouns as *abundance, half, part, plenty, rest* and *variety* take a singular verb or a plural verb according to the number of the noun in the *of* phrase which modifies the noun. The same rule applies to fractions used as subjects.

Plenty of apples *are* on the market now.
Two-thirds of the business district *was* destroyed.
Half of the members *are* absent today.

12. The word *number,* when modified by *the,* takes a singular verb; when modified by *a,* it takes a plural verb.

The number of students who failed *was* small.
A number of the workers *have* failed to get by the picket lines.

13. Foreign plurals require plural verbs.

The editor found that the *data were* inaccurate.

14. The nouns *all* and *most* and the pronouns *none, any* and *such* are ordinarily considered singular when they refer to quantity, but they are regarded as plural when they refer to number. A safe way is to regard them as collective nouns: If they refer to units, use a singular verb; if they refer to individuals, use a plural verb.

Most of the money *was* recovered by Deputy Player.	(Quantity)
Most of the members *were* there.	(Number)
All (of the cargo) *was* lost.	(Quantity)
All (of the crew) *were* saved.	(Number)

The pronoun *none* causes a great deal of trouble. Some authorities say that it means *no one* or *not one* and must take a singular verb. Others regard it as either singular or plural according to the meaning of the sentence. A majority of editors prefer the use of a singular verb with *none,* but there is a strong trend toward the use of a plural verb with it. The safest rule may be: Use a singular verb if *none* means *no one* or *not one;* in all other uses of *none,* you either may follow your newspaper's stylebook or determine the correct number by context, that is, according to the meaning to be conveyed.

None of the company's clients *was* lost.
None but the best *were* accepted.
None of the cars *was* (or *were*) wrecked.

You can play safe by writing: No cars were wrecked *or* Not a single car was wrecked.

15. The nouns *kind* and *sort* should be modified by the singular adjectives *this* and *that.* The plural forms *these kinds, those kinds* are correct, of course. The verb is singular after *kind* or *sort.*

This kind of sheets *is* selling well.

It is considered correct sometimes to use a singular noun in the *of* phrase after *these kinds.*

These kinds of apple are delicious.

Never say, "This kind of a . . . ." The article *a* or *an* is not needed.

16. Nouns like *breed, brand, class, group, herd, type, species* and *variety* are regarded as singular when they refer to a collection as a single unit, but plural when they refer to the individual members of a collection.

That *group* of soldiers *have* the best ratings of individual performance.

That *group* of soldiers *is* a top-notch fighting unit.
The *herd are moving* toward the sheds by twos and threes.
That *herd is* the healthiest the farm has had in some time.

17. The plural forms *kinds of* and *brands of* and so on may have a singular or a plural noun as the object of the preposition, according to the meaning to be conveyed.

Six brands of *paper* were tested.
Two kinds of *oil* were found in the area.
Six brands of *cans* were ordered.

18. In general, you should keep the same number throughout a sentence.

POOR: Buy some ordinary fishing corks, cover each one with cellophane, and attach sequins to them with short pins.
BETTER: Buy some ordinary fishing *corks,* cover *them* with cellophane . . . .

However, some sentences may use a singular noun with a plural possessive to make the meaning clear, thus:

The two pilots plunged to *their death.*
The publisher knew most of them by *their first name.*

19. The pronoun *you* always takes a plural verb.

Miss Dodge, *you are* wanted on the phone.
The teacher told the boys, *"You are early."*

20. A *gerund* used as a subject requires a singular verb.

Increasing their wages *has raised* the crew's morale.

Quiz Answers

1. is. 2. are. 3. were. 4. is. 5. were. 6. was. 7. were. 8. are. 9. were. 10. have, has. 11. was. 12. intends. 13. was. 14. are. 15. were. 16. were or was. 17. is. 18. was. 19. is. 20. enjoys. 21. varies. 22. is. 23. what are. 24. *Was* is preferred by newspaper editors but there's a strong trend toward use of the plural. 25. same as 24.

8

Using Pronouns Correctly

Journalists may find they have much "agreement" trouble in using pronouns correctly, particularly in the agreement of the subject with the predicate and in agreement with the antecedent.

In this chapter we consider the correct way to use each class of pronouns—personal pronouns, demonstrative pronouns, indefinite pronouns, distributive pronouns, interrogative pronouns and relative pronouns.

Test your knowledge of the correct use of pronouns by taking the following quiz.

Quiz

1. Each of the committeemen interviewed qualified (their, his) remarks to some extent.
2. "If you can learn to meet deadlines, it (might, may) be possible for you to hold your job," the city editor told the reporter.
3. The Dallas Cowboys won (their, its) first game of the season.
4. The Utah State team won (its, their) first game of the season.
5. The Oregon State University president spoke to the Chamber

of Commerce at (their, its) annual election banquet Friday night.

6. (Who, whom) did you think him to be?

7. The Asian flu has struck 26 persons, 11 of (which, whom) have died.

8. I thought it would be Dr. Delbert McGuire (who, whom) would be selected as journalism director.

9. McKissack is the only one of the three candidates who (have, has) conducted a hard campaign.

10. "We will nominate (whoever, whomever) you believe can make the strongest campaign," Rich declared.

11. Harlan Wetz is only one of many players on the team who (have, has) shown a top brand of sportsmanship on the gridiron this fall.

12. He declared that everybody must play (their, his) part.

13. Two nephews survive him. Neither (live, lives) in Montana.

14. The practice of setting low bail bonds is one of many evils which (tends, tend) to perpetuate (itself, themselves) under the present system.

What's wrong with the following sentences?

15. We hope that you will not be too disappointed about our failure to show up for you birthday, which we hope won't happen again.

16. Lewis told his brother that his car had been stolen.

17. Criminals pass in and out of jails as if they were equipped with revolving doors.

18. He thought it was necessary that it be given further study.

19. The future is bright for anyone, whether he is a high school graduate or a college graduate, who has the ability to better themselves.

20. To call defensive signals, the coach selected Jenkins, which the majority of the players did not like.

See end of chapter to find how well you did on this most important quiz.

PERSONAL PRONOUNS

Personal pronouns do not usually give the journalist much trouble in agreement. Study the following sections.

1. The pronoun *you,* even when singular, always takes a plural verb.

You, and only you, *are* to blame.

2. The pronouns *he, she* and *it* should not be used with *don't,* the contraction of *do not. Does* is the third person singular form of *do.*

Truman looks well, *doesn't he?*
The NLF's Mme. Nguyen Thi Binh said that *she doesn't* plan to play a secondary role to the North Vietnamese at the Paris peace talks.
"*It doesn't* hurt to try," the brash rookie declared.

3. The *reflexive pronouns* often give the journalist trouble. They are formed by adding *self* or *selves* to some of the personal pronouns. They should not be used alone as subjects or objects or as parts of a compound subject or object.

The money is for *you* (not *yourself*).
INCORRECT: My brother and myself will be there.
CORRECT: My brother and *I* will be there.
INCORRECT: Father gave the money to my sister and myself.
CORRECT: Father gave the money to my sister and *me.*

4. The reflexive pronouns may be used for emphasis, however, and are then called *intensive pronouns.*

Mayor Lindsay himself will conduct the arbitration sessions.
They expect to do the work *themselves.*

Note that the second sentence can also be written: *They themselves* expect to do the work. It is usually best to place the intensive pronoun close to the noun or pronoun it refers to. In the first sentence following it should be apparent that *itself* is misplaced:

INCORRECT: Any one of the books is a thorough treatment of the subject by *itself*.
CORRECT: Any one of the books by *itself* is . . .

Be careful not to use intensive pronouns unnecessarily. One intensive pronoun may be needed for emphasis, but the use of a second one in the sentence is often incorrect, as in this sentence:

The Saigon bureau chief himself should have interviewed President Nguyen Van Thieu and should have turned in the story himself.

The second *himself* is unnecessary.

And of course you know that there are no such words as "hisself," "theirself," or "theirselves." Use the objective forms of the personal pronouns in forming the reflexive pronouns.

DEMONSTRATIVE PRONOUNS

The *demonstrative pronouns* are *this* and *that* in the singular, and *these* and *those* in the plural. They are the pronouns that point out persons and things.

This is the book I mentioned.
That is what I meant.
These will be used rather than *those* over there.

Remember that *this, that, these* and *those* are adjectives if they are used with nouns: Those apples are winesaps.

INDEFINITE PRONOUNS

Indefinite pronouns point out indefinitely or vaguely. They may give trouble in agreement because some of them are singular, some are plural, and some may be either singular or plural.

1. The following indefinite pronouns always take a singular verb:

one	everyone	no one	anybody	another
anyone	everybody	someone	nobody	other

2. The following indefinite pronouns always take a plural verb:

both few many several

3. The following indefinite pronouns may be either singular or plural.

all some none

They are singular when they refer to a quantity. They are plural when they refer to a number. However, many editors require the use of the singular verb with *none* referring to number.

All his money *is* gone.	(Quantity)
All have arrived by now.	(Number)
None (of the money) *is* left.	(Quantity)
None (of the members) *have left* yet.	(Number)
or *None* of the members *has left*.	(Number)
Some (of the money) *is* left.	(Quantity)
Some (of the members) *are* still here.	(Number)

4. Most errors in the use of the indefinite pronouns occur when the writer fails to make a pronoun which comes later in the sentence agree in number with its indefinite pronoun antecedent.

Anyone (*Anybody*) in Des Moines may compete if *he* registers by May 15.

It would be an error to say "if they register." *He* must agree in number with its antecedent *Anyone* (or *Anybody*).

5. A common error is to use *anyone* or *anybody* when *anyone else* or *anybody else* is correct.

O. J. Simpson probably will score more touchdowns than *anyone else* (not *anyone*) this season.

6. Be careful to distinguish the difference between *anyone* and *any one*, *everyone* and *every one*, and *someone* and *some one*. Notice these sentences:

He will hire *anyone* who can type.
He will hire *any one* of the applicants who can type.
Someone must stand guard.
Some one of the soldiers must stand guard.

DISTRIBUTIVE PRONOUNS

The *distributive pronouns* are *each, either* and *neither*. They are always singular, and they are used to single out an individual from some group. Make sure that any other pronoun in the sentence is singular if its antecedent is the distributive pronoun.

Either (or *Neither*) of the two players *is* eligible.
Each of the members *was* in *his* seat when the session began.

Errors can be avoided if the adjective is used instead of the distributive pronoun, thus: *Each member* was in his seat. Another method is to use a plural subject and omit *each*, thus: *All members* were in their seats.

Don't write sentences like these:

Each of the three Minnesota quarterbacks *are* good runners, passers, and kickers.
Baylor and Arkansas *each have won* six games and lost two.

Correct:

Each of the Minnesota quarterbacks *is* a good runner, passer and kicker.
All three Minnesota quarterbacks *are* good runners, passers and kickers.
Both Baylor and Arkansas *have won* six games and lost two.
Baylor and Arkansas have won six games and lost two *each*.

It is considered good grammar to use *each other* and *either* in referring to two, and *one another* and *any one* in referring to more than two.

The two Smothers brothers admire *each other.*
All five members of the Crosby family admire *one another.*
Managing Editor Tom Simmons said he would hire *either* of the two men.
The managing editor said he would hire *any one* of the three men.

INTERROGATIVE PRONOUNS

The *interrogative pronouns* are *who—whose—whom, which* and *what.* They are either singular or plural, according to the meaning of the sentence.

Who is the nominative form, *whom* is the objective form, and *whose* is the possessive.

Whom, then, would the tax hurt? (Test it: The tax would hurt *whom?*)
Whose can that notebook be?
Do you know to *whom* it belongs?
Who is going with the reporter to get pix of the crash?

RELATIVE PRONOUNS

The common *relative pronouns* are *who—whom—whose, which, what* and *that. Who* and *whom* refer to persons; *whose* refers to persons and animals; *which* refers to animals and things. *That* may refer to persons, things or animals and is now usually used in restrictive clauses only. The good writer will guard against overuse of *that* as a relative pronoun.

Relative pronouns, especially *who* and *whom,* probably cause writers more sentence trouble than all the other kinds of pronouns put together. There are good reasons for this. First, a relative pronoun is one that has the power to make one sentence out of two; in other words, the relative pronoun introduces a subordinate idea, which increases the chance for errors.

Second, the relative pronoun performs a double function. It is a pronoun in the clause within which it stands, and it is a connective word that joins its own clause to an antecedent within the independent clause. Third, relative pronouns assume different forms to convey different meanings, thus leading to more confusion.

To prepare yourself to avoid incorrect usage of relative pronouns, study carefully the main points to be remembered about relative pronouns.

1. A relative pronoun introduces a *subordinate clause*—called also a *relative clause*—which is generally used adjectivally.

Henry Wade is the candidate *who will win.*
Most Republicans did not know the man *that Nixon named as communications director.*
The non-fiction *which Ramparts publishes* is largely controversial.

2. The word the relative pronoun refers to is outside the subordinate clause and usually immediately precedes the clause. It is called the *antecedent* of the pronoun. In the three sentences above, the antecedents of *who, that* and *which* are *candidate, man* and *non-fiction,* respectively. The relative clauses are used adjectivally to modify their respective antecedents.

3. The relative pronoun may be subject, object or predicate nominative in the clause in which it occurs.

Ask for the man *who directs the company's public relations.*
Is this the person *whom you want?*
I don't know *who he is.*

Who is the subject of the verb *directs* in the first sentence. *Whom* is the object of *want* in the second sentence. *Who* is a predicate nominative in the clause *who he is.* The normal order of the clause would be *he is who?*

4. The use of the relative pronoun *within its clause*—the subordinate clause—determines its case. A relative pronoun does agree with its antecedent in person, number and gender —but does not agree in case. Failure to recognize this principle results in many errors in using *who* and *whom*. Study these examples:

a) He is the player *who probably will play shortstop.*
b) He is the player *who was bought early in the season.*
c) He is the player *whom the Yanks bought this spring.*
d) Is he the player *for whom they paid a bonus?*
e) The manager already knows *who his best pitcher is.*

Note the use of the nominative *who* within the italicized relative clauses in (*a*), (*b*) and (*e*). In (*a*) *who* is the subject of *will play.* In (*b*) *who* is the subject of *was bought.* Many writers would mistakenly use *whom* in this sentence, thinking that since the subject is acted upon, the objective form is called for. But remember that *was bought* is a transitive passive verb, which means that the subject—not an object—receives the action. Therefore, *who* is correct. In (*e*) *who* is a predicate nominative. This is easily seen by revising the clause thus: . . . his best *pitcher* is *who.*

Note that the objective *whom* is correct in (*c*) and (*d*) because it is the object of the verb *bought* in (*c*) and the object of the preposition *for* in (*d*). To see this clearly, revise the order of the clauses: the Yanks *bought whom* this spring . . . ; they paid a bonus *for whom.* . . .

Note in (*e*) that there is no specific word in the independent clause to which the pronoun *who* may refer. In other words, there is no antecedent. In such constructions as this the pronoun often is called an *indefinite* relative pronoun, and the subordinate clause is regarded as a noun clause rather than as an adjectival clause. In (*e*) *who his best pitcher is* becomes the direct object of the verb *knows* in the independent clause. It answers the question: The manager knows what?

Analyze one more example: Sheriff White shot his deputy, *whom* he mistook for a burglar. Here *whom* introduces a non-restrictive relative clause that is set off by a comma. The clause is used adjectivally to modify *deputy,* a direct object in the independent clause. However, the objective form *whom* is not used because its antecedent is an object, but because it is the object of the verb *mistook* within the relative clause. Test it: He *mistook whom* for the burglar.

5. The relative pronoun *whose* and the contraction *who's*—for *who is*—should not be confused.

He's the man *whose* daughter is missing.

Whose introduces the subordinate clause *whose daughter is missing,* shows possession of *daughter,* and has the antecedent *man* in the independent clause.

AGREEMENT OF PRONOUN WITH ANTECEDENT

A pronoun agrees with its antecedent in number, person and gender. Its case, however, depends on the use of the pronoun in the clause or phrase in which it occurs. The *antecedent* of the pronoun is the word to which it refers.

Several constructions need to be watched closely to avoid errors in agreement of pronouns with antecedents, and in agreement in number of a relative pronoun with its verb.

1. Prepositional phrases which come between the pronoun and its antecedent often cause "false agreement" trouble.

Keyes is the only *one* of the players *who has* learned all the plays.

The antecedent of *who* is not *players* but *one,* which is definitely a singular pronoun here. Note that it is modified by *the only* (one). Therefore the singular verb *has* is correct.

Keyes is one of the few *players who have* learned all the plays.

Here the antecedent of *who* is *players,* a plural noun.

Walter Humphrey is one of those editors *who* always *take* (not takes) a leading role in *their* (not *his*) community.

In this sentence two errors in agreement, instead of one, could have been made. The antecedent of *who* is not *one,* but *editors* in the prepositional phrase. Therefore the plural verb *take* and the plural possessive pronoun *their* are correct.

2. The reflexive pronoun used after a relative pronoun must agree with the antecedent.

Dictatorship is one of the many *evils which* tend (*not* tends) to perpetuate *themselves.*

The antecedent of both *which* and *themselves* is *evils;* therefore both *which* and *themselves* are plural.

Note that if *the* is used before *one* in a sentence like the following, *one,* which is a noun here, becomes the *antecedent* of the relative and reflexive pronouns that follow; so, the pronouns are singular.

Selfishness is *the one* of her many faults *which* defeats *itself.*

3. When the pronouns *anyone, everyone, everybody, no one, nobody,* etc., are used as antecedents, the pronouns referring to them must be singular.

On the Boy Scout hike *everybody* was told by the scoutmaster to bring *his* own drinking water.
"Does *anyone* think *he* may be unable to attend?" the mayor asked.

4. Similarly, pronouns referring to *either* and *neither* are singular.

Neither of the women has brought *her* certificate.

5. A pronoun referring to a plural noun and a singular noun connected by *or* or *nor* sounds better in the plural form.

Neither the members of the cabinet nor the President will reveal *their* plans.

The plural possessive is preferred because the plans are being made by all the persons mentioned.

The rule for the agreement in number of the verb with the subject is followed for the possessive pronouns in other cases of reference to an antecedent. If the antecedent is composed of two singular nouns connected by *either . . . or* or *neither . . . nor,* the pronoun is singular. If the two nouns are plural, the pronoun is plural.

Either John or James, who are twins, has left *his* sweater.
Neither the twins nor their cousins have finished *their* courses.

6. If the antecedent of the pronoun may be either masculine or feminine in gender, the masculine pronoun is used. If the antecedent is a compound of a masculine and a feminine noun, it is considered correct to use a masculine pronoun.

Everyone is asked to do *his* part.
Every man and woman is asked to contribute *his* share.

In some cases, both the masculine and the feminine pronoun may strictly be required, as in the following sentence:

Every boy and every girl is called upon to do *his or her* part.

Such constructions should be avoided by the use of plural nouns:

All boys and girls are called on to do *their* part.

7. If the antecedent is a collective noun, the pronoun is singular if the noun refers to a unit, but it is plural if the noun refers to the individuals making up the collection.

The Ohio State *team* won *its* 1968 opener against SMU.   (Unit)
The defeated *team* hung *their* heads.   (Individuals)

8. Special care must be used when reflexive pronouns are used. The relative pronoun or personal pronoun and the reflexive pronoun must agree with the antecedent in number.

No editor should do for his *staff* what *they* can do for *themselves.*

Since the collective noun *staff* is considered as made up of individuals, the plural pronouns *they* and *themselves* are correct.

9. A personal pronoun is used correctly to refer to the antecedent *one*. Repetition of *one* now sounds stilted.

If *one* considers the plan carefully, *he* will find many flaws in it.

10. The antecedent of a pronoun must be made clear by the agreement of the pronoun with the antecedent. In the following sentences, for example, there is no clear antecedent of *This:*

POOR: Removal of the tax surcharge, lower social security payments and a drastic cut in federal funds for education are the issues. *This* is the platform of the new party.

The sentences can be combined to omit *This* in a better construction.

BETTER: Removal of the tax surcharge . . . and a drastic cut in federal funds for education all *are planks* in the platform of the new party.

11. When successive pronouns refer to the same antecedent in the sentence, the pronouns must all have the same gender.

The dog scratched *his* ear, shook *himself* and fell over on *his* back.

Do not say "fell over on *its* back" after using *his* and *himself* to refer to *dog*.

CONSTRUCTIONS TO BE WATCHED

In using pronouns, especially relative pronouns, there are some constructions which must be watched closely to avoid making errors.

1. Parenthetical clauses which come between the pronoun and its verb do not affect the case of the pronoun. Such confusing expressions or thrown-in statements, which may or may not be set off by commas, are: *they believe, they thought, it is believed, it is thought, he says,* etc.

The child who (not *whom*) *we thought* was lost was found in the next block.

We thought is a parenthetical phrase and has no effect on the construction of the clause *who was lost*. *Who* is the subject of the verb *was* in the dependent (relative) clause.

The woman *who* (not *whom*) *police believed took the jewels* was cleared.

The main clause is *The woman was cleared*. Note that the parenthetical expression *police believed* in the subordinate clause does not affect the case of *who*. *Who* is the subject of the verb *took*.

Note two more examples of this kind:

They will bring from Israel the one witness *who* (not *whom*) *the district attorney says* can give incriminating evidence. (*Who* is the subject of *can give*.)

The youth *who* (not *whom*) *they said* was the most advanced in the group did prove to be the leader. (*Who* is the subject of *was*.)

2. The case of the relative pronoun depends on its use in the subordinate clause, as you have seen. Note these sentences also:

The man *whom they arrested* confessed to the crime.

Whom is the object of the predicate *arrested* in the subordinate (relative) clause. Test it: They (subject) arrested *whom?*

That is a man *who may be president of the company some day*.

Who is the subject of the verb *may be* in the dependent clause.

I don't know *who it will be*.

Who is a predicate nominative after *will be*. (It will be who?)

He promised to support *whoever* (not *whomever*) *of the Republican prospects was chosen*.

Whoever is the subject of *was chosen.* In this construction the entire relative clause, not just the pronoun alone, is the object of the infinitive *to support* in the independent clause.

3. Some of the most glaring errors appearing in newspapers and magazines result from a careless misplacing of the relative clause. The relative clause should be placed near the word it modifies. Or, if possible, change the clause to a word or phrase.

WRONG: The boy held a doughnut in his hand which was coated with chocolate.

CORRECT: The boy held in his hand a doughnut which was coated with chocolate.

In his hand the boy held a chocolate-coated doughnut.

WRONG: Sylvia was given the four-poster bed with the canopy which had belonged to her aunt.

CORRECT: Sylvia was given her aunt's four-poster bed with the canopy.

WRONG: He showed the silver dollars to his friends which he found lying on the floor.

CORRECT: He showed his friends the silver dollars which he had found on the floor.

4. Be sure that pronouns like *he* and *it* do refer to a specific word—a clearly recognizable antecedent. Failure of a writer to keep his pronouns referring to the same person or thing throughout a sentence may lead to misunderstanding.

UNCLEAR: The governor promised Tompkins that he would hold his job if he won.

CORRECT: The governor promised Tompkins that he would hold his job if the governor won.

UNCLEAR: Cabbage contains this vitamin, and it is essential to sound teeth. (Does *it* refer to cabbage or vitamin?)

CORRECT: Cabbages contain this vitamin, and it is essential to sound teeth.

BETTER: Cabbage contains this vitamin, which is essential to sound teeth.

5. Change an indirect quotation to a direct quotation if that will make the statement clearer and avoid the use of several pronouns.

The governor promised Tompkins that he would hold his job if he should win again.

Governor Black told Tompkins yesterday, "You will keep your job if I win."

6. A pronoun should refer to the substantive which is central or uppermost in the writer's mind.

INCORRECT: The senator's *theory* of politics on the local level is interesting, and many citizens agree with *him*.

CORRECT: The senator's *theory* of politics on the local level is interesting, and many citizens agree with *it*.

The *theory* is the thing with which the citizens agree, not the *senator*. An even better way to express this would be to use two sentences.

BETTER: The senator's theory of politics is interesting. Many citizens agree with it.

Be sure to see that the pronoun *it* has a clearly recognized antecedent. Avoid writing sentences like those below.

Mr. and Mrs. Perkins have been generous contributors, and they will be recognized for *it*.

The girls will dance for the veterans; *it* will cheer them up.

The sentences could be recast as follows: Mr. and Mrs. Perkins have been generous contributors, and they will be recognized for their generosity. To cheer up the veterans, the girls will dance for them.

7. The antecedent of the pronoun should not be a possessive. In number 6 above, the first illustration given is incorrect for the wrong reference of *him* to *senator's*, as well as for reference to the wrong noun.

8. The indefinite use of the pronoun *they* can cause trouble.

POOR: Down in Texas they are noted for the telling of tall tales.

BETTER: Down in Texas the citizens are noted for the telling of tall tales.

Texans are noted for telling tall tales.

POOR: They say that it may be a hard winter.

BETTER: The prediction is that the winter will be a hard one.

The papers predict a hard winter.

If you use *they* in a sentence, ask youself, "Who are *they?*" If the meaning is not clear, rewrite the sentence.

9. Don't use *it* in such phrases as "It says in the paper. . . ." Revise the sentence to leave out the phrase.

POOR: It says here that the troops will be home by Christmas.

BETTER: The troops will be home by Christmas, according to to-day's newspaper.

10. The expletive *it* and the pronoun *it* should not be used in the same sentence.

POOR: It is best to keep the soap on hand for a few weeks so that it will shrink slightly before it is used for sculpturing.

BETTER: If possible, keep the soap on hand. . . .

11. Do not use a pronoun with a double reference, that is, reference to more than one antecedent in the same sentence.

INCORRECT: Beth telephoned Helen that *she* would be on the committee.

CORRECT: Beth telephoned Helen, "You will be on the committee." Beth telephoned Helen, "I will be on the committee."

Beth telephoned Helen that she, Helen, would be on the committee.

INCORRECT: He sent for Pollard and told him that when Edwards was added to the staff, *he* would serve as chief agent.

CORRECT: He sent for Pollard and told him that . . . Pollard would serve as chief agent (*or* Edwards would serve). . . .

12. Do not fail to have an antecedent for any pronoun you use.

INCORRECT: It was Amateur Night, and the program was presented by them.

CORRECT: Amateurs presented the entire program on Amateur Night.

In the first sentence, there is no antecedent for the pronoun *them.*

INCORRECT: Dr. Casey has visited these areas in Africa and knows what their customs are.

CORRECT: Dr. Casey has visited these areas in Africa and knows what the customs of the natives are.

In the first sentence *their* apparently refers to *areas,* but areas do not have customs.

    13. Construct sentences so that *which* and *that* will have definite antecedents to refer to.

POOR: Burkett was given the leading role in the play, which the other members of the cast did not like.

Which does not refer to the nearest noun *play,* or to *role* or to *Burkett.* It is best to completely recast such sentences, as shown below.

Selection of Burkett as the leading man in the play displeased the rest of the cast.

Burkett's being given the leading role displeased the rest of the cast.

The cast was displeased when Burkett was given the leading male role.

    14. Do not use the pronoun *them* as an adjective. The correct adjective is *these* or *those.*

Did Jack Taylor draw *those* (not *them*) cartoons?
No, but he drew *these* comic strips.

    But *them* is used correctly as a pronoun in the following sentence:

Jack Patton drew *them.*

15. Do not use a coordinate conjunction before a relative pronoun unless a similar pronoun is used earlier in the sentence.

INCORRECT: Sutton, a squad member for three years, keeps training rules and practices hard but who simply does not have the knack for playing the game well.

CORRECT: Sutton, who has been a squad member for three years and who keeps training rules and practices hard, simply does not have the knack for playing the game well.

Sutton has been a squad member for three years, and he keeps training rules and practices hard; but he simply does not have the knack for playing well.

16. Be consistent in the use of the person of the pronouns throughout the sentence.

If *any student* turns in *his* assignments late, *he* (not *they* or *you*) will get poor grades.

If *any students* turn in *their* assignments late, *they* will get poor grades.

17. Subjects, predicate nominatives, appositives, etc., should be consistent throughout the sentence.

POOR: Because *he* arrived early, *it* was easy for him to get the interview with the general.

CORRECT: Because *he* arrived early, *he* found it easy to get the interview with the general.

The subject *he* in the dependent clause and the expletive *it* in the independent clause of the first sentence are not consistent. It would be still better in the revision, also, to avoid the use of *it* by saying *he easily got the interview.*

POOR: Shuford is now a full professor, a rank which he has worked hard to obtain.

CORRECT: Shuford now holds a full professorship, a rank . . .

Rank, as an appositive, is incorrect in referring to *full professor.*

Quiz Answers

In sentences 1–14 the correct words are: 1. his. 2. may. 3. their. 4. its. 5. its. 6. Whom. 7. whom. 8. who. 9. has. 10. whoever. 11. have. 12. his. 13. lives. 14. tend, themselves. Correct sentences 15–20 as follows: 15. Make a sentence out of the misplaced phrase, to read something like this: We hope we won't ever miss another of your birthday parties. 16. Lewis told his brother, "Your (or My) car has been stolen." 17. Criminals pass in and out of jails as if the jails were equipped. . . 18. He thought it was necessary that the plan be given further study. 19. The future is bright for. . . who has the ability to better himself. 20. To call defensive signals, the coach selected Jenkins. The majority of the players did not like the coach's choice.

9

Using Verbs and Verbals Correctly

This is a "round-up" chapter with three main purposes: (1) to treat in more detail certain verb usages which have been called to your attention in previous chapters; (2) to present uses of verbs and verbals not already covered; (3) to provide further drill on correct verb usage.

In the quiz that follows, you may test yourself on the correct usage of verbs and verbals. Included in the quiz are examples of unnecessary splitting of verb phrases and infinitive phrases; incorrect use of mood; incorrect use of tense; and incorrect usage of future tense verbs such as *shall* and *will* and of other auxiliary verbs such as *may* and *can*. You may find some sentences to be correct.

Quiz

1. The mayor attempted without any fanfare to get the facts.
2. Johnson reiterated that the opposition would early in the campaign attempt to disprove all six charges.
3. He had never been able to find a discrepancy in Stinson's books.

4. You should read many books on feature writing, study the markets and then you ought to write, write, write.

5. We expected to have seen you at the Drake-Minnesota game.

6. They handed the new man a camera, showed him how to operate it, and he started down Main Street snapping pictures.

7. Until enlightened in today's session, Commissioner Jercks was displaying muddled thinking on the use of the new voting machines.

8. George Washington was said to be the originator of the first cherry pie.

9. Gradually Craig Morton learned to more skillfully conceal the ball, to feint with great deceptiveness and passing accurately to either left or right.

10. Lindbergh's solo flight across the Atlantic probably was the most dramatic performance in aviation history.

11. Mayor Johnson says he shall open the meeting promptly at 7:30 p.m.

12. Humphrey flies to California tomorrow.

13. Griffin asked Jercks, "Shall you resign if the plan fails to pass?" Jercks replied, "I shall not resign, come hell or high water.

14. If Griffin can slightly revise the plans for a municipal center and could persuade James and Peterson to reverse their stand, he can be in position to get the board's approval.

15. Miss Chadwick told the reporters, "I can swim the English channel in record time." A majority of the reporters agreed that she may do it.

Turn to the end of this chapter to see how well you did with this important quiz.

VERB PHRASES

Most newspaper editors frown upon the practice of needlessly separating the parts of the verb phrase. Adverbs and phrases used adverbially are sometimes placed between the words that make up the predicate for the sake of smoothness, but ordinarily these adverbs could have other positions in the sentence.

No editor can object to the use of the adverb *not* when it separates the words of the predicate.

The weatherman does *not* see any signs of rain for tomorrow.

It would be impossible to place *not* in any other place than between *does* and *see*.

Most editors do not object to splitting the predicate with the adverb *never*.

Coach Schwartzwalder had *never* anticipated having three star quarterbacks in one season.

Not many editors would prefer to have the sentence read: *never had anticipated*.

Most grammarians today say that the normal place for the adverb is between the auxiliary verb and the rest of the compound verb or after the first auxiliary verb if there are two auxiliaries.

The session was *needlessly* prolonged.
The delegation must *definitely* be pledged to support our man.

But the use of an adverbial phrase or a prepositional phrase or a subordinate clause to split the predicate is condemned by most editors.

INCORRECT: He predicted that the Lions would in the first quarter score two touchdowns.
   He predicted that the Lions would before the first quarter ended score two touchdowns.
CORRECT: He predicted that the Lions would score two touchdowns *in the first quarter*.
   Or: . . . before the first quarter ended.

Both the prepositional phrase and the subordinate clause can be placed correctly at the end of the sentence, and the sentence reads more easily then.

Variety in expression is important in journalistic writing, but readability is even more desirable. The position of the phrase or clause may be changed to the first part of the sentence, but in general it is best to keep the adverbial modifier close to the predicate.

Before the first quarter ends, he predicts, the Lions will score two touchdowns.

INFINITIVES

Newspaper tradition is strong against the splitting of the infinitive. However, as H. W. Fowler points out in his *Dictionary of Modern English,* example after example of the split infinitive may be found today in newspapers of high repute. Note these examples:

It will be found possible to considerably improve the miners' working conditions, the commissioner believes.
He seems to still be allowed to speak at Black Panther meetings.

The use of a single adverb to separate the infinitive, as in the examples above, may get by the copy editor, and a certain amount of emphasis is obtained by it; but most American editors would blue-pencil such constructions as *to carefully use* and *to soon return.*

Splitting the infinitive with several words or phrases is inexcusable.

INCORRECT: He will attempt to within the course of this year's campaign cover all 50 states.

The infinitive *to cover* should be kept intact.

CORRECT: Within the course of this year's campaign, he will attempt to cover all 50 states.

The safe rule to follow is to split the infinitive only if this makes the meaning clearer and keeps your writing from sounding artificial and awkward.

Summer internships are provided *to better equip* students for newspaper work.

It sounds artificial to say: *to equip students better. . . .*

In the following sentence the split infinitive is objectionable because it sounds awkward.

The city manager urged the council *to immediately enact* the zoning ordinance.

The adverb *immediately* fits easily at the end of the sentence.

CORRECT USE OF MOOD

The verbs in a sentence should not shift from one mood to the other.

POOR: The police captain told the youth, "Just sit there for an hour and think of the worry you have caused your parents; then you ought to think about mending your ways."

The verb *sit* is imperative; the verb *ought* followed by the infinitive *to think* is in the indicative mood.

CORRECT: The police captain told the youth, "Just *sit* there for an hour and *think* of the worry you have caused your parents; then *think* about mending your ways."

CORRECT USE OF TENSE

The verbs in a sentence should all be in the same tense unless there is some good reason for their differing.

1. The general rule is that the tense of the predicate verb in the independent clause determines the tense of the predicate verb in the dependent clause. Very often the tense is the same in both clauses, as in the following correct sentences.

Her friends *came* to comfort her when they *heard* of her misfortune.
Her friends *had come* to comfort her after they *had heard* of her misfortune.

The opposition *would react* vehemently if we *should change* our tactics without warning.

Had it not *been* for their foul tactics, we *would have had* a tighter contest.

2. Unless you are quoting someone who is deficient in grammar, avoid the use of the present tense to express past actions.

INCORRECT: He raced fifteen yards to his left, then stops dead in his tracks.

Kaline makes a difficult one-handed catch and then threw cleanly to home plate to catch Brock.

The verbs *stops* and *makes* should be past tense to agree with *raced* and *threw*.

CORRECT: He *raced* fifteen yards to his left, then *stopped* dead in his tracks.

Kaline *made* a difficult one-handed catch and then *threw* cleanly to home plate to catch Brock.

3. The present tense may be used occasionally to refer to future action. Most editors would advise using the future tense in such cases, however.

Humphrey *flies* (*will fly*) to California tomorrow.

This use is called the *historical present tense* and its use in newspaper headlines is standard practice.

4. Many journalism students puzzle over whether to use the present-tense form *is said, is reported,* etc., or the past-tense form *was said, was reported,* etc., in writing about past action. Most editors consider the present-tense form correct.

Yesterday the governor *is reported* to have told Californians . . .

The Secretary of the Interior left the train at Chicago, it *is said*.

5. It is also correct to use the present tense in referring to a universal truth or a permanent fact, that is, within a dependent clause.

He reminded his audience that slums *breed* (not *bred*) criminals.

He recalled that the two countries *are* not in the same hemisphere.

However, there is a strong trend toward using the past tense form in a dependent clause following the use of the past tense in the independent clause.

The lost girl told police that she *lived* in South Evanston.
Their experiments proved that yellow fever *was* transmitted by the bite of a mosquito.

Be sure, however, to use the past tense in the independent clause in referring to a universal truth.

Pasteur's discovery *was* (not *is*) of great economic value.

6. There is some controversy over the tense to be used in direct quotations and indirect quotations, but in general the following rule is accepted.

In an indirect quotation that follows a verb in the past tense, keep the present tense in the subordinate clause unless the past tense was used in the original quotation. In other words, retain the tense used in the original quotation in the indirect quotation.

The senator declared that the fear of Communists *is* a real fear.

However, many journalists use the past tense in both clauses: The senator declared that the fear of Communists *was* a real fear.

7. Many errors are made in using the perfect tenses. Recall the forms of the perfect tenses in the active and passive voice, and of the progressive forms of the verbs.

PRESENT PERFECT

Active	*Passive*
I have beaten	I have been beaten
you have beaten	you have been beaten
he, she, it has beaten	he, she, it has been beaten
we have beaten	we have been beaten
you have beaten	you have been beaten
they have beaten	they have been beaten

PAST PERFECT

I had beaten, etc.   I had been beaten, etc.

FUTURE PERFECT

Active	*Passive*
I shall have beaten	I shall have been beaten
you will have beaten	you will have been beaten
he, she, it will have beaten	he, she, it will have been beaten
we shall have beaten	we shall have been beaten
you will have beaten	you will have been beaten
they will have beaten	they will have been beaten

PROGRESSIVE FORMS

I am beating, I had been beating, I shall have been beating.

a) The *future perfect tense* must be used to indicate an action that will have been completed before some expressed time in the future.

By next year he *will have been* with the company twenty-five years.

Will be would be incorrect in this sentence. Avoid incorrect use of the future tense for the future perfect.

b) The *present perfect tense,* not the past tense, is used to refer to action that began at some indefinite time in the past and is continuing in the present; or to refer to some action that has been completed when the statement is made; or to refer to actions that happen frequently or continuously.

Up to now, he *has been floundering* (not *was floundering*) for a solution.
In his first month on the newspaper he *has learned* to turn out good copy.
The team *has been playing* well all season.

c) The *past perfect tense* refers to some action completed before the past time of the verb in the other clause.

He *had married* (not *married*) Irene before he got his inheritance.
After the deputy *had warned* the prisoner, he locked him in.

Because he *had turned* (not *turned*) in the story late, it missed the first edition.

You will note that in these sentences the past perfect refers to action definitely completed in the past, and that this past time preceded the other past event mentioned in the sentence.

You will not make errors in using verbs if you strive to be consistent in the use of tenses. Always remember to avoid needless shifting from one tense to another.

8. The *infinitive* used after a verb in the past or past perfect tense very often causes trouble unnecessarily when the writer tries to force the infinitive into the past tense. The infinitive is usually present tense.

The president intended *to present* the matter earlier.

The president intended to do what? He intended *to present* the matter. It would be incorrect to say "to have presented."

He would have liked *to obtain* a negative vote on the question.

It is especially necessary to watch this construction after *like* or a similar verb. The infinitive *to obtain* is correct after *would have liked*.

9. The *present perfect infinitive* is used, however, if the action was completed at the time indicated by the predicate.

Benjamin Harris is said *to have been* one of the most militant editors in the history of the press.
That book was said *to have been published* in the eighteenth century.

10. Participles also give trouble sometimes.
The *present participle* is used when the action it refers to has the same time as the main verb in the sentence.

Being first in line, he *is* entitled to a complimentary ticket.

The *past participle* is used when it refers to action that came before the time of the main verb in the sentence.

Having been (not *Being*) first in line, he *was given* a free ticket.

Check particularly the tense of a participle that follows a verb. In the following sentence, the main verb is in the present tense, but the action of the participle occurred before that time; therefore the past participle is used.

This *is* his most prized cup, *having been given* (not *being given*) him for winning the National Open Tournament.

11. Watch closely the tenses of compound verb phrases and of verbs used in compound and complex sentences. If the principal verb changes its spelling in its use later in the sentence, it must be repeated, not left to be understood.

Since her youth she always *has sung* and always *will sing* (not *will*) in the Lakeside Baptist Church.

Sing must be given after *will,* since this future tense form differs in spelling from *sung* in *has sung,* which is in the perfect tense.

12. When two or more predicates in the sentences have different tenses, the subject must be repeated with each verb.

He installed the split-T system at the university in 1949; *he has used* it every year since; and *he* probably *will continue* to use it this year.

13. Predicates used in clauses of equal rank, as in two or more independent clauses or in two or more dependent clauses, should agree in tense and in every other possible way. The predicates should have the same subjects unless retaining the same subject is impossible or extremely awkward. This is called using parallel construction. The following sentences illustrate parallel construction:

Namath *fakes* the ball well and *he passes* (not *is passing*) superbly. If *he can perfect* his left jab and *can put* (not *could put*) on more weight, *he may go* on to take the championship.

Awkward errors may result from failure to keep parallel construction, especially when equivalent clauses are joined by the coordinate conjunctions *and, but* or *or* in compound sentences.

AWKWARD: Quarterback Bobby Douglass sidestepped the charging tackle, and the ball *was snapped* to wingback John Jackson.

CORRECT: Quarterback Bobby Douglass sidestepped the charging tackle and *snapped* the ball to wingback John Jackson.

The awkward compound sentence above has been converted into a simple sentence with a compound predicate.

AWKWARD: Burgin *committed* two goal-line fumbles, but they *could not score*.

CORRECT: Burgin *committed* two goal-line fumbles, but the opposition *failed* to make a touchdown.

Note also that parallel construction forbids mixing of infinitives and participles or gerunds as equivalents within the same complete predicate.

WRONG: He tried *charging* the line fast and *to get* through the guard and tackle.

CORRECT: He tried *charging* the line fast and *getting* through the guard and tackle.

Or: He tried *to charge* . . . and *to get* through. . . .

SHALL AND WILL

Journalists now tend to disregard the distinctions which grammarians have made between *shall* and *will*.

Rudolf Flesch would have us abandon all rules for using *shall* and *will*. *Will* for the future tense is now standard, Flesch declares.

Roy H. Copperud, in *A Dictionary of Usage and Style*, states, "*Shall* and *should* have taken on a flossy overtone . . . and seem well on the way to extinction."

Yet Theodore M. Bernstein in *The Careful Writer* quotes Winston Churchill's defiant declaration of June, 1940, as a superb example of using *shall*, rather than *will*, to express determination: "We shall not flag or fail. We shall go on to the end. We shall fight in France, we shall fight on the seas and oceans, . . ."

Since many editors still feel that the more obvious distinctions should be made in using *shall* and *will* in the future tense, you will do well to familiarize yourself with the following simple rules.

1. Simple futurity or mere expectation is expressed by using *shall* with the first person—both singular and plural—and *will* with the second and third persons.

I shall attend if *you will go* with me.
We shall fly if *you will make* the reservations.
I doubt that *we shall* ever *succeed.*

2. The order is reversed to express determination, resolution, emphatic assurance, command, promise, obligation and the like. Use *will* with the first person and *shall* with the second and third persons. This type of construction is found in imperative sentences especially.

I will reach shore or die in the attempt.   (Determination)
You shall sing tonight or you will not be paid.   (Command)

3. In interrogative sentences the form that is expected in the answer is the correct one to use.

Shall we go?	We shall (not) go.
Will you pass math?	I am sure I will.
Will they arrive on time?	They probably will.
Shall he remain in jail, Judge?	He certainly shall (remain).

In the use of informal, colloquial English, as on radio or television, there appears to be no distinction any longer between *shall* and *will* or *should* and *would*.

SHOULD AND WOULD

Since *shall* seems well on the way to extinction, it is no longer necessary to differentiate between *should* and *would*.

Should is generally used now in the sense of *ought to.*

We *should* adopt the resolution or resign from the board.

CAN AND COULD

Present tense *can* and past tense *could* ordinarily express ability, power, and so on.

Bob Gibson *can* (or Walter Johnson *could*) throw the fastest ball in the majors.
He *can* fire you, remember. He said he *could* fire you.

MAY AND MIGHT

Present tense *may* and past tense *might* express permission or possibility. Don't misuse *can* for *may.*

May I take this assignment? You *may* (not *can*).
The instructor told the pupils that they *might* (not *could*) leave.
It is possible that I *may* be able to join you in London.

MUST AND OUGHT

The auxiliary verb *must* is used in the present tense to express obligation, necessity, etc.

The message *must* (not *should*) be delivered by seven o'clock.
Soldiers *must* obey the orders of their commanders.

The auxiliary verb ought is sometimes used to express duty or responsibility in the present tense. It is a stronger form than *should.*

You *ought* to keep an accurate set of books.
Gordon McLendon ought to run for Congress.

MISCELLANEOUS USES

1. As you have seen, the auxiliaries *shall, will, may* and *can* ordinarily are used in the subordinate clause if the governing verb in the independent clause is in the present tense. The auxiliaries *should, would, might* and *could* are used if the gov-

erning verb is in the past tense. However, *would* may now be used in place of *should*. Observe the following examples:

The captain *tells* us that we *may get* a ten-day leave.
The captain *told* us that we *might get* a ten-day leave.
The captain *told* us that we *would* get a ten-day leave.
The chairman *said* (that) he *would call* (not *will call*) a special
meeting Tuesday to consider the petition.
If Detroit *had* not *committed* four errors, the Tigers *might have
won* the game.
If Detroit *had* not *committed* four errors, the Tigers probably *would
have won* the game. (The auxiliary *would* has largely replaced
should, but either *should* or *would* is correct here.)

After a verb in the present perfect tense in an independent clause, *may* should be used in the dependent clause. After a verb in the past perfect, *might* is correct.

The captain *has said* that we *may take* a ten-day leave.
The captain *had said* that we *might take* a ten-day leave.

2. The auxiliary verb *do* is used in what is called the *emphatic form* of the verb. *Do, does* and *did* add emphasis to the main verb.

He *does intend* to come, doesn't he?
I *did do* the exercise, I tell you.
They really *did mean* what they said.

Do, does and *did* may be used in place of the main verb, as in this sentence:

They know that Jenks stole the money, although he maintains that
he *didn't* (steal it).

3. Keep in mind the fact that *has* and *have* are used as main verbs as well as auxiliary verbs.

The company *has* (*has obtained*) a franchise.

Avoid using *has* or *have* with *got.*

I *have* (not *have got*) two classes tomorrow.

Below, *has* is an auxiliary in the present perfect tense. Also, the use of *has got* is more emphatic.

The FBI *has* finally *got* Public Enemy No. 1.

Quiz Answers

1. Place *without any fanfare* either first or last in sentence. 2. Place *early in the campaign* last. 3. Correct. 4. Delete *you ought to.* 5. We expected to see you. . . 6. They handed the new man . . . and started him down. . . 7. Change *was displaying* to *had been displaying*. 8. George Washington is said to have been the originator. . . 9. Gradually Craig Morton learned to conceal the ball more skillfully, to feint with great deceptiveness and to pass accurately. . . 10. Correct; *was,* not *is,* in the independent clause. 11. Change *shall* to *will*. 12. Humphrey will fly. . . 13. Change first *shall* to *will;* second *shall* is now considered correct, although old rule says *will* in first persons is correct to express determination. 14. Change *could* to *can* and the final *can* to *may*. 15. Change *may* to *could* or *can* or *might*.

10

Using Adjectives and Adverbs Correctly

To put flesh on the skeleton, the framework of the sentence, the writer uses modifiers. Human skeletons look pretty much alike. But, except for identical twins, all persons look different. It is the flesh added to the skeleton which makes it possible to distinguish one human being from another. Just as flesh added to the skeleton gives a person an observably different appearance from that of his fellows, so do modifiers added to the skeleton of a sentence give individuality to that particular construction.

The modifiers—adjectives and adverbs—are very important grammatical tools which the journalist must learn to use with deftness. Verbs, nouns and pronouns are the important parts of speech that make the sense of the sentence, but try to imagine how flat the journalist's writing would be if he had to use them without any modifying elements.

Adjectives and adverbs are essential parts of speech because they present the reader with definite word-pictures of the persons, things and actions named in the sentence. Through the use of adjectives and adverbs the journalist can present facts

144

and ideas in more specific, concrete form. Such words are indispensable in stating exactly what the writer desires to say. For example, if the word *pear* is used, how much clearer your conception of it is if the writer uses one or more of the following adjectives with it: *ripe, green, yellow, bitter, sweet, luscious, juicy, large, Bartlett, dew-covered.* Similarly, a verb like *turned* conveys more meaning if it is modified by some such adverb as: *slowly, quickly, jerkily, painfully, hesitatingly, apprehensively, expectantly.*

The expert use of adjectives and adverbs will give color to your writing. It is not always possible to write colorfully in handling routine news stories, to be sure, but any journalist worth his salary strives to turn out colorful writing.

Do not confuse *colorful* writing with *colored* writing. Colored writing is biased writing, writing that is slanted to fit the editorial policy. Most editors and publishers do not condone or require writing that fits any one policy. But they do approve of *colorful* writing, writing that presents vivid pictures to the reader.

And, to produce *colorful* writing you not only must learn to use concrete nouns and verbs but also to use adjectives and adverbs expertly.

Since modifiers are such important tools for the journalist, he must be able to use them correctly. Before you take up the sections in this chapter, review pages 35 to 43 and make sure that you can identify the classes of adjectives and adverbs and recognize their various uses as modifiers.

Recall, too, that many adjectives and adverbs may be compared to show degree, and that many errors in the use of adjectives and adverbs result from lack of knowledge of the three degrees of comparison.

Test your knowledge of correct usage of adjectives and adverbs by taking the following quiz.

Quiz

1. When the police entered the room, an hysterical, thinly-clad woman rushed towards a rear door.

2. The trustees will consider the matter farther. The chairman, however, feels farther study of the complaint is likely to make the situation worst.

3. Gibson only allowed five hits as the Cards battered the Tigers, 10 to 1, in the rain.

4. He is more efficient at the free-throw line than anybody on the Lincoln University team. Cashing in on free shots very consistently, the coach pointed out, is one of the toughest, if not the most difficult, chore that a basketball player is called upon to perform.

5. He's an excellent prospect, and his passing is the more effective of all the backs, but surely he cannot hardly ever hope to equal the incomparable Sammy Baugh.

6. He began to run towards her, and he scarcely had covered half the distance between them than she recognized him.

7. The advantages and the disadvantages tend to almost offset each other.

8. The patrolman admitted, too, that he had failed to thoroughly check the door at the back of the building.

9. "Alright, I agree that every member of the starting freshmen quintet are good shot-makers," said Coach Prewitt, "but I think Phillips and Berg will prove to be the better sharp-shooters."

10. This kind of old-fashion mountings are some different than the type your mother's ring is set in. The medium-size mounting is as attractive, if not more so, than the larger size.

11. Sitting there with their shoes off, four black bears—a huge male, female and two cubs—rounded the bend in the trail suddenly.

12. Mayor Gibson feels badly about the investigation.

13. Horton's average slumped due to insufficient batting practice.

14. Doyle Dane Bernbach's copywriting techniques are the most effective of all advertising men in the United States.

15. The largest of the two bream barely weighed a half a pound.

How many did you miss? Turn to page 161 to find out.

THE ARTICLES

1. The indefinite article *a* is used before words that begin with a consonant or a consonant sound.

a table   a future year
a man   a historical novel

The *h* in *historical* is pronounced.

In the following words, the vowel *o* is sounded like the consonant *w*, and the vowel *u* is sounded like *you*.

a one-armed bandit   a union
a used automobile   a unique ring

2. The indefinite article *an* is used before words that begin with a vowel or a vowel sound.

an arrow   an illegal arrest   an heir
an orange   an airy manner   an hour

The *h* in *heir* and *hour* is silent; the words begin with a vowel sound.

3. Be careful to apply rules 1 and 2 in the case of *abbreviations* used in newspapers and magazines. Some abbreviations are read as letters and some are read as words. You must try to determine how the reader will use them.

It was *a* MS of 350 pages.
He received *an* M.S. degree in June.

The average reader will read MS as *manuscript*, but probably will read M.S. as letters rather than as *Master of Science*.

The same rule applies to figures used before nouns.

a $10,000 loss   *a* 10-ton load
a $50,000,000 deficit   *an* 11-man team

4. If two or more nouns in a compound subject or object refer to different persons or things, the article must be repeated before each noun. If the nouns refer to the same person or thing, the article is used before the first noun only.

We met *the* general manager and *the* editor.   (Two persons)
Edwards is the general manager and editor.   (One person)
The short story and *the* feature story are similar.

The exception to this rule is the compound subject or object that names two or more nouns which constitute a unit. A single article is used then. See the sentences which follow.

The farmer bought *a* wagon and team.
A horse and buggy appeared around the bend.

5. Only one *the* is necessary before two adjectives modifying a plural noun. If *the* is repeated, the noun must be singular.

The Irwin-Keasler and Socony-Mobil buildings were destroyed in an early morning fire.
The fifth and eighth chapters have been completed.
The fifth and *the* eighth chapter have been completed.

6. If adjectives in a series modify the same noun, the article is used only before the first adjective when the noun denotes one item; the article is repeated before the second adjective when the noun denotes two or more items.

He bought *a* rayon and nylon shirt.   (One shirt)
He bought *a* rayon and *a* nylon shirt.   (Two shirts)

Of course only one article is needed in: *a* tall, heavy-set, dark-complexioned man.

7. Use the article *the* before the title *Reverend* or its abbreviation.

the Rev. John Mathers
the Reverend Mr. Mathers

8. Be sure to include the article when it is part of the official title of a newspaper, a magazine, a book, a poem, etc.

The Dallas *Times Herald*
The Reader's Digest
A Midsummer Night's Dream

9. The article is repeated sometimes for *emphasis*.

The wealth and *the* riches of this land shall be yours.

10. Journalists must learn to avoid the use of superfluous articles. Omission of the article is common practice in the following cases, and such omission saves precious space.

Directors of the First National Bank voted to declare a dividend.
Johnson was gone only a half-hour.
The children have chicken pox.

Do not say *The directors* or *a half an hour* or *the chicken pox*.
11. Do not use *a* or *an* after *kind of* or *sort of*.

Jenkins invented a new *sort of* zipper.
That is the kind of (not kind of *a*) car I want.

12. On the other hand, be careful to use the article if it is necessary for clarity. Note how the meaning is changed in the following sentence if the article *a* is omitted.

He found *a little comfort* in the message.
He found *little comfort* in the message.

THE DEGREES OF COMPARISON

Many errors in the use of adjectives and adverbs result from failure to use the correct degree of the modifier.

Remember that the *comparative degree* is used when two

persons or things are compared, and the *superlative degree* is used when three or more are compared.

1. Most adjectives of one or two syllables form the comparative and superlative degrees by adding *er* and *est* to the positive degree.

high, higher, highest
pretty, prettier, prettiest

A few adverbs are compared in the same way.

slow, slower, slowest
soon, sooner, soonest

Adjectives of more than two syllables and most adverbs form the comparative and superlative degrees by using *more* and *most* or *less* and *least* before the positive degree.

ADJECTIVES: beautiful, more beautiful, most beautiful
             kind-hearted, less kind-hearted, least kind-hearted
ADVERBS: carefully, less carefully, least carefully
             easily, more easily, most easily

Some adjectives and adverbs are compared irregularly. They are called *irregular comparatives*.

ADJECTIVES: good, better, best
             bad, worse, worst
             little, less, least
ADVERBS: much, more, most
             far, farther, farthest
             well, better, best

Many of these words may be used both as adjectives and as adverbs.

2. The words *farther* and *further* have always given writers trouble. Within the next fifty years there probably will be no distinction between *farther* and *further*. *Further* likely will drive out *farther*. However, until this occurs, the journalist will do well to observe these two rules: (1) *Farther* is usually an

adverb and *further* an adjective, but it is not safe to assume that this is always the case. (2) Use *farther* to refer to distance and space; use *further* to refer to time, quantity or degree.

The retired judge lives on the farther side of the hill.	(Adjective)
Fran Tarkenton can throw the ball farther than Bart Starr.	(Adverb)
Further study of the committee's report is needed.	(Adjective)
The committee will discuss the matter *further*.	(Adverb)

Some authorities, including Copperud, think that choice of *farther* and *further* may best be governed by ear. Use the one that sounds better in the sentence, they advise. You may do best to rely on your publication's stylebook. Or, when you are in doubt, you may use *further* interchangeably.

3. There is now more permissiveness in using *last, latest* and *past*. Grammarians still insist that *last* can only mean *final,* and that *past* must be used for immediately preceding, as in *during the past week* or *the past year*. However, *during the last week* or *the last year* are now accepted.

You cannot be wrong if you still follow the old rules observed by many editors. Use *last* in referring to an object or person that follows all others. Use *latest* in referring to that which is nearest the present time.

It was his *last* dollar.
The council met *last* week.
The instructors came *last* in the commencement procession.
The article appears in the *latest* issue of the magazine.

4. Be careful not to compare anything with itself. Use *any other* and *anything else* to designate the other items in the comparison.

The Mississippi is larger than *any other river* in the United States.
His story on the hospital fire is better than *anything else* he has turned in.

It would be incorrect to say: larger than *any river* or better than *anything*.

5. Use the word *all* in the superlative degree to express comparison of a person, a place or a thing with the rest of its class.

Willie Davenport, Olympic champion, may develop into the fastest of *all* hurdlers in track history.

6. Be sure to compare things *within the same class*.

INCORRECT: Doyle Dale Bernbach's copywriting techniques are the most effective of all advertising men in the United States.

CORRECT: Doyle Dale Bernbach's copywriting techniques are the most effective of all those used by admen in the United States.

7. Do not confuse *as* and *than* in making comparisons. Always state the comparison fully before you add the qualifying expression.

INCORRECT: Theismann may be *as good,* if not better, *than* Hanratty (is) in the quarterback position.

CORRECT: Theismann may be *as good* in the quarterback position as Hanratty, if not better (than Hanratty is).

8. In comparisons, avoid using a singular noun that confuses the reader as to number.

INCORRECT: Supplying the city with sufficient water is one of the most difficult, if not the most difficult, *problem* that the city council has faced.

The singular noun *problem* is used incorrectly.

CORRECT: Supplying the city with sufficient water is one of the most difficult problems that the city council has faced, if not the most difficult.

9. Some adjectives and adverbs should not be compared. Such words as *unique, perfect, perfectly, square, round, absolute, absolutely,* and *supreme* represent a superlative degree in themselves; so one should not say "more perfect," "more unique" and so on. Avoid such expressions as: "the most per-

fect diamond," "the most perfectly executed play" and the like. To express degree with these words, use "most nearly perfect," etc.

MISCELLANEOUS RULES

To round out your review of correct usage of adjectives and adverbs, study the miscellaneous rules that follow.

1. Journalists should note that the trend is toward more frequent use of what are called *flat adverbs*. These are words that have an *ly* adverb form but are used in their adjective form to modify verbs. The following are considered correct usage:

Drive *slow* (or *slowly*). Work *fast*. Tell it *quick* (or *quickly*).

2. Be sure to use a predicate adjective—not an adverb— after such copulative (linking) verbs as *appear, become, feel, look, seem*. The adverb *badly* is correct after the verb *feel* only if it modifies the verb, as in this sentence: The youth feels *badly* the need for getting a college education.

Review of the three kinds of verbs, especially the linking verb, will be helpful here. See Pp. 54–59.

The mayor feels *bad* (not *badly*) about the investigation.
The patient looks *bad*.
We feel *safe* and *sound* here.
The sun shines *bright* today.

3. Remember that *well* may be either an adjective or an adverb, according to its use.

The patient feels *well* (not *good*).	(Predicate adjective)
His doctor says he is *well*.	(Predicate adjective)
He sits *well* in the saddle.	(Adverb)
He eats *well* (not *good*).	(Adverb)

4. Remember that *sure* is an adjective, *surely* is an adverb; that *real* is an adjective, *really* is an adverb; and that *very* is an adverb. Don't misuse *sure* for *surely* or *real* for *really*.

Crosby is *sure* of his facts.	(Predicate adjective modifying *Crosby*)
He *surely* (not *sure*) should arrive soon.	(Adverb modifying verb *should arrive*)
This is a *real* opal.	
I am *really* sorry about that.	(Adjective modifying *opal*)
He spoke *very* clearly over the telephone.	(Adverb modifying pred. adj. *sorry*)
	(Adverb modifying adverb *clearly*)

5. As a rule, the use of *very* before an adjective is unnecessary. Note these sentences:

The girl is very attractive.

Why not omit *very* and say she is *lovely* or *beautiful?*

The tramp was very offensive in appearance.

Why not simply say: The tramp was *repulsive?*

The pears were very rotten.

If the pears were rotten, the adverb *very* does not add anything to the meaning.

Other adverbs are sometimes used unnecessarily. Avoid such expressions as: perfectly beautiful, simply horrible, absolutely correct. The adverbs add nothing to the adjectives.

6. Remember that only adverbs may modify adjectives.

It was *extremely* (not *real*) warm in the courtroom.

Extremely is an adverb modifying the predicate adjective *warm.*

Dunning was considered an *ordinarily* reliable reporter.

The adverb *ordinarily* modifies the adjective *reliable.* If the adjective *ordinary* is used, it should be followed by a comma: *an ordinary, reliable reporter.* But note the difference in meaning. The first sentence refers to Dunning's being reliable under ordinary circumstances. The use of *ordinary* in the second sentence would describe the reporter as being an ordinary type.

7. Avoid the use of *mighty, awful, awfully* (for *very*) in your writing, if not in your speaking. Do not say: The lieutenant was mighty (or awfully) tired. Say he was *very tired*. Or if he was *exhausted*, say so!

8. Do not use the adjective *some* or the phrases *sort of* and *kind of* for the adverbs *somewhat* and *rather*.

Former President Johnson was reported *somewhat* better today. Johnson feels *rather* (not *sort of* or *kind of*) tired, though.

9. Use *almost*, not *most*, when the meaning is *nearly*.

Walker executed *almost* all his gridiron feats in the Cotton Bowl.

Almost in this sentence means *nearly*. *Most* in the sentence below has the meaning of "the majority."

Walker executed *most* of his gridiron feats in the Cotton Bowl.

10. Avoid the use of *above* as an adjective. Instead of saying: "Refer to the above section," have your sentence read: "Refer to the *foregoing* section," or less formally: "See *above*."

11. Do not confuse the preposition *to* with the adverb *too*. *Too* means "to an excessive degree" or "also."

The soldier was *too* tired to move. He was wet to the skin, *too*.

The adjective *two* will not give you difficulty.

12. Some writers have trouble in deciding what adverb to use with a past participle that is used adjectivally. This is not surprising, because there is no hard-and-fast rule to follow. Perhaps the best guide is this: (1) If the passive participle is used merely as a descriptive adjective, like *distinguished* or *tired*, use a single adverb like *very, too* or *so* as a modifier. (2) If the passive participle is a strong verbal form, that is, if it appears to be a part of the predicate and is used to express deep feeling or emotion or strong force, use *very much, too greatly* and so on. Note the following examples:

He is a *very* distinguished man.
He is *too* tired to go on.

The boy was *very much* depressed over his failure.
She was *too badly* frightened to remember the pistol.
He was *so much* (not *so*) overwrought that he decided to take his
life.

13. When they modify the singular *kind* or *sort,* the singular
this and *that* must be used even when the noun in the *of*
phrase is plural. Do not say: "these kind of dresses, those sort
of actions." Note the following correct usages:

He prefers *that kind* of pens.
Where can I buy *this sort* of shrubs?

14. Nouns modified by the adjectives *each, either, neither*
and *every* are singular and take singular verbs.

Neither Amanda nor her brother is married.
Every woman and child in Quang Ngai *was* saved.

15. Use *from,* not *than,* after the adjective *different* in most
instances. There are some strong arguments for *different than.*
The most logical argument is for using *than* when it introduces
a condensed clause: "It has possessed me in a different way
than (it) ever (did) before," Cardinal Newman declared. As
Bernstein points out, insistence on the use of *from* in the cardinal's quotation would result in some such monstrosity as this:
"It has possessed me in a different way *from* the way in which
it ever before did." Bernstein rightly recommends the use of
than to avoid awkwardness, cumbersomeness and elaborate
wastefulness with words. But, the writer who confines himself
to the use of *different from* will always be grammatically correct.

The colonel's answers were *different from* those of the major.
His copywriting style is quite *different from* Bernbach's (style).
Flying conditions are no *different from* yesterday's (flying condi-
tions). But: Flying conditions are no *different than* they were
yesterday.
The Dallas Cowboys today are a far *different* team *than* (preferred

to *from what they were*) when they started competing in the NFL ten years ago.

16. Journalism teachers agree that a common mistake of their students is the omission of the hyphen in compound adjectives which precede the nouns they modify. The hyphen is used correctly in the following:

an all-star lineup	a seven-foot pole
the three-year-old girl	an old-fashioned ring
a do-or-die expression	a well-developed figure
a pearl-handled revolver	a two-car garage

The hyphen also is used when the adjectives are appositives.

The cowboy, *raw-boned* and *weather-beaten,* hunched over the fire.

When the compound adjective follows the verb as a predicate adjective, however, the hyphen may be omitted, although some authorities sanction its use in some cases. It is always used in a compound predicate noun.

The little girl is only three years old.
She is a little three-year-old.   (Predicate Noun)
Her figure is well developed (or well-developed).

The hyphen is not used between an adverb ending in *ly* modifying a participle which modifies a following noun:

Several *smartly dressed* girls entered.
The *recently completed* bridge will be opened to traffic Friday.

17. *Size* is not an adjective and must not be used to form adjectives. The correct form is *small-sized,* etc.

They owned a *large-sized* ranch in California.
The hungry boy quickly ate the *full-sized* steak.

18. The numerals *twenty-one* through *ninety-nine* are always written with a hyphen, of course, and so also are the corresponding adjectives.

Only *twenty-four* persons were rescued.

19. "Alright" has not been accepted in formal writing. Use *all right*.

20. Use *due to* to modify a noun or a pronoun.

Cox's slump was *due to* insufficient batting practice.

Due modifies the noun *slump*.

It is better to use *because of* to modify a verb.

Cox's average slumped *because of* (not *due to*) insufficient batting practice.

Because of modifies the verb *slumped*. In time *due to* used adverbially, as a prepositional phrase, will be accepted. But, for the present it is better to write: *Because of* (not *Due to*) serious illness in his family, the senator could not attend the hearing.

21. Journalists should never be guilty of using a double negative. Two negatives make an affirmative; therefore, such expressions as "can't hardly" and "couldn't never" defeat their purpose. Use such words as *barely, hardly* and *scarcely* without another negative.

Unitas *can hardly* (not *can't hardly*) raise his throwing arm above his shoulder.
The fleeing convict *could scarcely* climb the river bank.
With only a high school education, he *could never* succeed in that job.

22. Another rule to remember in using the adverbs *barely, hardly,* and *scarcely* is to use *when,* not *than,* in completing the statement.

Hardly had he reached the gangplank *when* he saw her.

23. The adverbs *anywhere, somewhere,* and *backward* do not have an *s* on the end.

It is around *somewhere.*
The man fell over *backward.*

24. Use *anywhere* and *somewhere* instead of *any place* and *some place*.

You can place the desk *anywhere* in the room.

25. Many writers fail to place *only* near the word or element it modifies. Most editors will insist that you use *only* where it belongs in the sentence—immediately before the element it modifies. Note how the meaning in the following sentences is changed merely by moving *only*.

Red Shoendienst believes *only* Lou Brock can equal Eddie Collins' record for stolen bases in a World Series.

Only Red Schoendienst believes Lou Brock can equal the World Series record for stolen bases.

Red Schoendienst thinks Brock can *only equal* [cannot break] Collin's record.

Schoendienst *only supposes* [he doesn't *know*] Brock can equal the record.

Brock needs *only* one more stolen base to equal the record. (Not: *only needs*)

Note this other example of placing *only* in its normally proper position.

The trustees plan to spend *only* $500,000 on the building. (Not: The trustees *only plan* to spend)

Placement of *only* in other than a normal position may be defended when *only* is used as a sentence adverb to modify an entire statement rather than a word or phrase. In the following sentence *only* correctly precedes the verb because it modifies the entire statement:

The coach *only* felt that he was doing the right thing to substitute Morton.

Placing *only* just before the verb in the following sentence may be better than placing it in what would be considered the normal order, before *when*:

The purpose of the investigation only became clear when the district attorney asked the vending machine company to open its books.

The same rule holds for *ever* and *almost.*

Frank Howard does not hope *ever* to break the records of Ruth and Maris. (Not: does not *ever* hope)
Flood has *almost* the easiest swing I have ever seen in baseball.

26. The dangling participle is a common error of writers. If you begin a sentence with a participial phrase, remember that the phrase is used as an adjective and must modify a noun or a pronoun that follows it. Make certain that it modifies the correct word.

INCORRECT: Running at full speed, the ball was caught near the wall in right field.

Surely the ball was not doing the running!

CORRECT: Running at full speed, Kaline caught the ball near the wall in right field.

Be sure that you use a comma after the introductory participial phrase.

27. The split infinitive was discussed in Chapter 9. Remember that separating the parts of the infinitive with an adverb is sometimes permissible if emphasis is gained, if smoother writing results, and if the meaning is clear and correct. But do not split infinitives needlessly.

The professor advised his students *to search diligently* for the facts.

Nothing would be gained by writing *to diligently search.*

Informed that she had won the contest, Mrs. Mayhew called her husband *to happily tell* him of her good fortune.
Jorgensen was unable *to completely master Greek.*

The split infinitives in these sentences do add emphasis.

The position of the adverb gives sentences different meanings, as shown in these examples:

He told Smith *immediately* to come to the point. Or, He *immediately told* . . .
He told Smith to *immediately* come to the point.
He told Smith to come to the point *immediately.*
The corporal failed to *completely* comprehend the order.
The corporal failed *completely* to comprehend the order.

28. Certainly no journalist should make a mistake like this: The pond, froze solid overnight, was crowded with skaters by noon. Use the past participle form of the verb as an adjective modifier.

The pond, *frozen* overnight, was crowded with skaters by noon.
The challenger, badly *beaten,* went down for the full count.

29. Do not confuse such adverbs as *respectfully* and *respectively* or *formerly* and *formally.*

Lee Evans and Tommie Smith finished first and second, respectively, in the 400-meter finals.
The house was *formerly* owned by Black.
Dress *formally* for this important dinner.

30. You should never use the plural *freshmen* as an adjective. The singular *freshman* is the adjective form.

The Oklahoma *freshman* team beat the sophomores, 27 to 13.
The personable star of the Temple Owls was elected president of the *freshman* class.

But "The *freshmen* outnumber the sophomores" is correct.

Quiz Answers

1. When police entered the room, a hysterical, thinly clad woman rushed toward a rear door. 2. Use *further* for *farther* in both places. 3. Transpose *only allowed.* 4. Insert *else* after *anybody;* eliminate *very;* and make last of sentence read: is one of the toughest chores that . . . to perform, if not the most difficult. 5. He's an excellent

prospect, and his passing is the most effective of that of all the backs, but surely he can hardly hope ever to equal (the record of) the incomparable Sammy Baugh. 6. He began to run toward her, and he had scarcely covered half the distance between them when she recognized him. 7. Correct. 8. Correct. 9. "All right, I agree that every member of the starting freshman quintet is a good shot-maker," said Coach Prewitt, "but I think Phillips and Berg will prove to be the best sharp-shooters. 10. This kind of old-fashioned mountings is somewhat different from the type your mother's ring is set in. The medium-sized mounting is as attractive as the larger-sized (mounting). It may be even more attractive. 11. Sitting there with their shoes off, they looked up to see four black bears . . . suddenly round the bend in the trail. 12. *bad* for *badly*. 13. Use *because* instead of *due to*. 14. Bernbach's copywriting techniques are the most effective of all those used by advertising men. . . . 15. The larger of the two bream weighed barely (or barely weighed) half a pound.

11
Using Prepositions and Conjunctions Correctly

If verbs and nouns may be thought of as composing the skeleton of the sentence, and if adjectives and adverbs are visualized as forming the flesh on the skeleton, then conjunctions and prepositions may be compared to the ligaments, those bands of tissue that tie the parts together.

Prepositions and conjunctions are connecting or linking words. These two parts of speech are much alike in function, and many errors are made by confusing them. They are treated together in this chapter.

Turn back to Chapter 3 and review carefully the sections on prepositions and conjunctions. Make sure that you know how these two parts of speech are used in sentences and that you can identify the kinds of conjunctions.

To test yourself on the correct usage of prepositions and conjunctions, take the following quiz.

Quiz

1. It looks like the new system is going to result in better employer-employe(e) relations at Atlantic-Richfield.

2. He told police his wife was forced in a truck and later raped.

3. Gildersleeve said he would try and show where maintenance costs could be reduced without impairing service.

4. Neither County Judge Lew Sterrett or County Auditor Moore Lynn would comment on reports that the tax rate had been agreed on.

5. The inheritance of around $30,000 will be divided between he, Dolores and Hazel.

6. She said the man identified himself as an insurance salesman, nevertheless she was suspicious of him.

7. Matte had no sooner taken the hand-off from Morrall before Barnes spilled him for a four-yard loss.

8. Collins cut to far to the left, so the pass overshot him.

9. The actors had come to have little regard and appreciation of his ability to direct the cast.

10. An accomplice was waiting in a 1967 Pontiac in front of the bank with its motor running.

11. He demanded to know if the payment could be made by April 1.

12. He said he would dismiss the jury providing the attorney general can present evidence that certain jurors are biased.

13. He left no money or property to the youngest son.

14. He kept boring in relentlessly so La Cruz was kept off balance throughout the fight.

15. The director whispered to the producer, "Between you and I, I think Alan is ready for a leading role. Why, he acts just like Clark Gable!"

16. Frazier's footwork is equal, if not better, than the challenger's.

17. District Attorney Wade stoutly declared that he would see that Jack Ruby got the death sentence.

18. "I'll have to differ with you on that. I think his change of pace is different than Gibson's."

19. "Winston tastes good—like a cigarette should!"

20. Commissioner Price stated that he propose two possible solutions besides the one suggested by the county auditor.

How did you do on this very important quiz? Turn to end of chapter to find out.

PREPOSITIONS

Let us first consider the *preposition,* the word that shows the relation between a noun or pronoun and some other word.

1. It is not only correct, but desirable, to end a sentence with a preposition if such a construction sounds natural rather than stilted. And placing the preposition at the end of the sentence often gives the sentence a certain emphasis, as: He took the manuscript home and read it *through.* (Not: . . . read through it.) Note these other examples:

Norman Mailer is the writer the critic referred *to.*
Congressman Teague asked, "What is there for us to talk *about?*"
Dole is the only man they can depend *upon.*

Certainly such sentences sound more natural and also have stronger endings than to write: Mailer is the writer to whom the critic referred, *or,* Congressman Teague asked, "What is there about which we can talk?" *or,* Dole is the only man upon whom they can depend. Let's analyze two more examples:

Use of drugs by high school students is the biggest problem the school board must deal with. (Not: . . . with which the school board must deal.)
Council Roark called the Crime Commission's report "the most ridiculous thing I ever heard of." (Not: . . . the most ridiculous thing of which I ever heard.)

Placing the prepositional phrase at the beginning of the sentence calls attention to the phrase as containing the more important thought in the sentence.

To the victor belong the spoils.

2. Avoid ending a sentence with a so-called suspended phrase.

INCORRECT: Right now the council is concerned with the water-shortage problem and is anxious about its solution.

The phrase *about its solution* is suspended. The sentence should be reworded thus:

CORRECT: Right now the council is concerned with the water-shortage problem and is anxious to find the solution.
Or: Right now the council is seriously concerned with finding the solution to the water-shortage problem.

3. Remember that the *object* of the preposition is always in the objective case. Watch this construction carefully if the preposition has a compound object and especially when the object is a pronoun.

This matter must be settled *between you and him* (not *he*).
Just *between you and me* (not *you and I*), I prefer skating to skiing.

4. Be careful not to confuse prepositions with conjunctions. A common error of this type is using *like* as a conjunction. *Like* is a preposition and takes a noun or pronoun object. If you use a clause, the correct connective is the conjunctive *as* or *as if.*

This tastes *like a peach.*
His son looks *like him.*
It looks *like rain.*
It looks *as if it might rain today.* (Not: It looks like it might rain.)
All right men, do *as I tell you.*

Some editors consider it correct to use *like* as a conjunction if it is followed by a word that may be regarded as a simile.

Caruthers is only a sophomore, but he plays like a professional (plays).

Caruthers is not a professional baseball player, but he resembles one in ability. *Professional* has the force of a simile. And since *professional* is a noun, the prepositional phrase *like a professional* is correct. If you use the conjunction and say *as a professional,* you are saying that Caruthers actually does play as a professional in a baseball league.

Like as a conjunction has become popular in advertising ("Winston tastes good—like a cigarette should.) and also in colloquial usage, especially on the air: Example: "Tell it like it is, baby." *Like* also is used often in newspaper headlines. In time it may supplant *as* as a conjunction in journalistic writing, but for now you should use *like,* on the whole, only as a preposition.

5. Do not confuse the preposition *but* with the conjunction *but.* When *but* is used as a preposition, it means *except* and usually takes an object. Watch pronouns, particularly compound pronouns, that follow the prepositional *but.* Such pronouns must be in the objective case if they come at the end of the sentence.

The instructor dismissed everyone *but (except)* Myrick and *me.*
The instructor dismissed everyone *but him* and *me.*

However, if the pronoun comes elsewhere in the sentence other than at the end, it may be said to be grammatically attracted to the noun to which it is linked by the *but* and may be put in the same case as that noun, as Bernstein points out. Example: No one (nominative) but *I* (nominative) had the answer. Some authorities, however, still insist on use of the objective *me* in such a construction.

6. The conjunction *and* must not be used to follow the infinitive *to try. To try* is followed by another infinite phrase as its object.

It was up to Lolich *to try to keep* Detroit's hopes alive.

Do not say "try and keep." Use of *try and* colloquially, especially when it adds force to the meaning of the sentence, has gained some acceptance, as in this sentence: "Little one, you must *try and* be brave." But unless they are quoting someone, journalists working for newspapers and most magazines will always use *try to*.

Watch such errors as "Be careful and don't . . ." Say: "Be careful *not to* . . ."

7. Guard against using "in back of" for the preposition *behind. In front of* is correct, but there is no such phrase as "in back of."

He testified that he had slept on the ground *behind* the garage that night.

8. The preposition *in* implies position; *into* implies motion or change of place. Do not use *in* for *into*.

He lives *in* the last house on this street. He went *into* the house.
They forced the woman *into* (not *in*) a car and assaulted her.

9. *Between* refers to position or action of two persons or objects. *Among* usually is used when there are three or more mentioned.

It sat *between* the window and the door.
The boys divided the money *among* the four of them.

However, *between* may be used when three or more persons are thought of severally or individually, or when three or more objects are being considered in pairs.

A contract was drawn up *between* Leslie Shelton, Bill Orr and Charles Mayhew.
It is hoped that an agreement *between* the four governments will be reached at Paris.

10. Do not confuse *beside* and *besides. Beside* means "at the side of." *Besides* means "in addition to."

The car paused *beside* the gas pump.
Savage owns two (other) houses *besides* this one.

11. Do not confuse the preposition *to* and the adverb *too*. Remember that *too* means "also" or "to an excessive degree."

The family went *to* the beach today.
They met the Fields and the Browns, *too*.
It was *too* bad that it rained.

12. The more formal *upon* is rapidly being replaced by *on*. *Upon* is still used to indicate upward motion or to connote *on top of*, as in:

The cowboy leaped *upon* his horse.
The students piled the books one *upon* another.

In the following sentence, *upon* is more euphonious than *on* at the end of the sentence.

There is little for the FBI to go *upon*.

Although *on* is steadily shoving *upon* aside, it should not be permitted to run wild in replacing other prepositions such as *in, by, about, against, toward, of, from, at* and *for*. In the following sentences the parenthesized words are much better than *on*.

Discussing the question *on* (*about* or *concerning*) whether he agreed with the Crime Commission on the extent of drug addiction in the high schools, the superintendent declared that . . .
The Crime Commission registered a vigorous protest *on* (*against*) the laxity of school administrators in reporting drug addiction cases.
The Crime Commission sharply criticized the City Council *on* (*for*) its attitude *on* (*toward*) drug peddlers.
The Crime Commission chairman declared he would seek the public's support *on* (*of* or *for*) the proposal.
The chairman exploded with anger *on* (*at*) the city council's disapproval of the report.

Remember that *on* is unnecessary with days of the week:
They left (on) Friday.
13. In writing for the printed media, use *about* when you mean approximately and *around* when you refer to motion.

However, in electronic journalism the casual use of *around* for *about* is common:

The high should be *around* (*about*) 82 degrees.

Note correct usage of *about* and *around* in the sentences that follow.

The Braniff International plane arrived at *about* 10:45 a.m.
About (Not *Around*) 5,800 persons attended the Nixon rally.
As the wizened grandmother wound the wool *around* the ball, the ball dropped to the floor and rolled *around* and *around*.

Don't use *about* redundantly with ranging figures, as in: She described the robber as weighing (*about*) 165 to 185 pounds.

14. The preposition *on* implies position; *onto* implies motion or change of place.

The passengers walked *on* the deck.
Your book is lying *on* the table.
The sailor jumped from the wharf *onto* the deck.

Note the difference between *onto* and *on to*. In the phrase *on to*, *on* is an adverb and *to* a preposition.

He jumped *onto* the deck and then went *on to* the bow.

15. Discriminate between the meaning of *differ with* and *differ from*. Use *differ from* to indicate dissimilarity and *differ with* to indicate disagreement.

Mayor Gibson *differed from* Councilman Reilly in temperament, but he did not *differ with* him in local politics.

Usage of *different than* was discussed earlier. Its use is considered correct now if it introduces a clause: The situation is no *different than* it was last week.

16. The preposition may sometimes be omitted from a prepositional phrase, and the infinitive is sometimes written without the *to*. Make sure that the meaning of the sentence is clear if

you leave out words. The words in parentheses in the following sentences may be omitted without obscuring the meaning.

The twins are (of) about the same height and weight.
The baby resembles his father; he even laughs (in) the same way.
He will be eligible to play varsity football (for) three years.
He regards it (as) his own personal problem.
Steers are selling for (from) 32 to 38 cents a pound.
The name (of) Smith is listed 116 times in the directory.
The car ran (to) within six inches of the precipice.
He helped his wife (to) do the dishes every night.
Do you dare (to) say he did it?

NOTE. The use of unnecessary words is called *wordiness* or *redundancy*. It is treated in detail later.

17. There are some cases where omission of the preposition would be an error. The italicized words in the following sentences should *not* be omitted.

Hixon will pass the ball either to Levias or *to* Richardson.
The members of the Bonehead Club and *of* the Variety Club worked together on the plan.
He has great respect *for* and confidence *in* the city manager.
These men have little grasp of the importance of the problem or *of* its possible solution.
The mayor never wearied *of* telling the story of that fight.
He wanted to cooperate *in* every way he could.

18. Instead of a gerund with the possessive, a prepositional phrase is sometimes preferable. However, either is correct.

He discouraged *my singing* the aria.
He discouraged *me from singing* the aria.

19. Many journalists fail to use the correct preposition after a verb to convey the right meaning. Note the italicized phrases in these sentences:

The members of the two clubs *agree in* principle.
The two clubs *agreed on* a common objective.

The Variety Club *agreed with* the Rotarians.

One club *agreed to* the other's plan.

The members of our club have *agreed among* themselves to work with you.

There are hundreds of such combinations of verbs and prepositions. Use the dictionary to know which preposition expresses the exact meaning you want to convey. Many reference books have lists of these combinations, also.

20. Prepositional phrases are used as adjectives and as adverbs. They should always be placed as near as possible to the words they modify.

Compare the faulty sentences below with the improved sentences that follow them.

FAULTY: He recovered from a four-month illness at the end of July.

The couple will be at home after a brief trip in Springfield.

The Auxiliary will place flowers on the graves of members who have died on Memorial Day in Rosemount Cemetery.

CORRECT: At the end of July he recovered from a four-month illness.

After a brief trip, the couple will be at home in Springfield.

On Memorial Day the Auxiliary will place flowers in Rosemount Cemetery on the graves of members who have died.

Or: . . . place flowers on the graves of deceased members buried in Rosemount Cemetery.

You will have no difficulty in spotting the misplaced phrases in the following "bulls."

WANTED—Second-hand typewriter by young lady student with wide carriage. (Advertisement)

Sergeant Acquitted of Drunk Driving in Criminal Court (Headline)

A former highway patrolman drew a sentence of two years for operating a moonshine still in federal court at Knoxville.

The hostess chose a cerise dinner dress with a low, oval neckline for entertaining.

CONJUNCTIONS

Always keep in mind the fact that conjunctions are words that join or link two parts of the sentence.

COORDINATE CONJUNCTIONS

Coordinate conjunctions join words, phrases or clauses of equal rank. The common coordinate conjunctions are:

and   or   nor
but   yet   for

The conjunction *and* denotes addition or enumeration. *But* and *yet* denote contrast. *Or* and *nor* denote choice. You should readily recognize that the wrong conjunction is used in the following sentence: Schlesinger is the best substitute on the basketball squad, *and* his insertion into the starting line-up will definitely weaken the Ponies' attack. Obviously, *but* is the correct conjunction. Even better would be this sentence: Although Schlesinger is the best substitute on the squad, his insertion into the starting line-up will definitely weaken the Ponies' attack.

The words, phrases or clauses joined by a coordinate conjunction must be of equal rank.

INCORRECT: Reilly is well-educated and of moderate wealth.
CORRECT: Reilly is *well-educated* and *moderately wealthy*.
   Reilly is a man of *good education* and *of moderate wealth*.

In the first sentence *well-educated* is an adjective and *of moderate wealth* is a phrase. Change the sentence to have either two adjectives or two phrases.

INCORRECT: Jeffers was suffering physically and in mind.
CORRECT: Jeffers was suffering physically and mentally.

In the first sentence, *physically* is an adverb, *in mind* a prepositional phrase. Although the phrase is used adverbially to modify the verb, it differs too much in form from the adverb *physically* and makes the sentence less smooth and clear than the correct sentence.

In the following sentence the writer was thinking and writing loosely. He began with an independent clause, followed by a dependent clause beginning with the conjunctive adverb *as;* then he added to the independent clause.

INCORRECT: Brock stepped back from the plate as the pitcher shook his head negatively and called for another bat.

CORRECT: As the pitcher shook his head negatively, Brock stepped back from the plate and called for another bat.

In the correct sentence it is now clear that *and* joins the compound verb *stepped* and *called.* Of course, you could make two sentences.

CORRECT: The pitcher shook his head negatively. Brock stepped back from the plate *and* called for another bat.

CONNECTIVE ADVERBS AS CONJUNCTIONS

Independent or *connective adverbs* can be used as coordinate conjunctions. The following is a partial list of independent adverbs:

accordingly	hence	moreover	then
also	however	nevertheless	therefore
besides	indeed	still	thus

When they connect two independent clauses, a semicolon is used to separate the clauses, or a period is used to make two sentences.

Fort Worth is a friendly western city; *nevertheless,* I prefer Dallas. New York is an interesting place to visit. *However,* I prefer to live in a much smaller city.

CORRELATIVE CONJUNCTIONS

The *correlative conjunctions,* which are used in pairs, must be used carefully. Errors occur most often in using the correla-

tives *either . . . or, neither . . . nor* and *not only . . . but also*. To avoid making errors, learn the following four rules:
   1. Use *or* with *either, nor* with *neither;* don't mix them.

INCORRECT: *Neither* Bolton *or* Irwin will be nominated.
CORRECT: *Either* Bellmon *or* Monroney will be nominated.
   Neither Bolton *nor* Irwin will be nominated.

   2. *No* is not a correlative; therefore compound nouns modified by *no* should not be joined by *nor*. Use *or*.

He has *no* money *or* land. (Not: He has no money *nor* land.)
No man *or* woman in this room can say that he will run.

   3. Place correlative conjunctions as near as possible to the words they connect.

He possesses *neither* land *nor* money. (Not: He *neither* possesses
   land *nor* money.)
He possesses *not only* land *but also* money. (Not: He *not only*
   possesses land *but also* money.)

   4. Where a compound subject has a singular noun and a plural noun joined by *or*, or *nor*, the predicate agrees in number with the nearest noun.

Either the *trustees* or the *president is* to issue a statement.
Neither the *mayor* nor the *councilmen were* at the dinner.

SUBORDINATE CONJUNCTIONS
Subordinate conjunctions connect a dependent (subordinate) clause with an independent or main clause in the sentence. The common subordinate conjunctions are:

although	because	in order that	that
as	even if	since	though
as if	if	so that	unless

Some conjunctive adverbs used like subordinate conjunctions are: *before, how, when, whether, while* and *why*.
   If the dependent clause precedes the independent clause, it

is usually followed by a comma. The comma may not be necessary if the subordinate clause is very short or if the comma is not needed for clarity.

Although he fought on even terms early in the bout, Frazier managed to win only three rounds.
Because of the fog we could not leave. (The clause is very short.)
When you see Harry, hurry and let us know. (The clause is short, but a comma is needed for clarity.)
While he was there, they could not leave.
Because you were late, we missed a ride.

The dependent clause may begin the sentence if this does not make the sentence sound artificial.

Miscellaneous Uses of Conjunctions

1. Although some editors frown upon using a coordinate conjunction to begin a sentence, a majority approve the practice when it adds variety or emphasis to your writing, as in the following:

These men have robbed the city of millions of dollars. *And* I dare say they will not try to refute this charge. *But* if they do dare to come forth . . . .

2. The use of *so* as a coordinate conjunction is a general practice, but it is not really good usage. Other conjunctions will give a more exact meaning in most cases. Use of a subordinate conjunction or a connective adverb is often preferable. If you do use *so,* place a semicolon before it.

He neglected to study for the examination; *so* he failed.
BETTER: He failed *because* he neglected to study for the examination.
Or: He neglected to study for the examination; *consequently,* he failed.

Use *so that,* not *so* or *so as,* to introduce a clause of purpose. Do not use a comma before *so that.*

Jenkins kept talking for an hour *so that the motion would not be put to a vote.*

An infinitive is frequently used to express purpose.

Jenkins talked for an hour *to keep* the motion from being put to a vote.

3. The adverbs *where* and *when* are misused for *that* in some sentences.

INCORRECT: I read in today's paper where he died in Korea.
CORRECT: I read in today's paper *that* he died in Korea.

Do not use "is when" and "is where" in defining words.

INCORRECT: A debate is when two teams argue both sides of a question.
CORRECT: A debate is the discussion of a question by two teams.

4. Do not use *because* or *as* to introduce a noun clause.

INCORRECT: The reason why he failed was because he did not study.
CORRECT: He failed *because* he did not study.
The reason why he failed was *that* he did not study.

5. Do not overuse *that* in a sentence.

INCORRECT: The professor insisted *that* in learning to spell correctly *that* the students master four important rules.
CORRECT: The professor insisted *that* the students master four important rules in learning to spell correctly.

6. Use *than* instead of *until, before,* etc. after the comparative *no sooner.*

He had no sooner begun his speech *than* (not *until* or *before*) catcalls were heard.

7. The conjunctive adverb *while* is used to denote time. It should not be used in place of *although* and *but.*

While he was being groomed for the part, he grew a beard.

Although he had been groomed for the part, he failed to make good.

Although he found flaws in the suggested program, he admitted it deserved serious consideration.

Rucker prefers immediate action, *but* Alward advises going slow.

8. Be careful to use *whether*, not *if*, when an alternative choice is indicated.

The senator wanted to know *whether* (or not) the bill could be amended to provide larger sums.

9. The past participle *provided* is still considered preferable to the present participle *providing* when used as a conjunction in the sense of *if*. However, don't use *provided* or *provided that* incorrectly for *if*. Note correct usage in the sentences that follow.

A truce can be negotiated *provided that* a satisfactory plan for the exchange of prisoners can be agreed upon.

Summaries of the panel discussions can be made available *if* (not *provided that*) the delegates want them.

Summaries of the panel discussions can be made available *provided* (or *provided that*) the delegates pay for them.

Quiz Answers

1. Change *like* to *as if*. 2. He told police his wife was forced into a truck and (was) later raped. 3. Gildersleeve said (that) he would try to show that (preferred to *where*) maintenance costs. . . . 4. Change *or* to *nor*. *Upon* may be used for *on*. 5. The inheritance of *about* $30,000 will be divided between him, Dolores and Hazel. (Colloquial *around* is all right in electronic journalism or in quoting someone in the printed media.) 6. Change comma to a semicolon and place comma after *nevertheless*. 7. Change *before* to *than*. 8. Collins cut too far to the left; so the pass overshot him. Better: When (or Because) Collins cut too far to the left, the pass overshot him. 9. Need *for* after *regard*. 10. An accomplice was waiting in front of the bank in a 1967 Pontiac, with its motor running. 11. He demanded to know *whether* (or not)

the payment. . . 12. Change *providing* to *provided* and *can* to *could*. 13. Correct. 14. Change *so* to *so that*. 15. Change *I* to *me; like* is correct here. 16. Frazier's footwork is equal to, if not better than, the champion's. 17. Delete the first *that*. 18. Change *than* to *from;* differ *with* is correct. 19. Accepted as colloquial usage, at least in radio-television and advertising fields. 20. Correct.

PART 2

SENTENCE
CONSTRUCTION

12
What Good
Sentences Require

Much has been said and written about *readability*. Newspapers, press associations, newspaper groups and magazines have retained such experts as Robert Gunning and Rudolf Flesch to study how to improve the writing of their staffs.

The results have been extremely helpful to practicing journalists. First of all, these experts advise the writer that he must have something to say: writing without ideas and information is like trying to breathe in a vacuum. Second, they insist that the really capable writer will develop his subject in simple words and short sentences. What they urge, then, is *clear, concise* and *interesting* writing. They remind the would-be journalist that words and sentences are tools that one masters by constantly using them. The formula is: a good subject plus simple words plus short sentences.

All this is certainly sound advice. But perhaps the experts are making the task seem a bit easier than it actually is. For instance, they underestimate the amount of knowledge needed by the competent writer. Professor Roscoe Ellard of the Graduate School of Journalism of Columbia University has this to say about a chapter in Rudolf Flesch's book *How to Make Sense:*

> In his chapter on grammar in this book, the author worries me. An impression the unformed writer might get is that formal grammar is outdated, like a top-hat. Dr. Flesch quotes violations of grammar by Lord Bryce, Jane Austen, and a lovely opening sentence by E. M. Forster: "Do you like to know who a book's by?"
>
> Good for E. M. Forster. But it reminds me of a brash defense I made once to a Regular Army colonel who rebuked me for laxity in my lieutenant's uniform. I reminded him that Major General Howze was parading one of the same laxities a hundred feet away.
>
> "A major general," Colonel Julian E. Gaujot reminded me as my eyes fixed on the ribbon of his Congressional Medal of Honor— "a major general can do a hell of a lot of things a lieutenant doesn't know how to get away with."
>
> Which is something to remember in counselling amateur stylists. Jane Austen, Rudyard Kipling and E. M. Forster know how to take liberties with formalities effectively. There are times to split infinitives for clarity—and times not to. This danger often lurks: The young writer who reads in a book that grammar is top-hat may turn up with sentences that force both copy desk and readers to conclude: "That reporter slept through high school. He ought to go back to one and stay awake." [1]

In an earlier book, *The Way to Write*, Flesch and his co-author Lass give full recognition to the fact that writing well and using good grammar are essentially equivalent.

The argument over the importance of formal grammar is endless. But one must face the fact that the journalist cannot hope to produce clear, concise and interesting writing until he learns how to put sentences together and *knows what he is doing.* This is a roundabout way of saying that he must know good grammar and apply it.

[1] By permission from Roscoe Ellard and *Editor and Publisher* magazine.

A BRIEF REVIEW OF THE SENTENCE

Let us try to tie together some of the points brought out in earlier chapters and add some pointers on sentence structure and word usage.

Make sure that you can always tell the difference between a complete sentence and a fragment of a sentence. The fragment should never be punctuated as though it were a whole sentence.

One body was recovered last night, that of William G. Seymour.

You know that it would be incorrect to make the second part (*that of William Seymour*) a separate sentence.

By now you should also be able to avoid the run-on sentence, in which two complete sentences are run together needlessly; in other words, you will not make the comma blunder —the use of a comma instead of a semicolon to separate two independent clauses when the conjunction is omitted.

You must be able to distinguish: (1) between independent clauses and dependent clauses; and (2) between coordinating conjunctions and subordinating conjunctions, including conjunctive adverbs.

If you have trouble telling the difference between an independent clause and a dependent clause, review Chapter 2. If you have difficulty with prepositions and conjunctions, review Chapters 2 and 11. The conjunction is an important part of speech and you should know how to use conjunctions correctly to say exactly what you mean.

Another important piece of knowledge for the writer to have is the distinction between the simple subject and the complete subject, and between the simple predicate and the complete predicate. Without such knowledge you may commit many errors. With such knowledge you should be able to write correct sentences.

Complete understanding of the four types of sentences—

simple, complex, compound, and compound-complex—will enable you to give your readers the variety of sentence structure which the readability experts stress. True, you can obtain variety through other methods, but varying the sentence forms is important to good writing.

Note how the use of a variety of sentence forms makes the following excerpt from a World War II story by Hal Boyle highly readable. [S] at the end of a sentence denotes a simple sentence; [Cd] denotes a compound sentence; and [Cx] denotes a complex sentence.

AT SEA WITH A U.S. TASK FORCE EN ROUTE TO NORTH AFRICA, Nov. 3. (AP)—

Water rings the gray-clouded horizon, and winds trouble the sea. [Cd]

Scores of tiny dots slug slowly through the never ending waves, like determined ants painfully inching across a furrowed field. [S]

The little dots are ships, and each is carrying thousands of American men to battlefields far from home. [Cd]

Life on a troopship is like wearing a tight shoe. [S] You don't mind it for a few minutes. [S] But on a transport, it may endure a week, two weeks, perhaps longer. [S]

The packed quarters are the chief cause of grousing among the troops, who wouldn't be American if they didn't complain about the lack of elbow room. [Cx]

Water is available for showers, washing and laundry less than three hours out of the 24. [S] Officers bunk four to a room. [S] The men are quartered in holds which become hot and fetid within a few hours. [Cx]

Part of the voyage the officers sleep with the troops in the crowded holds to show [that] they can take it, too. [Cx]

Said one private when his officer showed up in the hold at bedtime: "Why are you sleeping here, sir?" [Cx]

"Oh, just for morale," replied the officer. [S]

"Sir," said the private worriedly, "What is wrong with the officers' morale?" [Cx] . . .[2]

2 By permission from AP Newsfeatures.

You should be ready now to take a closer look at some of the principles of sentence structure. You should have already mastered some of the rules. Those that have been treated in previous chapters are repeated for emphasis; others are added to make sure that you have a fairly complete review of the fundamentals of grammar and composition. You are urged to devote major attention to those principles which you have not yet mastered. Be honest with yourself. You know whether or not you are thoroughly familiar with any principle or rule and whether or not you need drill on it.

UNITY, EMPHASIS AND COHERENCE

In your study of grammar and composition, have you ever heard of "the trinity"? Many older editors were drilled thoroughly in it, but this was before the advent of "progressive education." These editors will tell you that, no matter what it is called, a thorough understanding of "the trinity" of grammar and composition is of primary importance to the journalist. Younger editors will agree when it is explained that "the trinity" is a term once used to refer to *unity, emphasis* and *coherence* in the sentence.

To produce effective sentences and paragraphs the writer must apply the three primary principles of *unity, emphasis* and *coherence. Coherence* is usually treated in today's grammar textbooks as a subdivision under the broader heading "clearness" or "clarity." Clearness is fundamental in all good writing, and it matters little if grammarians classify coherence as a subdivision of clearness as long as the journalist recognizes the need of coherence—as well as of unity and emphasis—in his writing.

If you add *variety* to *unity, emphasis* and *coherence,* you have the four essentials of effective sentences and paragraphs.

13

Sentence Unity

As far as grammar and composition are concerned, unity means simply oneness of thought. A sentence is supposed to express a single complete thought. In other words, the sentence must be unified.

To test yourself on sentence unity, take the following quiz. Correct errors that violate sentence unity. Watch particularly for such errors as: fragmentary sentences; omission of a word, phrase or clause which is needed for sentence unity and clarity; omission of transitional devices needed for unity and clarity; lack of unified thought in the sentence; choppy sentences; failure to subordinate minor ideas by using subordinate clauses or prepositional, participial and infinitive phrases; use of the wrong conjunction; and using the incorrect sentence form.

You may take the quiz by copyediting each sentence or by completely rewriting it.

Quiz

1. One auto was recovered. That of William Truehart.
2. Seven men were lost and one saved in the crash.

3. He maintained the girl is a prostitute.
4. He asks us to read, to meditate and write.
5. The most famous temple is Vishwanatha, so be sure to visit it.
6. Dorsey, W. Waring, who was a retired army officer, age 81, who was a first lieutenant in the Kentucky National Guard and a captain of the 50th Artillery Brigade in World War I, and who, incidentally, was awarded an honorary LL.B. degree last year by the University of Kentucky, died here Friday night.
7. The city manager may be compared to the manager of a big department store. He has the power to appoint employees. He has the power to fire employees. He supervises the work of the employees in the various departments.
8. He is neither interested nor concerned about the problem.
9. The farmer, together with his wife and two children, were swept two miles down the swollen river.
10. The jury of ten men and two women were dismissed this afternoon by Judge Chamberlain.
11. The man was booked for investigation of burglary, rape and indecent exposure; he is 24 years old.
12. You can now read all afternoon at the public library; the Woman's club has just installed a brand new wash room.
13. We watched them from a sightseeing boat, but we could hardly believe what we saw.
14. He had the services of the nation's top lawyers, but he failed to win the suit.
15. Coach Landry said that if Hayes had been available, that the Cowboys could have won the game.

COMPLETENESS OF THOUGHT

Since a sentence should express a single complete thought, *completeness of thought* must be stressed as an important part of sentence unity. The main points of sentence completeness may be summarized as follows:

A. Do not put a period at the end of a phrase or a subordinate clause that stands alone.

A phrase is a group of related words without a subject or a predicate. It modifies some other word in the sentence. Obviously it cannot be written as a complete sentence.

A subordinate clause depends on some other clause for its meaning. It must be connected to the independent clause, even though the subordinate clause has a subject and a predicate, if the sentence is to comply with the principle of completeness.

In the examples that follow, the italicized portions might have been incorrectly punctuated as separate sentences. In fact, they were so punctuated in a metropolitan newspaper.

One body was recovered last night, *that of T/Sgt. William G. Seymour.*

Rex never won a round on the United Press score sheet, *although he fought on even terms in the first session.*

These sentences are correct, but the writer of the following sentence became so involved in his construction that he forgot to complete the sentence:

Twittle was a raw recruit who, hailing from the mountains of Tennessee, with only a fourth-grade education, but with a "shooting eye" that was to bring him fame as a sharp-shooter in World War I.

B. Do not omit any word, phrase or clause which is needed for sentence clarity and unity.

You have been warned not to omit articles that are necessary to the meaning. Study these examples of the omission of other words, phrases and clauses and the resultant clouding of the meaning of the sentence.

1. A main verb is sometimes omitted in error.

INCORRECT: Patti launched her career by singing the type of songs that many other girl singers have and still are singing.

CORRECT: Patti launched her career by singing the type of songs that many other girl singers have *sung* and still are singing.

Just to make sure that this point is clear, consider one more example.

CORRECT: Forrester *has* never *done* any quarterbacking and never *will do* any. (Not: and never *will.*)

Both verbs should be given in full, as shown.

2. Do not omit a necessary auxiliary verb.

INCORRECT: Four dazed airmen were recovered from rubber rafts after they bailed out.
CORRECT: Four dazed airmen were recovered from rubber rafts after they *had* bailed out.

The auxiliary verb *had* is necessary to show the correct tense, the past perfect.

INCORRECT: Seven crewmen were lost and one saved in the crash.
CORRECT: Seven crewmen were lost and on *was* saved in the crash.
INCORRECT: The wrecked car was rolled off the highway, a wrecker called and other drivers told to proceed cautiously.
CORRECT: The wrecked car *was* rolled off the highway, a wrecker *was* called and other drivers *were* told to proceed cautiously.

NOTE: An auxiliary verb may be omitted if it is in the same form as the other auxiliary verbs in the same sentence. The auxiliary is said to be understood. For example, it is correct to write:

Six crewmen *were* lost and three saved in the crash.

Were is understood before *saved.*

3. Do not omit a necessary relative pronoun.

INCORRECT: Collier manages a professional football club which played well on both offense and defense and drew well throughout the season.
CORRECT: Collier manages a professional football club which played well on both offense and defense and *which* drew well throughout the season.

The second relative pronoun *which* is needed to make the meaning clear.

INCORRECT: The reply followed a reminder on a South Vietnamese station the Viet Cong had not yet mentioned the proposed truce.

The reporter who wrote the sentence failed to note that the omission of the relative pronoun left the meaning of the sentence cloudy.

CORRECT: The reply followed a reminder on a South Vietnamese station *that* the Viet Cong had not yet mentioned the proposed truce.

NOTE: The relative pronoun, particularly *that,* may sometimes be omitted without clouding the meaning of the sentence. The writer should make sure that the omission does not make the sentence difficult to comprehend. The pronouns given in parentheses in the following sentences could be omitted.

The senator said (that) he thought (that) the legislature "wanted the regents to run a pretty conservative university."
The President ticked off a dozen actions of Congress and said (that) they seem bewildering at first glance.

Compare the sentences above with the following sentence:

Obviously, the wild things are now living jammed up so close to human beings *that* they are beginning to learn human tricks.

If the writer had omitted *that,* readers might think that *they* refers to *human beings* instead of to *wild things.*

A good rule to follow in using *that* or omitting it is this: If its omission would cause the reader to assume that the subject of the dependent clause is the object of the preceding verb, the pronoun should be used. Recall the following example that was used in Chapter 2:

He maintained the woman is a prostitute.

At first glance *woman* might be taken to be the object of *maintained.* And think of the embarrassment—and the possible libel suit—if a typesetter set "He maintained the woman *as* a prostitute" and the proofreader let the error get by. It would certainly be safer to write:

He maintained *that* the woman is a prostitute.

On the other hand, be careful not to use *that* twice in a sentence for one subordinate clause.

INCORRECT: The coach said that if Kirkpatrick had been available for service, that the team could have won the game.

The second *that* is wrong and should be omitted.

However, the relative pronoun needs to be repeated in a series of clauses like those in the following sentence.

The City Plan Commission Wednesday advised the City Council *that* Dallas should stay strictly within its 260-square-mile drainage area in annexing new territory, [*that* it should] adopt a flexible annexation policy, and [*that* it should] head off undesirable residential developments.

Some editors would advise you to write the sentence this way: ". . . advised the City Council to stay . . ., to adopt . . . and to head off. . . ."

4. Do not omit a necessary preposition.

In the sentences below, the prepositions that are set in italic type are necessary to the sentence. They should not be omitted.

He never worried *about,* nor tried to help with, her problems.
He admits that he is more apprehensive for his own safety than *for* that of (*for* the safety of) his family.
The strange writings were found on the box, which had been broken open, and *on* the wrappings that had been torn away.

Make sure that you do not omit prepositions which are needed to make the sentence clear. Many prepositions are little words. Don't judge their importance by their size!

5. Do not omit the *to* of any of the infinitives in a series.

He wants us to write letters, *to* present our arguments and *to* convince the council of the necessity for this action.

The student must learn to read extensively, *to* analyze what he reads and *to* summarize the main points presented.

6. Do not omit the conjunction before the final item in a series. Using a comma in place of *and* is not sufficient.

Read extensively, analyze what you read *and* summarize the main points.

7. Do not omit the participle in a phrase, especially when the main verb contains a different idea from that of the participle.

In addition to *having* a nose for news, the good reporter must possess integrity.

But note that the participle may be omitted when the phrase follows the independent clause with the same verb:

That reporter has integrity as well as a nose for news.

8. Do not omit other words, phrases or clauses that are needed to make the meaning clear and to unify the sentence.

Because the demonstrative pronoun *that* is omitted, the incorrect sentence below has a *main point* and a *man* coinciding, an impossible feat.

INCORRECT: The main point made by the first speaker and the man who followed him on the panel coincided.

CORRECT: The main point made by the first speaker and *that of* (*that made by*) the man who followed him coincided.

The words italicized in the following sentences are needed:

A revaluation of gold at $52.50 *an ounce* instead of the present $35 would best achieve the Gaullist purpose.

Twenty armed soldiers and seventeen People's Police escaped to West Berlin from *the duty of* enforcing a government ban on free United States food for East Germans.

Two of the five critically injured rioters were found *to be* dead on arrival.

The kind old woman gave us a sight-seeing tour to talk about *when we got* back home.

Try omitting the italicized phrases and clauses to see whether you think the reader would get a clear meaning of the sentences without these.

9. Do not omit transition words, phrases or clauses that help make the connection between the parts clear to the reader.

This is a common fault of newspaper reporters. Persons handling news are usually warned to use transition devices sparingly, it is true, but the writer should not leave too great a gap between sentences or clauses or even between paragraphs. Otherwise, the reader will be unable to "follow" the writer.

In the sentence that follows, omission of the transition word *however* would make the meaning obscure.

Colby is protected in his job under the Civil Service Act. *However,* he is (He is, *however,*) subjected to tremendous pressures.

The *conjunctive adverbs* are especially useful in helping the reader to grasp more readily the true meaning of sentences and paragraphs. Look back to pages 48–49 for a list of some important conjunctive adverbs. In addition to this list, the words and phrases below are frequently used:

otherwise	meanwhile	for this reason
consequently	furthermore	for example
immediately	in contrast (with)	for instance
later	in addition (to)	as a result

Use of any of these words and phrases establishes the connection between the sentence in which it occurs and some previous sentence.

10. Do not use two sentences if the use of one sentence is clearer.

Two sentences often can be combined by making one sentence a subordinate clause introduced by a subordinating conjunction; for example, *if, unless, although, even if, in order that, so that, because,* or *since.* Let's look at some examples of this.

> Streaming north through Panmunjom were North Korean Communist prisoners. They were transported in closed ambulances. They did not appear to be sick or wounded.

Why were the prisoners being transported in ambulances? Were they sick or wounded? Use of a subordinate clause to introduce the second sentence would answer the questions at once, and the addition of a phrase at the end of the construction would further clarify the meaning. Read the following sentences and compare them with those in the previous illustration.

> Streaming north through Panmunjom were North Korean Communist prisoners. Although they did not appear to be sick or wounded, they were being transported in closed ambulances, apparently to prevent incidents.

Often the omission of a necessary sentence makes it difficult to keep pace with the writer, as in this excerpt:

> The ROK's moved cautiously as they began the ascent of Old Baldy. At the summit they found only a remnant of the North Korean division that had defended the mountain for 21 days.

The writer asked his readers to make quite a jump from the foot of Old Baldy to the top of the mountain! At least one transition sentence is needed between these two sentences, something like: "It took them two hours to work their way to the summit." Or the second sentence might be started with the subordinate clause: "When they reached the summit, . . ."

Sometimes you may find that you need to use transitional devices throughout a series of paragraphs, or at least between several paragraphs within a story. Do not hesitate to do this if these expressions make it easier for the readers to follow the meaning of the paragraphs and of the complete story. In the following Associated Press story note how the italicized transitional devices help hold the story together and make it easy to read.

Panmunjom, Aug. 11 (AP)—A bitter band of die-hard Americans came back from their Red prison camps today—vowing vengeance on weaker comrades who turned to communism under pressure.

They spat out "progressive" as a dirty word, and wore with honor the badge of "reactionary" fastened on them by Red Chinese who clubbed and tortured them but did not break their spirits.

One of these tough Americans had to be held back by force when he spotted a "progressive" at the Freedom village reception center.

"I'll get him when I get home," *he* said.

One hundred Americans came back from the North, along with 24 British, 25 Turks . . .

Meanwhile, 328 Americans repatriated earlier sailed from Inchon aboard the troopship Gen. Nelson M. Walker, . . .

At the same time a plane bearing 17 seriously ill *Americans,* all litter patients, landed at Honolulu for a night of rest, . . .

OTHER PHASES OF UNITY

Besides completeness, there are many other phases of unity which are important. The fact that unity means oneness of thought and that a correct sentence expresses a complete thought does not mean that a sentence can contain only one statement; if it did, we would not have complex, compound and compound-complex sentences. What the journalist needs to remember is this: If the sentence is composed of two or more parts—two or more statements—the parts must be closely related. In other words, make sure that the parts of a sentence fit together to make up one unified larger thought or idea.

If this kind of unity is to be obtained, consideration must be given the main principles that are discussed below.

1. Keep each sentence to one unified thought. The statements or ideas of the sentence must be related.

Study these examples:

POOR: The blaze spread rapidly through the sprawling plant, which is of modern, functional design.

BETTER: The blaze spread rapidly through the sprawling plant. The brick structure is of modern, functional design.

INCORRECT: War damage totals more than $1,000,000,000, with one building in every six having been destroyed, and industry and agriculture are almost dormant.

CORRECT: War damage totals more than $1,000,000,000, with one building in every six destroyed. Industry and agriculture are almost dormant.

The thoughts in each case are not closely related. They should be put into separate sentences, as shown.

Certainly the two statements in the following example do not go well together as independent clauses. You might get past the sports editor if you made a subordinate clause of the second statement.

INCORRECT: A majority of Pacific Coast Conference players have the ability to graduate to the professional ranks, and most of them come from California.

CORRECT: A majority of Pacific Coast Conference players, most of whom came from California, have the ability to graduate to the professional ranks.

If you make the change of putting the idea in one independent clause into a subordinate clause, make sure that the idea does have some relation to the idea in the main clause. This subordination of one idea to another is an important phase of coherence.

2. Avoid going to the other extreme and chopping your sentences into small units.

Although the reporter is urged by readability experts to use as many simple sentences as possible, he should avoid the choppy writing that sometimes results from this practice.

If the ideas expressed in two or more short sentences are evidently related, they may be put into one unified sentence. This usually means subordinating one idea or ideas to another.

CHOPPY: The city manager may be compared to the manager of a big department store. He has the power to appoint employees. He has the power to fire employees. He supervises the work of the employees in the various departments.

BETTER: The city manager may be compared to the manager of a big department store, as he has the right to appoint and to fire employees. He also supervises the work of the employees in the various departments.

There are times, of course, when the stringing together of short sentences is permissible. The sports writer may employ the style to express fast action. Writers use it sometimes for emphasis. If you use it, make sure that it serves a legitimate purpose.

Here is a good example of a sports writer's reporting:

Hardy backtracked several paces. He feinted to the left. He hesitated another few seconds. Then he rifled a 20-yard pass, straight over the middle, into the arms of Schnellenberger.

3. Prospective journalists do not need to be reminded that the childish habit of stringing clauses together with the conjunction *and* will not be condoned in any publication office. However, some of you may need to be reminded that you must keep superflous details out of your sentences.

In the following sentence, some of the details—possibly including birthplace, birth date, parents and education—belong in separate sentences. Some of the details might be omitted, unless this is an obituary.

Rathbone Deberry, born in New Orleans Dec. 1, 1894, the son of James and Stella Deberry, received a B.E. degree from Tulane in 1916, and has served as assistant city engineer in New Orleans, as assistant location engineer for the Illinois Central Railroad, and has engaged in architectural practice since 1926.

4. You may be failing to use enough subordinate clauses or prepositional, participial and infinitive phrases.

If you study the writings of professional journalists, you will find that they have learned to subordinate minor ideas in their sentences, using dependent clauses and, in many instances, phrases to express the less important ideas. When you have mastered this technique, you will be well on your way to becoming a first-rate writer.

Here are examples of poor sentences and the way to improve them.

POOR: We harvest raw sap and the water content is reduced from two-thirds to a third by a centrifuge similar to a cream separator, and then the concentrate is treated with ammonia to prevent souring and shipped.

BETTER: We harvest raw sap, whose water content is reduced from two-thirds to a third by a centrifuge similar to a cream separator. After the concentrate is treated with ammonia to prevent souring, it is ready to be shipped.

POOR: Treating the concentrate with ammonia to prevent souring is the next step in the process, and it is the most important one.

BETTER: Treating the concentrate with ammonia to prevent souring, the next step in the process, is the most important one.

The important idea is stressed in the better sentences, as it should be.

POOR: The third season of the television show, "Bewitched," has been completed, and the producer is planning to send Elizabeth Montgomery and Agnes Moorehead, the first socially acceptable witches, on a personal appearance tour.

BETTER: With the third successful season of the television show, "Bewitched," (having been) completed, the producer is planning to send Elizabeth Montgomery and Agnes Moorehead, the first socially acceptable witches, on a personal appearance tour.

The main idea—that the two TV stars will make a personal appearance tour—is given the emphasis it deserves by changing the first independent clause to a phrase.

Take care to subordinate the minor ideas, not the principal statement. Notice this sentence:

POOR: The firemen were laying the first hose line when the roof caved in.

BETTER: The roof caved in while the firemen were laying the first hose line.

The important idea is the caving in of the roof.

Putting a *when* clause at the end of a sentence may result in faulty subordination, as shown in the first sentence about the firemen. Sometimes the subordinate clause needs to come first in a sentence, for emphasis, as in the following example:

POOR: The vote on letting the bridge contract was taken when Commissioner Price arrived.

BETTER: After Commissioner Price arrived, the vote on letting the bridge contract was taken.

The following are other examples in which the main ideas were incorrectly subordinated by being placed in dependent clauses or phrases:

POOR: The blackmailer hesitated several minutes before he opened the post office box, which gave the officers sufficient time to spot him and to make the arrest.

BETTER: When the blackmailer hesitated several minutes before opening the post office box, the officers were given sufficient time to spot him and to make the arrest.

POOR: He looked like a tramp, although he is a multimillionaire.

BETTER: Although he looked like a tramp, he is a multimillionaire.

POOR: The governor glanced across the lobby to see two senators taking pokes at each other.

BETTER: When the governor glanced across the lobby, he saw two senators taking pokes at each other.

POOR: Wainwright lapsed into a coma, dying 24 hours later.

BETTER: After lapsing into a coma Tuesday, Wainwright died 24 hours later.

5. Earlier you were warned to be habitually on the alert against committing the comma fault, or comma splice.

You should recognize that the comma fault is a violation of the principle of unity. The following examples should be sufficient to demonstrate how to correct this fault.

INCORRECT: The water content in the raw sap is reduced from two-thirds to a third, then the concentrate is treated with ammonia.

The second clause should be preceded by a semicolon because *then* is not a coordinate conjunction.

CORRECT: The water content . . . to a third; then the concentrate . . . .

The sentence would have even more unity if the minor idea were expressed in a subordinate clause:

BETTER: After the water content in the raw sap is reduced from two-thirds to a third, the concentrate is treated with ammonia.

A common error of the worst type is illustrated by this sentence:

INCORRECT: Richardson hit the middle of the line three times, he failed to make a first down.

The error can be corrected in several ways: (*a*) by use of a coordinate conjunction; (b) by use of a subordinate clause; (c) by conversion of one clause into a phrase; (*d*) by making two sentences.

a) Richardson hit the middle of the line three times, *but* he failed to make a first down.
b) *Although* Richardson hit the middle of the line three times, he failed to make a first down.
c) *After hitting* the middle of the line three times, Richardson failed to make a first down.

d) Richardson hit the middle of the line three times. He failed to make a first down.

The following sentence violates the principle of unity even more seriously because the two clauses are not so closely related as those in the foregoing example.

INCORRECT: Gene and Lynn Phillips are brothers, they will both be in the starting line-up for the Ponies this fall.

The error is corrected below in three ways: (*a*) by making two sentences; (*b*) by use of a subordinate clause; (*c*) by use of a prepositional phrase and an appositive.

a) Gene and Lynn Phillips are brothers. They will both be in the starting line-up for the Ponies this fall.
b) Gene and Lynn Phillips, who are brothers, will both be in the starting line-up for the Ponies this fall.
c) In the starting Pony basketball line-up this fall will be two brothers, Gene and Lynn Phillips.

Which type of construction you use will depend upon where you wish to place the emphasis.

Avoid the comma fault. If the two statements are not closely related, use separate sentences. Otherwise, you will not achieve unity in your sentence.

The comma fault is often committed when *so* is used to introduce the second clause. This results in a weak construction in most cases.

WEAK: Johnston is needed, so he will go.

Even with a semicolon before *so*, this sentence is weak. Unity may be achieved in the following ways:

CORRECT: Johnson is needed. He will go.
Because he is needed, Johnson will go.
Being badly needed, Johnson will go.
Johnson is needed, and he will go.

Many editors prefer the conversion of one statement into a subordinate clause as the solution.

6. Exercise care in the choice of the conjunction.

Use the conjunction which expresses exactly the meaning you intend to convey. There is a wide variety to choose from, and there is no excuse for violating the principle of unity.

INCORRECT: Bernard Buckheit entered politics and became governor, and his twin brother became a peanut vendor.

The conjunction *and*, which implies addition, is wrong; the correct conjunction to use is *but*, which expresses contrast.

INCORRECT: Bobo is not observing training rules, and his batting average is dropping sharply.
CORRECT: *Because* Bobo is not observing training rules, his batting average is dropping sharply.
INCORRECT: The victim was given two blood transfusions, but he died.
CORRECT: *Although* the victim was given two blood transfusions, he died.

7. Do not violate the principle of unity by using the incorrect sentence form.

As a rule, the compound-complex sentence finds little place in journalistic writing. Conversion of these sentences into complex sentences is often the best way to achieve better unity.

POOR: Bruce Portillo was especially good at backing up the line, and later the coach found that he was even more effective at fullback on the offensive.
BETTER: Later the coach found that Bruce Portillo, who was especially good at backing up the line, was even more effective at fullback on the offense.

The second sentence has greater unity and places the emphasis where it belongs—on the fact that the coach found Portillo more effective at fullback.

Of course, two ideas which are truly coordinate should be written as a compound sentence. Don't try to force a coordinate idea into a subordinate clause.

POOR: Bowers and McCloud brought in a third detective, with whose help they solved the murder of the councilman.

The second idea is as important as the first, if not more important. It belongs in an independent clause.

BETTER: Bowers and McCloud brought in a third detective, and with his help they solved the murder of the councilman.
OR:
After Bowers and McCloud brought in a third detective, they solved the murder of the councilman.

The exercise for this chapter contains many types of sentence errors that violate sentence unity. Be on the alert to detect run-on sentences and fragmentary sentences. Look closely at any connective adverbs, like *so*, which introduce a second independent clause. Make sure you can distinguish between clauses and phrases and between independent clauses and dependent clauses. You must be able to find the simple predicate and the simple subject and make them agree. Some of the sentences need to be separated; others need to be combined. Some need to have independent clauses converted into dependent clauses or into phrases; others need to have dependent clauses changed into independent clauses. In several constructions a dependent clause should be converted into a phrase. Look for use of the wrong conjunction and for omission of necessary conjunctions like *that*. Be especially alert to find omissions of necessary prepositions or the *to* in an infinitive, or omission of needed transition words, phrases or sentences. Some main verbs need to be repeated, and some auxiliaries are missing. If you can change these sentences so as to make them correct, unified sentences, you have learned the lesson of this chapter.

Quiz Answers

1. One auto was recovered, that of William Truehart. 2. Insert *was* before *saved*. 3. Insert *that* before *the*. 4. Insert *to* before

write. 5: Change comma to semicolon or make two sentences. 6. Break up into more sentences; be sure to have the honorary degree fact in a sentence by itself. 7. Combine into two sentences, preferably. 8. He is neither interested *in* nor concerned about . . . 9. Change *were* to *was.* 10. Change *were* to *was.* 11. The man, 24, (or The 24-year-old man) was booked. . . 12. Two sentences, by all means! 13. Change *but* to *and.* Could convert first sentence to a subordinate clause: As we watched. . . 14. *But* is correct conjunction; however, this would be better: Although he had . . . top lawyers, he failed to win the suit. 15. Delete the second *that.*

14

Sentence Coherence

Coherence means logical consistency or agreement. Whether we call it sentence coherence or sentence clearness makes little difference. If a sentence has coherence, then it has clarity; its meaning is immediately clear to the reader because the parts of the sentence are logically arranged and related.

Sentence coherence is gained in various ways. Some of the essentials of coherence are discussed in this chapter.

First, however, why don't you test your knowledge of the essentials of sentence coherence by taking the following quiz?

Rewrite or copyedit the sentences to correct errors that violate sentence coherence or clarity. Watch for such errors as: misplaced modifiers, misplaced dependent clauses, needlessly split phrases, wrong correlative conjunctions, incorrect reference of pronouns, and dangling words and phrases. Also, correct all violations of parallelism and consistency—unnecessary shifting of voice, subject, person, number and tense.

Quiz

1. He only had two dollars.

2. While climbing the fence, his pants caught on the barbed wire.

3. Revise: He tripped and fell forward into the mud when he hit the last hurdle.

4. Charles Johnson of Abilene caught 11 black bass on a black Hula Popper lure, the biggest one weighing five pounds.

5. He neither owns land nor cattle.

6. He is honest, a hard worker and has confidence in his ability to make good.

7. Bring the mixture to a boil, and then it should be stirred briskly.

8. Revise: Her sister told her that she had won the prize.

9. Each salesman will be allowed a commission also.

10. To provide the city with more water and finding more parking space downtown are the two big problems facing the city council.

11. Coach Shula began to listen to his assistants, and the team's morale was improved.

12. There is no panacea either for farm market problems or dwindling profits ahead, Dr. Timm told the vocational agriculture teachers.

13. The dark-eyed senorita dangled a basket on her arm that was filled to the brim with bright-colored flowers.

14. Morrall hid the ball for a few seconds, then he tossed it to his left end as he cut off to the right sideline.

15. He gunned the motor while it veered sharply to the left.

PLACING THE PARTS CORRECTLY

Modifiers should be placed as near as possible to the words they modify or in such a way that the meaning of the sentence is clear to the reader. Guard against misplacing word, phrase or clause modifiers.

ADVERBS

You know that such adverbs as *only, nearly, hardly, scarcely, even, almost, also* and *not* can change the meaning of the sentence if they are placed near different words in the sentence. The word *only*, which can be used as an adjective or an adverb, must be watched particularly.

Note the difference in meaning of the following sentences because of the change in position of the word *only:*

Patterson *only* won three fights in 1968.
Patterson won *only* three fights in 1968.
Only Patterson won three fights in 1968.
Patterson, *only*, won three fights in 1968.

Study the different meanings of the following sentences also. *Almost* and *ever* should always be placed carefully.

Jenkins *almost has* a perfect batting stance. (Incorrect)
Jenkins has an *almost perfect* batting stance.
The manager said he didn't *ever think* the recruit could learn to play first base. (Incorrect)
The manager said that he did not think the recruit *ever could* learn to play first base.

Many adverbs can be used at different places in the sentence: (1) to gain variety; and (2) to give the exact emphasis desired. Be sure that the adverb is not used ambiguously, however. Study the following sentences to see the difference in meanings.

He was *even polite* to his mother-in law.
He was polite *even to his mother-in-law.*
Even he (of all persons) was polite to his mother-in-law.
Surely the Tigers will win this one.
The Tigers will win this one, *surely.*
The Tigers *will surely win* this one.

Beware of using a "squinting adverb," one that may modify either of two words, one preceding and one following the adverb. Such adverbs usually modify an infinitive. Note these sentences.

To miss batting practice *often* results in suspension from the team.

Does *often* modify the infinitive *to miss* or the verb *results?* To avoid confusion, it would be permissible to split the infinitive in this case and say: *to often miss.*

Another case would be an adverb placed between a verb and an infinitive, like this:

The players were told *constantly* to concentrate on the fundamentals.

Does *constantly* modify *were told* or *to concentrate?* The probable intention is to have it modify the infinitive, and this may be made clear by saying: *to concentrate constantly* or *to constantly concentrate.* The first form is preferable.

PHRASES AND CLAUSES

1. The *prepositional phrase,* used either adjectivally or adverbially, must be watched closely.

POOR: They found him beneath the overturned car with a broken left leg.

BETTER: Beneath the overturned car they found him, *with a broken left leg.*

BEST: They found him beneath the overturned car. He had a broken left leg.

Of course you would know that the first sentence did not mean that the car had a broken leg, but the phrase should be near the word *him* which it modifies. However, this may make a rather stilted sounding sentence. The best solution is to make two sentences.

Consider this lead that the United Press International editor called to the attention of telegraph editors: His rejected mistress confessed today that she stabbed the man *with the bushy mustache* who died of his wound on a midtown street yesterday, police said.

2. Participal *phrases* used at the ends of sentences are often dangling phrases; they have no word to modify. The error may be corrected by placing the phrase at the beginning of the sentence or by rewording the sentence entirely.

INCORRECT: Funeral services will be held at Keever Chapel at 10 a.m. Thursday, the Rev. W. J. McCawley, pastor of the First Christian Church, officiating.

The phrase *the Rev. . . . officiating* is a dangling participial phrase. Such phrases may be used to introduce sentences occasionally. The following sentence has a correct participial construction at the beginning of the sentence. This construction is called the nominative absolute (see page 86).

His shirttail flying in the breeze, the boy raced down the street.

In the incorrect sentence above, the correction could be made in several ways:

CORRECT: Funeral services will be held at Keever Chapel at 10 a.m. Thursday *with* the Rev. W. J. McCawley, pastor of the First Christian Church, officiating.

Or: Funeral services . . . Thursday. The Rev. W. J. McCawley . . . will officiate.

Or: Funeral services will be conducted (read) by the Rev. W. J. McCawley, pastor of the First Christian Church, at Keever Chapel at 10 a.m. Thursday.

3. *Elliptical expressions* that dangle are sometimes found in sentences. Such expressions usually begin with *when* or *while.*

INCORRECT: While making an entrance from the wings, the actress' feet became entangled in her long dress and she sprawled on her face.

CORRECT: While *she was* making an entrance from the wings, the actress' feet became entangled. . . .

Or: While making an entrance from the wings, *the actress* got her feet entangled. . . .

An elliptical expression is really an incomplete clause, that is, a clause from which one or more important parts have been omitted. The error can be corrected by supplying the missing parts. If that is not done, care must be taken to see that the phrase modifies the correct word, such as *actress,* not *feet,* in the last example given.

Here are other examples of the dangling elliptical expression:

INCORRECT: When idling, the noise of the motor becomes louder.
CORRECT: When *the motor is* idling, the noise becomes louder.
INCORRECT: The old man's 1955 pick-up always seems to stall when making an important delivery.
CORRECT: The old man's 1955 pick-up always seems to stall when *he is* making an important delivery.

Some editors would pass the following sentence:

Candidates failing to report regularly for practice cannot make the team, the coach declared.

However, the meaning would be clearer if a relative clause were used:

Candidates *who fail to report for practice* cannot make the team, the coach declared.

Surely most editors would require you to revise this sentence:

Candidates failing to report for practice by the deadline which will be observed by all schools in the conference will be ruled ineligible for varsity competition.

The meaning of the sentence is vague. It might be revised thus:

All candidates who fail to report by the deadline set by conference officials will be ruled ineligible for varsity competition.

Do not confuse dangling elliptical expressions with the transitional devices often employed by good writers to connect sentences or paragraphs. A sentence like the following is correct. The transitional phrase *speaking of taxes* is used independently.

Speaking of taxes, what does Chairman Mills think of the new income-tax proposal?

4. Most editors would call the introductory *when* clause in the sentence below a dangling clause because it does not modify the main verb *can look* in the independent clause.

When the Mississippi Rebels opened the season in such high spirits, their supporters can look back now and see that they were certain to have a successful season.

The sentence would be better this way:

Supporters of the Rebels can look back now and see that when the players entered the season in such high spirits, they were certain to have a successful season.

5. Guard against misplacing a dependent clause. Both relative clauses and adverbial clauses are often placed incorrectly in sentences.

INCORRECT: Sidden apparently had put the gun into the car *while it was loaded.*

CORRECT: Sidden had apparently put the gun, *while it was loaded,* into the car.

BEST: Sidden apparently had failed to unload the gun before placing it in the car.

INCORRECT: He tripped and fell forward into the mud *when he hit the last hurdle.*

CORRECT: *When he hit the last hurdle,* he tripped and fell forward into the mud.

You can avoid this type of error if you arrange the parts of the sentence in chronological order—in the logical time sequence in which they occurred. In the last example above what was the sequence in the hurdler's accident? He first hit the hurdle; then he tripped; then he fell forward into the mud. Note this further illustration:

INCORRECT: His car hurtled over the 25-foot embankment when Johnson reached the slick pavement and lost control.

CORRECT: When Johnson's car reached the slick pavement, he lost control, and the automobile hurtled over the 25-foot embankment.

It is always safest to place a relative clause next to its antecedent.

POOR: All girls and boys are eligible for prizes who (that) send in the box tops.

CORRECT: All girls and boys *who send in the box tops* are eligible for prizes.

POOR: The soldier pulled a bar of chocolate from his pocket, which he fed to the South Vietnamese waif. (He did not feed his *pocket* to the waif!)

CORRECT: The soldier pulled from his pocket a bar of chocolate, which he fed to the South Vietnamese waif.

6. Do not place a phrase or a clause where the reader cannot tell whether it belongs with what precedes it or with what follows it. As we observed earlier, such a construction results in what is called a "squinting" modifier—a modifier that looks both ways.

POOR: The manager when he was fouled repeatedly protested to the referee.

There are two misplaced modifiers in this sentence. The clause *when he was fouled* seems to refer to the manager, and the adverb *repeatedly* squints—it may modify either *fouled* or *protested*. The sentence should be written this way:

CORRECT: When his fighter was fouled repeatedly, the manager protested to the referee.

Note one more example:

POOR: Tell him, if he is in his office, I will see him this afternoon.
CORRECT: If he is in his office now, tell him I will see him this afternoon.

Or: Tell him I will see him this afternoon if he is to be in his office then.

7. Avoiding the misplacing of a modifier is simply a matter of refraining from the needless separation of these sentence parts: (*a*) subject and verb; (*b*) verb and object; (*c*) a compound verb; (*d*) a verb phrase; (*e*) an infinitive phrase.

Study these examples:

a) INCORRECT: The Braves, in their first game after moving from Milwaukee to Atlanta, scored a stunning upset.
CORRECT: The Braves scored a stunning upset in the first game they played after moving from Milwaukee to Atlanta.

b) POOR: His car careened to the right and hit hard and almost demolished the abutment.
BETTER: His car careened to the right and *hit* the *abutment* hard. The abutment *was* almost *demolished.*

c) POOR: His car careened to the right and, traveling at almost a 45-degree angle, smashed into the abutment.
BETTER: His car careened to the right. Traveling at almost a 45-degree angle, it smashed into the abutment.

The parts of the compound predicate, *careened* and *smashed,* are too widely separated in the first sentence.

It is correct to separate a verb phrase with adverbs if this makes the meaning clear. It is also considered correct to place the adverb after the first auxiliary verb, thus:

Gibson had *definitely* been chosen to pitch the first game of the series.

It is also permissible to split the infinitive with an adverb if the construction is clear and reads smoothly.

He was able to *slowly* cross the ledge.

But needlessly separating the parts of a verb phrase or of the infinitive is an error.

d) INCORRECT: He declared that he would, despite strong opposition, continue his project.

CORRECT: He declared that he would continue the project despite strong opposition.

e) INCORRECT: He is far too slow afoot to within three days' time switch from guard to halfback.

CORRECT: He is far too slow afoot *to switch immediately* from guard to halfback.

CONJUNCTIONS

The *correlative conjunctions* should be placed correctly in the sentence. *Either . . . or, neither . . . nor, both . . . and,* and *not only . . . but also* should be placed so that each conjunction immediately precedes the word it connects with another word.

INCORRECT: He *neither* possesses land *nor* money.

CORRECT: He possesses *neither* land *nor* money.

INCORRECT: The Gibsons raise *not only* geese *but also* a herd of goats.

CORRECT: The Gibsons *not only* raise geese *but also* keep a herd of goats.

PRONOUNS

Correct *reference of pronouns* is an essential of coherence.

If necessary, review Chapter 6. Remember that it must always be clear what word is the antecedent of the pronoun. Avoid having a double reference.

POOR: Johnson told Hall that his car had been stolen.

Whose car had been stolen, Johnson's or Hall's?

CORRECT: Johnson told Hall, "*My* car has been stolen."
Or: Johnson told Hall, "*Your* car has been stolen."

Make sure that the pronoun has a definite antecedent to which to refer. For example, there is no antecedent for *it* in this sentence:

INCORRECT: He offered to advise the councilmen, but they refused it.

CORRECT: He offered his *advice* to the councilmen, but they refused *it*.

Or: He offered *to advise* the councilmen, but they refused *to hear him.*

Avoid the use of the pronoun *which* to refer to the entire clause used as the antecedent.

INCORRECT: Aaron Spelling was given the leading part, which the other actors did not like.

The reader might think that *which* refers to *part* or even to *Spelling,* when actually the intention was to have it refer to the entire independent clause. The sentence will be clear if changed like this:

CORRECT: Spelling's being given the leading part displeased the other actors.

Or: The other actors were displeased at Spelling's being given the leading part.

In most cases, the pronoun should refer to a specific word, and that word should be an important word in the sentence. The pronoun should not refer to a parenthetical expression or to a word in the possessive case.

POOR: Baseball is a difficult game to master, one that requires a good *physique* and more *skill* than most other games, and *they* must be developed while you are young.

BETTER: Baseball is a difficult game to master, one that requires a good physique and more skill than most other games. You should develop a sound body and baseball skill while you are young.

poor: The face leered at her in the semidarkness. It looked like a *murderer's* face, *which* made her swoon.

better: . . . It looked like the face of a murderer. At the sight, she swooned.

Make sure that the pronoun has the correct antecedent, and place the pronoun as near that antecedent as possible.

incorrect: He introduced the car-inspection bill early in the session, which was promptly acted upon.

correct: Early in the session he introduced the car-inspection bill, which was promptly acted upon.

poor: The youngest daughter in the Scarborough family, who was both beautiful and popular, was Vicki.

better: In the Scarborough family the youngest daughter was Vicki, who was both beautiful and popular.

poor: Jocko was merely a puppet in her hands that was controlled by expertly manipulated wires.

better: In her hands Jocko was merely a puppet that was controlled by expertly manipulated wires.

The pronoun *it* may be used as an expletive to introduce a sentence, but this construction should be employed sparingly and carefully.

Note these sentences:

correct: It is snowing hard.

faulty: It says in today's paper that Premier Abdullah Yafi may be replaced by a pro-Egyptian former premier, Rashid Karami.

The same rule applies to the impersonal pronouns *they* and *you.*

faulty: They take a siesta every day in Mexico.

better: *Mexicans* take a siesta every day.

faulty: All play and no study makes you a dullard.

better: All play and no study makes *one* a dullard.

USING VERBALS CORRECTLY

PARTICIPLES

Participles that "dangle" make the sentence incorrect. Journalists, of all people, must not be caught in this error. The participle must have a word to modify, and it must modify the correct word to make sense.

Remember that a participial phrase is always used as an adjective. If the participle introduces the sentence, the word modified is almost always the subject of the sentence.

INCORRECT: Having only a month to live, they gave him his Christmas presents early.

CORRECT: *Having only a month to live,* little *Tommy* was given his Christmas presents early.

INCORRECT: Being a dissenter, the committee probably will not invite him.

CORRECT: *Being a dissenter, Ferguson* probably will not be invited by the committee.

Or: As Ferguson is a dissenter, the committee probably will not invite him.

In the following incorrect sentence, there is no specific word in the independent clause for the participial phrase to refer to. This is a violation of coherence. The sentence should be recast as shown in the correct version.

INCORRECT: Highway 80 is much too narrow to accommodate present-day traffic, causing unnecessary traffic casualties.

CORRECT: Unnecessary traffic casualties are occurring on Highway 80 because it is much too narrow to accommodate present-day traffic.

The past participle may be used incorrectly, also. The reference is vague in the following sentence. Note the revision of it.

FAULTY: Unnecessary traffic casualties are occurring on Highway 80, caused by the narrowness of the road.

CORRECT: Unnecessary traffic casualties, caused by the narrowness of the road, are occurring on Highway 80.

The dangling past participle phrase may introduce the sentence, thus:

FAULTY: Caught in the late-afternoon traffic on Main, it was impossible for Maxwell to get his wife to the hospital before the baby arrived.

CORRECT: *Caught* in the late-afternoon traffic on Main, *Maxwell* found it impossible to get his wife to the hospital before the baby arrived.

Placing *thus* or *thereby* before a participle does not keep it from dangling if there is no specific word for it to modify.

FAULTY: Abandonment of the two-platoon system required coaches to use men who could play on both the offense and the defense, thus largely eliminating the football specialist.

CORRECT: Since abandonment of the two-platoon system required coaches to use men who could play on both the offense and the defense, the football specialist was largely eliminated.

The misplaced participial phrase often violates correct use of tense.

FAULTY: The injured man was rushed to the hospital, entering the emergency operating room at 8:30 p.m.

CORRECT: The injured man *was rushed* to the hospital for emergency treatment and *was wheeled* into the operating room at 8:30 p.m.

Or: The injured man, *rushed* to the hospital for emergency treatment, *was wheeled* into the operating room at 8:30 p.m.

In the sentence above the participle *entering* not only is too far removed from the word it modifies (*man*) but the idea expressed in the participle phrase needs to be in the same tense as the predicate *was rushed*.

Another example of faulty tense is the following:

FAULTY: Olivares died in a rest home here Tuesday at the age of 113, being born March 9, 1840, in Rosario, Argentina.

The sentence can be corrected by changing *being born* to *having been born*.

GERUNDS

A *gerund* has the properties both of a verb and of a noun. It may be the object of a preposition, the object of a verb or the subject of a sentence. It can have the same kind of modifiers that a noun can have—adjectives and pronouns—but unlike a noun it can take an object. The phrase in which the gerund is used is called a gerund phrase and, like the participial phrase, it must not dangle.

INCORRECT: After considering the problem from all angles, a vote was taken.

CORRECT: *After considering* the problem from all angles, *the committee* voted.

The gerund phrase cannot modify *vote*. The noun *committee* must be used.

INCORRECT: In jumping from the plane, the parachutist's head banged against the door.

CORRECT: *In jumping* from the plane, *the parachutist* banged his head against the door.

INCORRECT: By terracing his fields, erosion may be avoided by the farmer.

CORRECT: *By terracing* his fields, *the farmer* may avoid erosion.

Errors in the use of the gerund usually result from failure to use the active voice rather than the passive voice, that is, failure to have the subject doing the acting rather than being acted upon. The following sentence is another example.

INCORRECT: The feature article should be outlined before attempting to write it.

CORRECT: *Before attempting to write* a feature article, *the author* should outline it.

The dangling gerund phrase occurring at the end of the sentence is corrected by placing it at the beginning of the sentence and having the correct noun in the main clause for it to modify. Note, too, use of the active voice.

INFINITIVES

An introductory *infinitive phrase* must properly refer to the subject of the sentence. Make sure you have a true subject in the active voice for the infinitive phrase to modify. Study these sentences:

INCORRECT: To become a champion swimmer, the shoulder muscles should be developed while you are young.

CORRECT: *To become* a champion swimmer, *you* should develop the shoulder muscles while you are young.

INCORRECT: To prevent soil erosion, terraces should be built and crops should be rotated.

CORRECT: *To prevent* soil erosion, *the farmer* should build terraces and rotate crops.

Note that the subjects in the correct sentences are doing the acting; in other words, the verb in the main clause is in the active voice.

PARALLEL STRUCTURE

Parallel structure is an important element of coherence. It is simply the principle of placing ideas which are parallel (alike) in thought or meaning into grammatical forms or constructions that are alike (parallel).

Parallelism is not called for or even possible in much journalistic writing, but knowledge of the principle will keep journalists from writing sentences that are not uniform and not clear in meaning.

The most common violations of parallel structure occur when there is an unnecessary interchange of: (*a*) an infinitive with a gerund; (*b*) a noun with a gerund or with an infinitive;

(*c*) a noun with a dependent clause; (*d*) an adjective with an independent clause; (*e*) an adjective with a verb; and (*f*) an infinitive or a gerund with an independent clause. These errors are illustrated in the following sentences:

a) INCORRECT: To provide the city with more water and finding a solution to the downtown parking problem are the two big matters to be discussed tonight.

CORRECT: *Providing* the city with more water and *finding* a solution to the downtown parking problem are the two big matters to be discussed tonight.

Or: To provide . . . water and *to find.* . . .

b) INCORRECT: The council must consider two matters: the shortage of water and finding a solution to the downtown parking problem.

CORRECT: The council must consider two problems: *providing* a sufficient supply of water and *solving* the downtown parking problem.

INCORRECT: The answers to the water-shortage problem may be to tap Red River and stricter enforcement of lawn-watering regulations.

CORRECT: The answers to the water-shortage problem may be *to tap* Red River and *to enforce* more strictly the lawn-watering regulations.

c) INCORRECT: Mayor Tisdale announced his candidacy for a second term and that he would conduct a campaign based on his present platform.

CORRECT: Mayor Tisdale announced *that he would run* for a second term and *that he would conduct* a campaign based on his present platform.

d) INCORRECT: The bank robber was dark-eyed, sharp-nosed, and he had an olive complexion.

CORRECT: The bank robber was *dark-eyed, sharp-nosed* and *olive-complexioned.*

Or: The bank robber had *dark eyes,* a *sharp nose,* and an *olive complexion.*

e) INCORRECT: Cindy was graceful, well-dressed and had charming manners.

CORRECT: Cindy was graceful, well-dressed and *well-mannered*.
  Or: Cindy had grace, she dressed well, and she had charming manners.

f) INCORRECT: The city council is considering two possible solutions: to tap Red River, or it can drill a large number of artesian wells.

CORRECT: The city council is considering two possible solutions: *tapping* Red River or *drilling* a large number of artesian wells.

INCORRECT: The committee of businessmen offered two alternative proposals: raising the parking-meter charge to ten cents, or more of the downtown streets could be converted into one-way thoroughfares.

CORRECT: The committee of businessmen offered two alternative proposals: *raising* the parking-meter charge to ten cents or *converting* more of the downtown streets into one-way thoroughfares.

By now you have observed that there are three important principles to follow to obtain parallelism. (1) See that coordinate conjunctions join constructions which are alike. (2) See that correlative conjunctions join constructions that are alike. (3) See that the parts of a series are alike in construction.

1. Do the coordinate conjunctions *and, but* and *or* join constructions that are alike in these sentences?

To provide the city with more water and *to find* more parking space downtown are the two big problems.
Raising the parking-meter charge or *widening* the streets may be the solution.
Not wider streets but *more one-way thoroughfares* may be the answer.

2. Do the correlative conjunctions *either . . . or, neither . . . nor* and *not only . . . but also* join constructions that are alike in the sentences below?

The driver was either *asleep* or *drunk*.
Neither the *car* nor the *driver* was harmed.
He was wise not only *in slowing down* but also *in sounding* his horn.

3. Are the parts in the series in each of these sentences alike in construction?

The mayor is *honest, cooperative* and *tenacious.*

A policeman has no legal right *to make* you talk or *to force* you to answer questions you do not choose to answer or *to prevent* your lawyer from talking with you or *to keep* you in jail on mere suspicion.

The mayor has fought hard *for* better *streets, for* adequate *parks, for* lower utility *rates* and *for re-election.*

CONSISTENCY OF STRUCTURE

Consistency in sentence structure is an important element of coherence. Do not change the point of view within a sentence without a good reason for the shift, or your sentences will lack unity, coherence and forcefulness.

1. Do not shift from one *voice* to another.

POOR: Under the proposed plan the engineering student would study three years at Baylor, and then he would be admitted to Texas Tech for two years and a summer session.

BETTER: Under the proposed plan the engineering student *would study* three years at Baylor and then *would attend* Texas Tech for two years and a summer session.

POOR: The head coach began to accept the advice of his assistants and the morale of the team was improved sharply.

BETTER: The head coach *began* to accept the advice of his assistants, and the morale of the team *improved* sharply.

POOR: Trout had been employed by the bank since 1945, and he became chairman of the board of directors in 1952.

BETTER: Trout *had been connected* with the bank since 1945, and *had been* chairman of the board of directors since 1952.

Or: Trout *joined* the staff of the bank in 1945 and *became* chairman of the board of directors in 1952.

Always keep in mind this rule: Use the *active voice* rather than the passive voice as far as possible. Of all the parts of speech, the one that will make your copy sparkle brightest is the active verb. Use of the active verb gives a sentence concreteness, forcefulness, life, vividness, originality and variety. Only the concrete noun comes close to matching the action verb as the most indispensable tool for the journalist.

In cultivating the use of the active verb, however, do not forget that the passive voice is sometimes useful in your writing. A fairly safe rule to follow is this: If the person or thing receiving the action is more important than the person who is acting, use the passive voice rather than the active voice. A review of Chapter 5 will refresh your memory on this point.

2. The *subject* of the verb should not be shifted unnecessarily.

POOR: Conrad established the business in 1956, and most of the firm's commercial loans were handled by him until 1964.

BETTER: *Conrad established* the business in 1956, and *he handled* most of the firm's commercial loans until 1964.

POOR: In the last minute Moore went in at fullback, and the game was won.

BETTER: In the last minute *Moore went* in at fullback and *won* the game.

POOR: Baugh played professional football longer than any other man, and practically all the league's records in forward passing were set by him.

BETTER: *Baugh played* professional football longer than any other man and *set* practically all the league's records in forward passing.

Or: Baugh, who played . . . , *set* practically all the league's records. . . .

3. The *person* of the pronoun should not be shifted unnecessarily.

POOR: You should keep your eyes on the players in the middle of the line, for one cannot learn to appreciate the fine point of football by watching only the backfield.

The error can be corrected by changing *one* to *you.* A better change would be to alter the construction of the sentence, thus:

BETTER: To learn to appreciate the fine points of football, *you* (*the spectator*) should keep *your* (*his*) eyes on the players in the middle of the line instead of watching only the backfield.

4. Unnecessary shifting of *number* should be avoided.

INCORRECT: The big Ohio Wesleyan fullback grinned and replied, "Each player was informed at the beginning of spring practice that we must learn to block first of all."

Each player is third person singular, and *we* is first person plural. The error will be corrected if *we* is changed to the third person singular *he*.

5. Do not shift the *mood* without good reason for the change.

INCORRECT: Grasp the ball firmly with all five fingers; then you flick your wrist slightly as you throw.

Grasp is in the imperative mood. *Flick* is in the indicative mood. Make both verbs imperative.

CORRECT: *Grasp* the ball firmly with all five fingers and *flick* your wrist slightly as you throw.

6. The *tense* of the verb should not be shifted within the sentence.

INCORRECT: Douglass threads his way down the east sideline and fell over the goal line for the winning touchdown.
CORRECT: Douglass *threaded* his way down the east sideline and *fell* over the goal line for the winning touchdown.

Remember that the past tense is used in most new stories, which are largely reports of events which have already taken place. Consistent use of the past tense in the story makes for clearer writing. Also, if each sentence and each paragraph is kept in the past tense, the copy editor has more leeway in cutting the story or in changing the order of the paragraphs. This is often necessary to fit the story into the space available for it.

For example, it would be better writing to say, "Moore *did* not *play* against Notre Dame because he *was* crippled" than to say "is crippled," even though Moore may still be crippled when the story is written. Here is another illustration:

CORRECT: A middle-aged woman was arrested Tuesday and is being questioned about the robbery.

BETTER: A middle-aged woman *was arrested* Tuesday and *was held* for questioning about the robbery.

The first sentence is grammatically correct, but most editors would prefer the consistent use of the past tense. Also, this insures accuracy of facts, as the woman may have been released before the story is printed.

Quiz Answers

1. He had only two dollars. 2. While climbing the fence, he caught his pants on the barbed wire. 3. When he hit the last hurdle, he tripped and fell forward. 4. Use second sentence: The biggest one weighed five pounds. 5. Transpose *neither owns*. 6. He is honest, hard-working (or industrious) and confident of his ability to make good. 7. Bring the mixture to a boil; then stir it briskly. 8. Her sister told her, "You (or I) won the prize." 9. Each salesman also will be allowed a commission. 10. To provide the city with more water and to find more parking space . . . 11. Change *was improved* to *improved*. Better: When Coach Shula began . . . assistants, the team's morale improved. 12. There is no panacea ahead for either farm market problems or dwindling profits, Dr. Timm told . . . 13. The dark-eyed senorita dangled on her arm a basket that was . . . 14. Morrall hid the ball for a few seconds; then he tossed it to his left end as the latter (or *the end*) cut off to . . . 15. He gunned the motor while the car (or the boat) veered sharply . . .

15

Sentence Emphasis

Emphasis, the third member of "the trinity," is a rhetorical principle which the journalist must recognize as a most important one in the practice of his profession. Closely associated with emphasis is variety of expression, another essential of distinctive writing.

Emphasis is the principle of stressing a certain word or words within a sentence or a paragraph. Emphasis is obtained by arranging the words in a sentence so that they give prominence to the central idea, with the minor details subordinated.

However, the journalist must bear in mind that his public reads silently—and often under hurried and distracting conditions. The newspaper reader may not even bother to complete the reading of every sentence. Thus, the beginning of the journalistic sentence is the best place for emphasizing a point. For the same reason a news story must register its important facts at the beginning and let the finer details fall into place later.

With radio and television copy the case is different. Here the copy is spoken aloud and must therefore be in a style that is more informal, more conversational than that of the newspaper. Also, since the audience is less hurried and distracted, the copy may build up to its important points more gradually —this is particularly the case with dramatic writing.

One cue may certainly be taken from the radio and television media: the readability experts urge newspaper men and women to write "like you talk." If this advice is taken, as a rule clearer writing results. But Gunning and Flesch recommend that you do not go all the way in writing as you talk. They recognize that their rules are not always applicable, and they suggest a compromise between formal written English and informal spoken English for newspaper writers. Every journalism student should read what these two authors have written on the subject of readability.

Before you begin your study of sentence emphasis, take the short quiz to test your knowledge of this important rhetorical principle.

Rewrite the sentences to obtain emphasis of major ideas.

Quiz

1. It is impossible to enforce the ordinance.
2. Before he died he had lost his property, his family and his friends.
3. The general lapsed into a coma, dying 24 hours later.
4. The sheriff carried a John Doe warrant which he served on the suspected robber.
5. The roof caved in and six firemen were seriously injured.
6. After he was shot six times following a midnight argument at another tavern in the 2100 block of Northwest Highway, a tavern owner died at 5:05 a.m. Thursday.
7. The boy was running across the street near his home at 8:45 p.m. Wednesday when he was struck and killed.
8. The driver of the runaway car is going to have to show up with greenbacks clutched in hand, if he wants his car back, because Mrs. Price chained the vehicle to a tree.

LOOSE SENTENCES VERSUS
PERIODIC SENTENCES

The basic sentence in most news writing is the declarative sentence with its parts arranged in normal order: subject—predicate—object. Grammarians term this type of sentence the *loose sentence.*

The *periodic sentence* is one that builds to a climax, with the important matter coming at the end. This type of sentence is best adapted to fiction writing. It is used in news writing largely for variety.

The loose sentence, in which the facts are recorded simply and straightforwardly, is the newspaperman's workhorse.

LOOSE SENTENCE: Miss Selma Adele Ullman wrote two checks for $2,100 the day she was murdered in her fashionable Highland Park home at 3605 Mockingbird Lane.

PERIODIC SENTENCE: The day she was murdered in her fashionable Highland Park home at 3605 Mockingbird Lane, Miss Selma Adele Ullman wrote two checks for $2,100.

In the loose sentence, normal sentence order is followed: subject (*Miss Selma Adele Ullman*)—predicate (*wrote*)—object (*two checks*). Placed last are the minor details, which many readers will not bother to read in a follow-up story such as the one this lead was taken from. The periodic sentence would be all right in fiction, but the newspaper copydesk would probably blue-pencil it. Newspaper editors insist that you "put first things first" in most of the sentences you write.

Do you think a copy editor would pass the following sentence as the lead for a follow-up news story?

Police Chief W. H. Naylor said Tuesday that Miss Selma Adele Ullman wrote two checks for $2,100 the day she was murdered in her fashionable Highland Park home at 3605 Mockingbird Lane.

The sentence would be turned down because the beginning of the sentence is devoted to the minor detail that the police chief was the source of the information. The important news was *what* the police chief divulged.

In his zeal to put first things first, the journalist must not forget that the end of the sentence is also a good spot in which to place interesting or important information. If the sentence is not too long, the reader will read it through and will get this piece of information.

Elimination of sex or robbery motives from the killing, he said, virtually removed male suspects.

The sentence ends with an idea that is as important as the idea which begins the sentence. This emphasis is achieved by placing the source of information—a minor detail—between the important ideas. Note how much weaker the sentence would be if *he said* were placed at the end of the sentence.

WEAK: The questioning of the woman got negative results, as did the lie-detector test.

Why not shift the concluding phrase to the middle of the sentence, giving the sentence a stronger ending?

BETTER: The questioning of the woman, as well as the lie-detector test, got negative results.

In the following sentence, likewise, the idea placed at the end should be tucked into the middle of the sentence.

WEAK: The mayor will request the city council to raise parking meter rates in his first attempt to solve the downtown traffic problem.
BETTER: The mayor, in his first attempt to solve the downtown traffic problem, will request the city council to raise parking meter rates.

The journalist should use the periodic sentence occasionally in news stories, and he should find much use for it in feature stories and editorials. In the following sentences, observe that the periodic sentence, with the emphasis at the end, is more effective than a loose construction would be.

Walter Williams, as head of the committee in its fight, was able to state facts and to sell his idea to the mayor.

The next sentence was taken from an editorial. Note how the sentence builds to a climax.

So long as Texas agriculture is bankrupt in the sense that it can not stand alone without government control and subsidy, the supreme contribution of the A & M System will be to show Texas farmers and ranchers how to make a living from the yield of ther own acres, *under their own efforts and with their own capital.*

The writer of the feature story from which the following sentence was taken used one of the most common devices for writing a periodic sentence—the introductory subordinate clause.

Although he was far beyond the regular age limit for membership in 20-30 International, Shimen's avid interest in the group's activities *led to his nomination as its first "honorary member and ambassador of good will."*

The periodic sentence given next comes from a feature article.

Though he has planned the make-up of his newspaper every week for 36 years, the editor of The Watkins Glen Express has never seen his front page, *for since the age of eleven he has been totally blind.*

This periodic sentence builds to a forceful climax.

The following sentence illustrates how the reporter sometimes can give a news story lead emphasis at the end of the sentence.

A man who looked down on the earth from a height of some 16 miles today told how his tremendous momentum in a Douglas Skyrocket enabled him *to climb almost another one and one-half miles without fuel.*

The beginning of a news story lead must be interesting and important, but do not overlook any opportunities to make the end emphatic as well.

SUBORDINATION OF MINOR IDEAS

You have observed by now that emphasis is achieved by placing the main idea at the beginning or at the end of the sentence and by subordinating the minor ideas.

The subordination of minor ideas is achieved by placing the ideas in subordinate clauses or phrases. If you wish to be a first-rate writer, you must learn to use subordinate clauses and phrases correctly.

You have been warned to be careful that you subordinate the *minor* ideas, not the principal statement of the sentence. You have been given special warnings not to place the main idea in a clause beginning with *when* or *which,* or in an infinitive phrase or in a participial phrase. If you feel that you need to review subordinate clauses, turn back to Chapters 2, 3 and 11, and study the sections that deal with subordinate conjunctions. Then study these additional illustrations of good use of subordination of minor ideas.

The important idea may be at the beginning or at the end of the sentence. The minor idea is put into a subordinate clause or phrase.

After being in a coma for 24 hours, Wainwright died. (Not: Wainwright had been in a coma for 24 hours when he died.)
He died after being in a coma for 24 hours. (Not: He lapsed into a coma, dying 24 hours later.)
If you could sell the months of the year, August would carry the lowest price tag.

Do not overlook the element of reader interest in determining what goes into the principal clause.

The bank, which recently moved into its new building on Avenue E, plans to hold open house Tuesday.

The element of timeliness makes the idea of holding open house more important than the fact that the bank recently moved into the new building.

Do not hesitate to use the introductory subordinate clause— even in straight news stories—if you are sure that such a construction helps make your sentence more effective. Although the device can be employed in straight news leads on occasion, its more frequent use will be in the body of the story. This type of construction can help you give your writing variety.

Five other main devices for obtaining emphasis in the sentence are as follows: (1) use of the active voice rather than the passive voice; (2)repetition of words; (3) use of balanced sentences; (4) arrangement of a series of words, phrases or clauses in the order that builds to a climax; and (5) use of separate sentences for important ideas.

1. Note the use of the active rather than the passive voice.

Foss *carried* the state by an overwhelming majority. (Not: Foss was elected by an overwhelming majority throughout the state.)
Governor D. X. Buchanan *shot* and *killed* a burglar Friday night. (Not: An unidentified burglar was shot and killed by Governor D. X. Buchanan.)

Readers are far more interested in reading that their governor killed a man than they are in finding out that an unidentified burglar was shot.

2. What better example of the effectiveness of the repetition of words can be given than this excerpt from Lincoln's Gettysburg Address?

. . . and that government of the people, by the people, for the people shall not perish from the earth.

3. Emphasis is obtained by balancing two clauses which are similar in structure and of approximately the same length.

The Tarheels could finish first, or they could finish last.
The spirit is willing but the flesh is weak.
Get it first, but first get it right.

The balanced sentence should be used only occasionally, usually to emphasize two ideas that are strongly contrasted.

4. Effective climax can sometimes be obtained in a sentence merely by arranging events in the order of their importance.

CLIMACTIC: He gambled recklessly and lost his friends, his family and finally his life.
WEAKER: Before he died he had lost both his family and his friends.

5. Certainly you will have no trouble seeing that the following sentence should be broken up into two or more sentences in which emphasis can be given to the main ideas.

A colorful array of exhibits, which will include antiques, paintings and leathercraft, will go on display for the three-day event, and poultry and livestock will be shown in the main barn, with judging in all events scheduled for 8 p.m. Saturday.

Note how much better the emphasis on the main ideas is in this revision:

A colorful array of exhibits—including antiques, paintings and leathercraft—will go on display for the three-day event. Poultry and livestock will be shown in the main barn. Judging of all events will take place at 8 p.m. Saturday.

The news writer should be particularly careful to separate any *direct quotations* he uses from important explanatory material. Study the following example:

You might say the Lone Star Steel Company dug into the pension files to build a top-notch fire department.
But Vice-President L. D. Webster puts it this way:

"We wanted experience—and got it. Back of the five veterans on our eight-man force are 160 years of fire-fighting know-how."

The inexperienced writer might have crowded into one paragraph the information contained in the three paragraphs above. Such a crowded paragraph would be difficult to read and would not put the emphasis where it belongs—on the quotation. Look at another example, which shows the *wrong* way to do it:

"My baby is dead; my baby is drowned!" cried the young woman, Mrs. William A. Varnell of Arsenal, Ark., as she ran screaming to the curb, with an unconscious child in her arms, and stopped Mrs. Drake, who was driving along Grand. "Take us to the hospital."

See how an expert reporter separated the direct quotation from the explanatory material in handling this story:

Mrs. Drake was driving along Grand when a young woman with an unconscious child in her arms ran screaming to the curb and stopped her.

"My baby is dead, my baby is drowned!" cried the young woman, Mrs. William A. Varnell of Arsenal, Ark. "Take us to the hospital."

In using fairly long quotations, it is best to place *he said* or its equivalent in the middle of the sentence or paragraph, rather than at the end.

"A hobo is a transient worker of varied occupations. So many people misconstrue the word," Zollner says. "It's used by the men themselves, but they sometimes resent others' using it, particularly when they are identified with tramps. These men don't want charity, but occasionally they may have to ask for it."

Note the position of *Zollner says*. Remember that you must not keep the reader in the dark too long as to the identity of the person speaking.

Even in the report of a speech or of an interview, you should bring the name of the person quoted into your report often, particularly in a lengthy quotation.

Quiz Answers

1. Enforcement of the ordinance is impossible. Or, To enforce the ordinance is impossible. 2. Before he died he had lost his property, his friends and his family. (Build to a climax.) 3. The general died 24 hours after lapsing into a coma. Or, The general, after lapsing into a coma, died 24 hours later. 4. The suspected robber was served with a John Doe warrant which the sheriff carried with him. Or, Taking along a John Doe warrant, the sheriff served it . . . 5. Six firemen were seriously injured when the roof caved in. 6. Begin with the independent clause: A tavern owner died at 5:05 a.m. Thursday after he was shot six times . . . 7. The boy was struck and killed at 8:45 p.m. Wednesday while running across the street near his home. 8. Begin with: If he wants his car back, the driver of the runaway car . . . clutched in hand, because Mrs. Price chained . . .

16
Variety of Expression

Variety is the spice not only of life but also of good writing. You can keep a reader reading by varying sentence structure and by using other devices to obtain variety in the expression of your ideas.

The subject of variety of sentence structure has been treated throughout this book. Remember that you can avoid monotonous writing in the following ways:

1. By varying the beginnings of sentences and of paragraphs

2. By using varied kinds of sentences of varied lengths

3. By using direct quotations

4. By using fresh figures of speech

5. By using simple, concrete words

Study the examples of these methods given in the sections that follow. Many of the illustrations were taken from news story leads and from the bodies of the stories.

Before you begin your study of the methods of obtaining variety in your writing, test your comprehension of this most important subject by taking the quiz that follows.

Quiz

Rewrite the following sentences so as to eliminate stereotyped words and expressions (cliches); unnecessary slang; wordiness, especially circumlocutions; provincialisms; unacceptable colloquialisms; non-idiomatic expressions, including misused prepositions in phrases; jargon or gobbledygook; and vulgarisms.

1. It was around the year 1898 when he and his small family located in the little village of Wilton.
2. His outlook on life is quite different than his partner.
3. Mme. Curie first discovered radium.
4. One would never has suspicioned that his Brigham Young team had finished up clear down at the bottom of the list in the 1967 conference race.
5. All of a sudden the walls caved in, and despite the gallant efforts of the hook-and-ladder heroes, the hungry flames completely destroyed the warehouse.
6. With the agreement finalized, the two firms will now be merged together.
7. The average tuberculosis patient has a real good chance today to recuperate in a healthy climate.
8. He lurched drunkenly towards the man who held onto a knife.
9. It was plain to see that she was fixing to raise a ruckus.
10. He had one car in front of and one in back of two brand new Lincolns.
11. The police quickly threw out a dragnet. The drunk hit-and-run driver was caught around one hour later. He had a half-emptied bottle of hooch in his car. He was promptly booked and tossed into the jug.

In the following four sentences you are to obtain variety of expression by rewriting so as to use the type of grammatical beginning called for:

12. Combine the two sentences and begin with a *present participle phrase*: Directors of the GI Transportation Company Thursday

announced they would continue their fight to win a city taxi-cab franchise. They declared they had the cabs necessary to public operation.

13. Revise to begin with a *gerund:* Juan Mason's business is understanding people.

14. Revise to begin with an *infinitive phrase:* The PTA's chief goal has become bringing the home and the school closer together.

15. Combine the two sentences and begin with an *adverbial clause of concession*—a dependent clause: The number of deaths from Hong Kong influenza may rise sharply this week, City Health Officer Tav Lupton said. However, he feels that the epidemic is now under control.

VARYING THE BEGINNINGS OF SENTENCES

Although the lead for the straight news story most often begins with a noun (the subject), do not overlook the opportunity to begin with any other part of the sentence if it will get the attention of the casual reader. However, you should be sure to begin the lead with an idea or a fact which is an important and interesting element of the story, and no conscientious newspaper editor will permit you to forget that rule.

What has been said about the lead applies equally to other sentences in the story. Strive to give the majority of the sentences interesting beginnings.

The following rhetorical devices—grammatical beginnings—are used by the skillful writer to play up the features in the lead or in any sentence.

1. Beginning with a *noun* (subject).

A *mother* was killed yesterday in Albuquerque in a futile effort to save her five-year-old daughter from death under the wheels of an automobile.

The subject *mother* is modified by the article *a* in this lead. As far as possible, it is best to avoid using *the* or *a* or *an* in leads. If the article is needed, however, use it. Here the article is unnecessary:

Jurors in the criminal assault trial of Gerald David Knight heard opposing arguments Saturday night as the case moved toward a conclusion.

2. Beginning with a *prepositional phrase*.

With a pinstriped railroad man's cap cocked on his blond head, young L. M. Crannell Jr. deftly engineered his way into the finals of the Public Links Golf Association championship Saturday with a surprising 2-and-2 upset of George Bennett.

In Boston next day, Ted took up his self-imposed task of fund raising to pay off the $3,500,000 in debts run up by Robert Kennedy's presidential campaign.

Before an audience that overflowed Municipal Hall Friday night, the rival candidates debated the issue of liquor by the drink.

After a few years in Washington, most politicians can detect the faint hiss of escaping gossip the way bird dogs can hear whistles pitched too high for the human ear.

Of all the disappointments the Mustangs suffered last season, the greatest, probably, was their inexcusably poor showing as they were shut out, 26 to 0, in the Cotton Bowl by Kansas.

At key points in Sout Viet Nam, allied forces last week were placed on alert in anticipation of a new enemy offensive.

By their own efforts, the students have rejected the lethargy and alienation inherent in their ghetto lives.

Among the seizures of enemy stores was a cache of 3,200 rounds of heavy machine gun ammunition, 82 mortar rounds and 2,700 pounds of rice.

For nearly a month, Greece had been gripped by a bitter and highly significant struggle.

As a judge on Hitler's dreaded wartime People's Court, Hans-Joachim Rehse signed 231 death sentences. (*As* is a preposition in this construction.)

In one or the other of two signed confessions read at her trial, Mrs. Dennison told how she gave Shirley Dianne the lethal potion.

3. Beginning with a *present participial phrase*.

Clicking off a one-over-par 72, Clark Haley, Tenison ace, took the lead Sunday in the qualifying test for the Texas Public Links championship which officially opens Thursday at the Cedar Crest Country Club.

Avoid the dangling participle! Be sure that any participial phrase you use properly modifies the noun or pronoun which follows the phrase. Don't write a sentence like this: "Falling down the elevator shaft, Smith's leg was broken." After all, Smith accompanied his leg in the fall!

Here are correct examples from news leads:

Honoring Miss Pat Hilbun, bride-elect of Dr. M. T. Braswell, Mrs. Tom Perkins of McKinney and Mrs. Cleve Hames of Henderson entertained with a luncheon Tuesday in the Century Room of the Adolphus hotel.

Inaugurating a new policy of summer productions using student directors, the Arden club will present "The Royal Family" in the Schuessler Garden July 7–9.

Rattling 15 hits to all sectors of the Astrodome, the Houston Astros overcame an early St. Louis lead to whack out a 10–3 triumph before 22,148 fans Saturday night.

Racing toward earth today on a near-perfect course, the Apollo 8 astronauts were to splash down in the Pacific Ocean a thousand miles southwest of Hawaii Friday.

Passing and pounding in impressive fashion, San Jose State crushed Fresno State, 28–0, in their annual football game here Sunday.

Note the use of the compound present participle *passing and pounding.*

4. Beginning with a *past participial phrase.*

Urged by Grogan "to take off your ties and remove the chains around your necks," the New Leftists refused to go along with the Yippie leader.

Plagued by a students' strike, France was also threatened today by another serious labor situation as factory workers walked off the job in Paris plants.

Bound for South Viet Nam to meet their husband and father, Mrs. Archie L. Mount, 3408 San Jacinto, and Betty Jean, 3, were preparing Tuesday for departure.

Injured in saving their baby from an oncoming automobile, a young man and his wife are in critical condition in City-County Hospital today.

Note the use of the compound past participle in the following opening phrase:

Delayed by bad weather and half hidden by mist over the harbor, the 83,673-ton Queen Elizabeth arrived in New York late yesterday with 1,758 passengers.

Here is another example of the use of a compound past participle. We hope that other journalism students will not, like Donald Withers, assume that journalism is an "easy racket" offering easy riches!

Caught and *booked* on robbery charges for an attempted holdup, Donald Withers of New York City told police he was studying journalism "because it's an easy racket and I want some easy dough."

5. Beginning with an *infinitive phrase.*

To match the razzle-dazzle politicking of Premier Maurice Duplessis, Quebec's Liberals had to set off some pre-election fireworks of their own.

Note that the infinitive phrase is used adverbially to modify the predicate *had to set off.* It plays up purpose by answering *Why?*

To write a biography of William Allen White took courage, for he left behind one of the great American autobiographies.

Note that this infinitive phrase is the subject of the verb took.
Remember that the infinitive phrase placed at the beginning of the sentence is used either as a *noun* or as an *adverb.* Note the following:

To believe in Christ has always been, as Kierkegaard put it, an inexplicable leap of faith.

The infinitive phrase *To believe in Christ* is used as the subject of the verb *has been*. That is, it is used as a noun.

To bring the home and the school closer together, the Idaho Congress of Parents and Teachers is cooperating in four workshops this summer over the state.

The infinitive phrase *To bring . . . together* modifies the predicate *is cooperating.* It is used as an adverb.

The infinitive phrase that is used as an adverb must be set off with a comma. When the phrase is used as a noun, no comma is needed.

6. Beginning with a *noun clause.*

What advertising can mean to the future of America is the theme of an essay contest for students of senior high schools under the sponsorship of the Advertising Federation of America.

The entire clause *What . . . America* is the subject of the verb *is.*

Avoid overuse of the noun clause to begin news leads. Some editors do not permit its use because it may make the lead run too long. But you will find you can often use it to begin sentences in the body of the news story, the feature article or the editorial.

Here are good examples of the use of noun clauses to begin sentences:

"That we must rebuild the Republican Party somewhat closer to the Democratic Party has always been one of my passions," said Robert Finch.

Whether the tax hike and hold-down in government spending will cool off the American economy as they're intended to do is the big question experts are pondering.

What was thought might be human hair under the fingernails of the murder victim was cat fur, Chief Naylor said.

That the Voice of America broadcasts need a stronger dose of Texas brag was the Saturday diagnosis of Rep. W. R. Poage of Waco.

If the beginning noun clause runs too long, it is better to break up the parts and make two sentences.

AWKWARD: *That the United Nations could be used "to settle little conflicts that might grow into big ones" like the conflict between India and Pakistan but could not be used effectively to settle conflicts in which major nations were involved* was the senator's conclusion when he appeared before the committee Thursday.

BETTER: The United Nations could be used "to settle little conflicts that might grow into big ones" like the conflict between India and Pakistan, but could not be used effectively to settle conflicts in which major nations were involved. That was the conclusion reached by the senator when he appeared before the committee Thursday.

7. Beginning with a *subordinate clause of cause.*

Because it became convinced that the Justice Department would not act against IBM, Control Data went ahead last week to file suit.

Since (Because) he didn't get his new suit back from the cleaners in time and was forced to get married in a "soiled and unkempt" gray ensemble, Thomas J. Mitchell of Shreveport has filed suit for $2,500 against the Shreveport Laundries, Inc., and its agent.

Often a phrase beginning with *Because* may be used rather than a cause clause. It is shorter, of course, and often just as effective as a clause: *Because of its size,* U.S. Steel has far less flexibility than its smaller counterparts.

8. Beginning with a *subordinate clause of concession.*

Although (Though) they have managed to reassert Soviet dominance with the Warsaw Pact countries and force the troublesome Roumanians back into the fold, the Russians still face serious economic dislocations within Comecon, the Communist equivalent of the Common Market.

Though the South Vietnamese army and police have some 7,700 female volunteers in staff and clerical jobs, a proposal to draft women outright was turned down.

While (Although) he was considered one of the top university ad-

ministrators in the nation, he simply could not deal successfully with the rioting students.

Note that *While,* usually used to mean *at the same time as,* is used here in the sense of *Although.* Use it in this sense sparingly, and only as a *while* clause preceding a main clause.

9. Beginning with a *subordinate clause of condition.*

If another widespread coal strike takes place in the next few weeks, the entire country will suffer, and diggers of coal will be among those who feel the pinch most sharply.

If the President-elect adopts the advice of President Johnson's Kappel Commission Report, Blount will be the nation's last Postmaster General.

If the young chick hatched by a Rhode Island hen in the back yard of Ernest Horn, 4141 Odessa Street, grows to maturity, it will be able to furnish four drumsticks for the dinner table.

Unless such steps are taken to provide greater equality of opportunity for higher education, an important reservoir of talent will go untapped, the commission argues.

If there was such a message from Hanoi to Washington, it was not getting through.

10. Beginning with a *subordinate clause of time.*

When the battle for Shinjuku station was over, authorities totted up damages of close to $1,000,000, with 140 person hospitalized and more than 700 in jail.

When Dallas' Neiman-Marcus department store set out to pretty up for the holidays, somebody thought it would be fun to have Christmas trees decorated to the specifications of various celebrities.

While investigators today sought the cause of an Army air tragedy on Hawk Mountain, authorities at Davis Monthan Airfield at Tucson reported that three of 12 persons killed in the crash had been identified definitely.

As their spaceship dashed ever nearer to home, the three tired Astronauts caught as much sleep as they could, resting for the critical re-entry through the earth's atmosphere.

As soon as they seized power 18 months ago, Greece's ruling colo
nels began waging a compaign to secure international acceptance
of their stern rightist regime.

Since Robert Lee Pauling was born five days ago, there are now
five generations living and present in the baby's family.

Often a time phrase, rather than a time clause, may be used
effectively and sometimes with a saving of space.

After his candidate had nailed down the nomination, Nixon confi-
dant John Mitchell was asked if he had enjoyed campaigning.

*Since the conditional resignation of Chief Justice Earl Warren six
months ago,* the queston of naming his successor has been an
imbroglio of partisan politics and personal enmities.

Before the end of the first inning, the White Sox had chased home
eight runs.

In one 24-hour period last week, 31 U.S. fighting men died in Viet
Nam.

Make sure that you know how to punctuate introductory
subordinate clauses and phrases.

A *comma* is needed to set off introductory subordinate cause
clauses, concessional clauses, conditional clauses and time
clauses.

A *comma* is used after a beginning present participial phrase
and after a beginning past participial phrase.

A *comma* is needed with an infinitive phrase used adverbially but not with an infinitive phrase used as the subject.

Unless they run very long or need a comma after them for
clarity, introductory prepositional phrases do not need a
comma. Such a sentence as this would require one to avoid
confusion: "After a few years in Washington, politicians can
detect. . . ."

An introductory noun clause that is used as the subject of
the verb is not followed by a comma.

There are other types of grammatical beginnings which may
be used by the journalist. Most of these devices can be easily

overused. You should learn to use them only for special effect or for the purpose of giving variety to your writing.

11. Beginning with a *gerund.*

Spying is tough these days, as the crew of the Pueblo unfortunately found out.

Finding the right man to be Secretary of Defense was a more difficult chore.

The gerund *Spying* is the subject of *is.* The gerund phrase, *Finding the right man to be Secretary of Defense,* is the subject of *was.* Here's another example: *Protecting the channel* is a dirty job.

Note the use of the compound gerund in the next sentence.

Knitting socks and learning to whittle were just two steps in the liberal education of Miss Laura L. Stickney, newest employee at Woodlawn Hospital.

12. Beginning with a *nominative absolute.*

Her right hand still paralyzed from a snakebite, 13-year-old Fay Nolan fondled the rattlesnake which had bitten her while 6,000 persons watched atop Little Black Top Mountain.

The nominative absolute is a phrase, you will recall, in which a noun precedes the participle, as in *hand . . . paralyzed.* The nominative absolute is used like a participial phrase and modifies the noun or the pronoun that follows it.

13. Beginning with a *verb.*

Look for the Buckeyes to blast any doubts that they are the No. 1 team in the nation when they clash with the Trojans in the Rose Bowl Wednesday.

Bring out the most extravagant fashion-adjectives, strew them with an Olympian hand from the tip of Alaska to the Horn, and you've just begun to cover the colossal fashion extravaganza which the Los Angeles Fashion Group staged this past week at the Statler hotel.

14. Beginning with an *adjective.*

Blonde little Nancy Gayle Swenson celebrated her second birthday Monday.

The thin, graying, condemned woman, clad in a black dress, sat stoically.

Jubilant over their unexpected World Series victory, the Tigers whooped it up in the locker room.

Subdued and pleasant, Maurice H. Stans, 60, fits into the sprawling Department of Commerce as unobtrusively as a wastebasket.

15. Beginning with an *adverb.*

Suddenly the hold-up man pulled a pistol and fired three shots at the liquor store manager.

Inevitably, the latest installment in the monetary crisis brought increased pressure for basic reform of the system.

Suddenly, unbelievably, Soviet tanks were in the streets of Prague.

Then General Dean, caked with dust, got out of the jeep without help.

Still later, the confession continued, the aunt watched doctors cut open the body for the autopsy that revealed the presence of arsenic.

Now and then her face twitched and she swallowed, but she held her composure until the verdict was rendered.

Scarcely less impressive than Morral's passing performance was that of the sore-armed Unitas.

Note that the adverb *scarcely* modifies the adverb *less,* which in turn modifies the adjective *impressive.*

16. Beginning with a *pronoun.*

None of Sikes' quarterbacks has played a minute of a varsity game.

This will be Sikes' sixth season at Lawrence after moving up to head coaching ranks from the University of Georgia.

You can't win for losing in this tough league.

"I shall not step out of character," said Coke Stevenson when asked if he would reply to the charges.

17. Beginning with an *expletive.*

It was Christmas Eve.

It was the first time a woman had been executed in Alabama.

It was Kern's two touchdown passes in the fourth period, after he had the shoulder snaapped back into place, that gave Ohio State its margin of victory in the Rose Bowl game.

It's still nip and tuck whether the tax hike and hold-down in government spending will cool off the American economy as they're intended to do.

There is no more than a quarter of a yard to go in the women's swim-suit industry.

There was a time when Ponelle seemed to be more concerned with chi-chi than with character.

18. Beginning with a *conjunction.*

But key fumbles by Simpson and quarterback Steve Sogge put the Buckeyes in scoring position in the fourth period, and Kern took advantage of them.

And in those five seasons the Jayhawks have been shut out only one time.

VARYING THE BEGINNINGS OF PARAGRAPHS

For the journalist, the *beginning* of a paragraph—like the beginning of a sentence—is the most important part. The newspaper reader, remember, reads silently and hurriedly. Just as he may fail to finish many sentences, he may fail to finish even more paragraphs.

Naturally, you cannot get the most important part (idea or fact) of every paragraph into the first line or two. However, you must strive to do this as far as possible. You must make the opening of every paragraph interesting if you expect the reader to go on with your story. Try, then, to begin each paragraph with an arresting fact or idea—if not with the most important fact or idea—and then devote the remainder of the paragraph to building the details.

Use *key words* to begin as many paragraphs as possible.

Avoid beginning paragraphs, as far as possible, with the articles *the, a* and *an* or with the expletives *there* and *it*.

Use the greatest possible variety of grammatical beginnings for paragraphs, just as you do for sentences. Variety in paragraph beginnings, in fact, is even more important than variety in sentence beginnings. You will use the subject for paragraph beginnings more often than any other kind of grammatical beginnings, just as in beginning sentences; but give the reader as much variety as you can manage.

Of course, you know that you must keep paragraphs short if you are writing for newspapers. Since you can get only five to six words in a narrow newspaper column, and as lengthy paragraphs will slow up and discourage the hurried newspaper reader, the newspaper journalist must write shorter paragraphs than the magazine journalist or the book writer. He will find himself writing many one-sentence paragraphs.

Remember that the paragraph is used simply as a mechanical, visual device to break up the subject matter into units and to facilitate readings. Since unity is desired in the paragraph, this may best be obtained by confining the paragraph to one idea or fact, rather than to two or more. Thus, the writer will achieve better unity by keeping paragraphs short.

You were told earlier that *transitional devices* must not be overworked in news writing, but you should not hesitate to use a transitional word, phrase or sentence that is really needed to tie a paragraph to a preceding paragraph or paragraphs. Use the transitional device to begin a paragraph whenever you feel that the meaning otherwise would not be clear to your readers.

Note how the use of transitional words, phrases and clauses in this report of William Anthony Toomey's winning of the Olympic decathlon in 1968 in Mexico City makes it easier for the reader to continue with the story.

Of all Olympic competition, *the decathlon* most closely reflects the original Greek ideal of all-around athletic excellence.

An entire track and field meet in miniature, its ten events in two days add up to the toughest individual test of speed, stamina, strength and spirit ever devised.

The man who wins the Olympic decathlon well deserves to be known as the finest athlete in the world.

That man last week was William Anthony Toomey, a 29-year-old school-teacher from Santa Barbara, Calif., who not only captured the gold medal but set an Olympic record in the process.

Toomey modestly insists that "behind every good decathlon man there's a good doctor," and indeed the demands of the brutal competition are enough to strain the strongest body.

Meanwhile, Kurt Bendlin, West Germany's world record holder, arrived in Mexico City complaining of two sore knees and tendonitis in one elbow. Toomey had a pulled hip muscle for which he was being treated with cortisone.

Even so, in the first test, the 100-meter dash, Toomey hit the tape in 10.4 seconds, best time of the day. . . .

Then, a soaring 25-ft. 9¾-in. long jump, best of Toomey's career, gave him another 994 points and kept him in the lead.

After that, a poor 45-ft. 1¼ in. shotput and a disappointing 6-ft. 4¾ in. high jump dropped him to second behind East Germany's Joachim Kirst.

Next came the grinding 400-meter run, and after ten straight hours of competition, Toomey somehow managed to sprint the distance in 45.6 sec.

It was the fastest time ever recorded in the decathlon and it put him back in the lead as the first day ended.

The second day's competition began with the 110-meter hurdles . . .

Now the gold medal was riding on the last event, the 1,500-meter run. If he could beat Toomey by 10 sec. or so, Bendlin could still win.

But Bendlin never came close . . .

Gasping in the thin air, every muscle rubbery with fatigue, Toomey led all but a few strides of the way and drove to victory by 30 yards . . . "That was the worst competition I've ever been in," said Toomey. "I've never had to endure anything so intense. They shouldn't call this the Olympic Games. It's not a game out there."

Here's an example of the use of a transitional device in a news lead:

Differences between Russia and the United States threatened today to stall world peace-keeping machinery on all fronts.
This was underlined sharply by Soviet and American deadlocks in the United Nations.

Only one word may be needed to make the transition clear, as in the following example:

Airport opponents intend to meet within two weeks at the home of one of their leaders, Reveau Bassett of 4705 Cedar Springs.
Meanwhile, the City Council will consider complaints from Love Field residents.

A prepositional phrase may be used to make the transition clear:

In addition, Mayor Johnson will ask the Council to visit the airfield and look over the situation.

VARYING THE KINDS OF SENTENCES

The journalist's workhorse is the declarative sentence, but he should use interrogative, imperative and exclamatory sentences occasionally to give his writing variety. Note these examples:
1. Using *interrogative sentences.*

Did you ever start down a strange staircase in pitch darkness? That is something like the way the pilot feels coming in on GCA.
What are little atoms made of? Nothing to be afraid of! Neutrons, protons and little electrons. That's what little atoms are made of.
Do you feel tired? Run down? Have you tried blood? The folks down at Kenya, Africa, have, and it works fine.

Note the effective use of a series of questions in the last example.

2. Using *imperative sentences.*

Cut the chatter, Buster! Halt your weeping about how you blew
that four-footer on the second hole. Forget that you almost suffered a fractured elbow getting out of those weeds off the first
fairway.

Just lie in bed, pick up your telephone receiver and hear a Sunday
morning sermon by your favorite pastor.

Relax! Kick off your shoes and stretch out on the sofa some Sunday
afternoon. Wriggle your toes if you want to, but don't go to
sleep.

Note that some of these imperative sentences may be classed
as exclamatory sentences also.

3. Using *exclamatory sentences.*

Earthquakes to order! That's the business of Geophysical Service,
Inc., and Saturday it had a new half-million-dollar instrument
with which to do the job.

Don't push the call button! The sudden *ping* in the cockpit might
startle the jet hijacker and provoke him to fire his pistol.

You might save a life—and it may be yours!

One of the most effective ways to obtain variety in your
writing is to use a judicious mixture of simple, complex, compound and compound-complex sentences. The newspaper
writer will find himself using the simple sentence most often,
followed by the complex, the compound and the compound-
complex sentences, in that order. Just be sure to mix them up!

4. Using *simple sentences.*

The low-fat diet of his North Korean captors helped John Higgins
shed unwanted weight—about 70 pounds.

Both the nine Roman Catholic pacifists on trial in Baltimore federal
court last week and their lawyer, William Kuntsler, conceded
immediately that the nine had broken the law.

In these supposedly lawless times and certainly orderless times, it
is tempting to see Norman Mailer's second film, *Beyond the
Law,* as a running commentary on dubious police practices.

5. Using *complex sentences.*

While organizations like Barr's and Tate's maintain a tenuous hold on power, the party's real strength has been slipping away.

The captain figured that the fire had started in a pile of rubbish underneath the cellar stairs.

The Democratic leadership has succeeded so well in stifling young talent that there may be nobody around capable of picking up the pieces.

At the end of the battle, the double flag-raising ceremony on two denuded palms had to be delayed several hours because no one could find a Union Jack.

6. Using *compound sentences.*

"They've gotten tired, but they've done a tremendous job in performing this mission."

Rage gripped Israel today at the Arab guerilla attack on an Israeli airliner, and the Israeli press warned of "a suitable reprisal" in due time.

Last week the trustees met and ordered Smith to reopen the campus at once; they also took a hard line on student protests.

7. Using *compound-complex sentences.*

There is a legitimate argument as to which reaction is more appropriate in today's world, and that may be what the 1968 presidential election is all about.

It took a Japanese woodcut artist to do it, but then perhaps he saw that the adventurous Commodore Matthew Perry was, in his way, the Yankee equivalent of a shogun.

It will be seen that the use of different kinds of sentences makes for varied *sentence lengths,* a device which lends interest and variety to any writing.

USING DIRECT QUOTATIONS

The use of *direct quotations* is popular in journalistic writing. Study news stories and features written by top-ranking journalists and note how they obtain variety by this device.

Here are some examples of the value of using direct quotations.

"This is the Bible for the Democratic Party," said a White House intimate.

"The child is just as dead as if the crime had been committed by a man," the governor told newsmen in announcing that he had rejected Mrs. Dennison's final plea for mercy. "The law does not contemplate any difference between a man or woman convicted of murder."

Note how the source of this longer quotation is placed in the middle of the quotation. Remember that you should not give too much of the quotation before letting the reader know the source of the excerpt.

After he had passed sentence, the judge paused just a few seconds. And then he said: "God have mercy upon your soul."

The second sentence may be written as another paragraph, of course, setting off the quotation in its own paragraph. The use of a colon is particularly necessary when it precedes several paragraphs of quotations.

"I expect to win quick!"

That was the comment today by Champion Griffith concerning next week's title bout at Yankee Stadium.

Note the separation of the quotation from the source, which is given in the second paragraph.

ANALYZING A FEATURE STORY

Here is an example of a capably written feature story. The author was Louis Cook, Jr., and the piece appeared in *The Des Moines Register*. We shall use the story to review the methods of varying the grammatical beginnings of sentences and paragraphs, varying the kinds of sentences and varying the length of sentences. Also, note the writer's fresh figures of speech, which are italicized.

S.U.I. ATOM BUSTER NEARLY READY
By Louis Cook Jr.
(Register Staff Writer)

(1) Iowa City, Ia.—Deep in the earth just east of the physics building on the State University of Iowa campus, scientists are preparing to give an atom the surprise of its life.

(2) The final phase in the construction of the University's new $23,000 device to bust atoms now is under way.

(3) Since the golden age of Greece the atom has been a subject for guessing and theorizing, and it still remains one of the enigmas of modern physics.

(4) Within a few months, researchers at the state university will be able to take an atom apart, see what makes it do the things it does, and, perhaps, put it back together.

(5) The atom buster is *an unromantic-looking job of plumbing, resembling an overgrown water heater* more than anything else.

(6) Made of inch-thick boiler plate, it rests in an underground concrete vault connected to the basement of the physics building by a zigzag tunnel *somewhat like the entrance to a world war dugout.*

(7) It's 50 feet over-all in length, 8½ feet in diameter. *Two grown men could run foot-races in it.* At either end is a round door of 3-inch-thick steel, held in place by 32 1¼-inch bolts.

(8) It takes a substantial piece of apparatus to bust up something that for centuries has been regarded as the smallest possible subdivision of matter.

(9) Thirty thousand volts of direct current, produced by an ordinary transformer and rectifier system, will start things going in the atom buster.

(10) An ordinary 22-inch-wide woven cotton belt, *like those used on a threshing machine,* will run on pulleys from one end of the apparatus to the center.

(11) A positive charge of electricity will be placed on the end of the moving belt by *a business that looks like a rake with the handle removed.* Electrons will be sprayed on the belt *just like water from a lawn-sprinkler.*

(12) The belt will carry the charges to the center of the buster. There another rake proposition, oppositely charged, will hold the electrons back, *as a dam stores up water.*

(13) When the mass of electrons becomes great enough—about five million volts worth—they will then flow onto a piece of metal in a 22-foot-long vacuum tube *similar to a regular radio tube except in size.*

(14) That's where the fun begins. The number of volts in an electrical circuit *is the same thing as the number of pounds of pressure behind the flow from a water faucet.* Volts are merely a measure of electrical pressure.

(15) When an electron is kicked down the 22 feet of empty space in the vacuum tube by five million volts, it's really traveling. Electrically charged plates surrounding the path of the electronic beam will keep it moving along.

(16) The electrons stream into the far end of the atom buster *like a watermelon seed squirted out from the fingers of a small boy*— but at an inconceivable speed.

(17) What will happen when this stream of electrons beats upon a substance placed in its path is anybody's guess, but previous experience with a lower-powered device at the university indicates many possibilities.

(18) For one thing, X rays, neutrons, alpha rays and beta rays *will spray out like sawdust when a saw whirls into a log.*

(19) Observers, peering through a periscope arrangement working through a water-filled six-inch pipe extending into a chamber 40 feet away, won't see much.

(20) But delicate counters will record the number and distribution of the rays emitted.

(21) An atom is made up *like a solar system.* In the center is *something like our sun, of great mass—the nucleus.* Around it revolve the electrons, *as the earth revolves about the sun.*

(22) Electrons will be ripped away from the orbits they have held since the beginning of things. Nuclei will be driven from their complacent positions *as heads of little universes.*

(23) Actually, sodium will be changed into magnesium; platinum to gold—but not lead into gold. . . .[1]

[1] By permission of *The Register and Tribune,* Des Moines, Iowa. (Italics and numbers supplied.)

First, note that there is great *variety in the grammatical beginnings of paragraphs and sentences.* Grammatical beginnings for paragraphs alone include the following: adverbs (1, 23); prepositional phrases (3, 4, 18); past participle phrase (6); pronouns (7, 14); expletive (8); adjectives (9, 19); subordinate clauses of time (13, 15); noun clause (17); subjects (19, 22); and conjunction (20).

You will note that seven paragraphs in the story do begin with articles (*a, an, the*)—which are not regarded as interest-arousing words. However, remember that the journalist must begin many paragraphs—and sentences—with articles. As long as the journalist strives to begin a *maximum* number of paragraphs and sentences with something other than an article, he will not draw the ire of the editor. In the story Louis Cook has given the reader plenty of variety in paragraph and sentence beginnings.

Second, check the *variety in sentence lengths.* The lead is the longest sentence—as is often the case in news writing. It runs 31 words. The opening sentence in the fourteenth paragraph is the shortest—six words, counting the contraction as two words. You will find sufficient variety in sentence length.

Third, note the *variety of sentence forms.* The reporter followed the advice of the readability experts in making maximum use of the *simple* sentence. Of the 33 sentences in that part of the story which is quoted, 22 sentences—two-thirds of the sentences used—are *simple.*

Also, note that the next most commonly used type of sentence is the *complex* sentence—not the compound. Eight complex sentences are used, unless you want to call the sentence composing paragraph 5 a complex rather than a simple sentence by reading into it some words that are not there. Only two *compound* sentences appear, and, as you might expect, but one *compound-complex* sentence.

You are urged to check the sentence forms used, which may be easily done by following this numbering system. Where a paragraph contains but one sentence, the sentence is given the number of that paragraph; where two or more sentences make up a paragraph, each sentence is given the paragraph number plus an *a, b* or *c* designation.

Simple sentences: 1, 2, 4, 5, 6, 7*a*, 7*b*, 7*c;* 9, 10, 11*b*, 12*a*, 14*a*, 14*b*, 14*c*, 15*b*, 16, 19, 20, 21*a*, 21*b*, and 22*b*. Complex sentences: 8, 11*a*, 12*b*, 13, 15*a*, 18, 21*c* and 22*a*. Compound sentences: 3 and 23. Compound-complex: 17.

When you first look at the sentence making up paragraph 16, you may be inclined to classify it as something other than a simple sentence. As you analyze it, however, you will note that the lengthy expression modifying atom-buster is composed of a prepositional phrase (like a watermelon seed), followed by a participle (squirted), followed by a prepositional phrase (from the fingers), which in turn is modified by another prepositional phrase (of a small boy); and you will find that the conjunction *but* is not followed by a clause but by a prepositional phrase. This sentence, then, is a good illustration of the use of phrases rather than independent and dependent clauses. This makes for tighter writing, and remember that any editor will bless the reporter who saves newspaper space.

The saving of space by the use of phrases instead of clauses is well illustrated in many of the other simple sentences in the story. For example, you should note in paragraph 2 that an infinitive (to bust) is used rather than a dependent clause, such as *that will be used to bust atoms*. In 4 the writer uses a triple predicate, rather than three independent clauses, to save space. In 6 the introductory past participle phrase not only gives the sentence an interesting beginning but takes less space than a subordinate clause like : (The atom buster) *which is made of inch-thick boiler plate*. Note the use of a past participle phrase at the end of paragraph 7, rather than the use of a space-wasting subordinate clause like: *which is held in place*. A prepositional phrase used appositively in the middle of 10 is very effective and saves space. In 12 note the use of the phrase *oppositely charged* in place of a subordinate clause. Finally, notice how space is saved in 23 by dropping the verb from the last two clauses: *platinum to gold—but not lead into gold.*

Fourth, observe that the reporter does not begin *every* sentence in the story with the most important or most interesting idea. Some of the sentences are periodic, rather than loose, in their construction; that is, *they build to a climax.* The lead itself in paragraph 1 is an excellent illustration of the periodic sentence. "Deep in the earth just east of the physics building on the State University of Iowa campus, scientists are preparing to give an atom the surprise of its life."

The sentence that makes up the third paragraph of the story is another good example of the periodic sentence, and one of the best examples in the story is sentence 4. "Within a few months, researchers at the state university will be able to take an atom apart, see what makes it do the things it does and, perhaps, put it back together."

You should observe that much of the superior quality of this piece of writing results from the reporter's deft use of *figures of speech.* Remember that the four elements of writing style are words, sentences, paragraphs and figures of speech.

In case you have forgotten, the main figures of speech are these:

SIMILE: The boy was as nervous as a cat on a windy day.

A simile is an expressed comparison. In the sentence above, the word *as* expresses the fact that the boy's nervousness is being compared to a cat's. Here's another one: As subtle as a sailor with a six-hour pass.

METAPHOR: Before his first solo flight, he had butterflies in his stomach.

A metaphor is an implied comparison. Reading the above sentence you will find that a disturbed, uneasy feeling is being compared to butterflies in the stomach. The comparison is implied, that is, not plainly stated, since the word *as* or *like* is not used to signal the comparison. Here's a second example: To the ski novice a molehill is a mountain.

PERSONIFICATION: The dishes in the sink cast dirty looks in my direction.

Personification consists in speaking of an abstract quality or something else not human as if it were a human being. Here's another one: Streaks of light probed from room to room and dived under chairs and tables like thieves.

Original and appropriate figures of speech will contribute clearness, concreteness, vividness and conciseness to your writing. Well-chosen figures of speech help the reader to grasp ideas quickly because they present a new idea by comparing it with something with which the reader is familiar.

In writing about the atom-buster, Cook is aware that he is dealing with a highly complicated apparatus which hardly anyone can have seen and about which the readers know little or nothing. He knows that he cannot use the technical terms of the scientists. Therefore, he employs figures of speech profusely, likening the parts of the atom-buster and its functions to things familiar to most readers.

Note how he did this with such figures of speech as the following: "resembling an overgrown hot water heater"; "like those used on a threshing machine"; "a business that looks like a rake with the handle removed"; "similar to a radio tube except in size"; "like a watermelon seed squirted out from the fingers of a small boy"; "made up like a solar system"; "as the earth revolves about the sun."

You can't become a first-class writer like Mr. Cook, who today is a top-flight journalist in New York City, until you learn to use expertly the fourth element of writing style, the *figure of speech*. Remember that your use of the four elements—words, figures of speech, sentences and paragraphs—determines your writing style.

In our analysis we have considered the handling of sentences in great detail. We have not devoted much attention to the development of paragraphs, but it will be well for the student to note how cleverly Cook manages these larger elements. There is sufficient variety in paragraph length, for instance; yet no paragraph is too long. In fact, sixteen of the twenty-three paragraphs are composed of single sentences.

The last thing to note about Cook's fine little story is its vocabulary. The most casual reading of the piece will convince the student that the words used by this reporter are sharp and vigorous. The subject of words is so important that it is worth close attention.

USING SIMPLE, CONCRETE WORDS

Many excellent textbooks on English which stress diction are available. You will do well to read some of them and to refer frequently to an unabridged dictionary, a thesaurus and a book of synonyms. The journalist must never stop developing his vocabulary, since every year brings new words into our language.

USING SIMPLE WORDS

The readability experts stress the use of *simple words*. You must follow their advice in most straight news writing, but you must not write *down* to the reader. The educational level of the average reader is rising, and his *reading* vocabulary is larger than his *speaking* vocabulary. But don't use words that are beyond the comprehension of the average reader, because he seldom will bother to keep a dictionary beside him as he reads his newspaper. If you must use a word that is big or technical, explain it to the reader; in other words, do a bit of interpretative reporting.

On the whole, then, you must use a simple vocabulary for

clearness. Can you find in the atom-buster story a single word which the average newspaper reader would not comprehend? I doubt it. And this story deals with a highly technical subject.

USING SPECIFIC, CONCRETE WORDS

In addition to using words that are clear to the reader, you should strive to use *specific, concrete words*—not general, abstract words. For example, don't use the verb *said* if the man actually *exclaimed, shouted, bellowed, thundered, ranted*—or perhaps *whispered.* Be sure, of course, that the person *did* shout or bellow or thunder or whisper before you use a synonym for *said.* You will use *says* or *said* far more often than you will use synonyms for this verb, but don't fail to employ the specific and more concrete term where it is appropriate.

Instead of using the general term *walked,* you should use, if appropriate, such specific, concrete verbs as: *strode, hurried, raced, dashed, strutted, strolled, limped, shuffled* and so on.

In the atom-buster story note the use of concrete verbs and verbals in the indicated paragraphs: (8) *to bust up;* (11) will be *sprayed;* (12) *stores;* (15) is *kicked;* (16) *squirted;* (17) *beats;* (18) will *spray;* (19) *peering;* (21) *revolve(s);* (22) will be *ripped* away, will be *driven.*

The nouns you use should also be concrete and specific. You will most often call a house a house, to be sure, but there may be times when you could appropriately use such words as *shack, shanty, lean-to, cabin, bungalow, duplex, apartment house, mansion* and so on.

The readability experts also advise the use of a maximum number of *human-interest words.* Human-interest words are words that appeal to the emotions. Grammarians would say that such words are those that are used for their *connotation,* which is defined as the suggestive emotional content or significance which a word has in addition to its explicit literal meaning. Words like *mother, sweetheart, home* and *Old Glory* are simple examples of words that have rich connotations for different readers.

USING CORRECT WORDS

The journalist must learn to avoid three things: (1) use of stereotyped words and expressions; (2) unnecessary use of slang; and (3) wordiness. Let's take a look at these three incorrect, improper and inappropriate usages.

1. *Stereotypes* are words or phrases that have been worn out through overuse. They are often referred to as trite or hackneyed words or expressions, bromides or clichés.

In the atom-buster story, the only expression which might be called a stereotype is *golden age* in the third paragraph. The writer of that feature story has learned what *you* must learn— that the use of stereotypes in newspaper, magazine and radio-TV writing is a fault to be avoided.

Since the use of bromides constantly crops up in news writing, the journalism student should be particularly alert in recognizing trite words and phrases and in eliminating them from his working vocabulary for the most part.

Most editors recognize that use of stereotypes cannot be avoided altogether and that, in fact, a cliché may be used effectively at times. However, editors will expect you to realize what you are doing when you use a stereotype, and you certainly should make it clear to the readers that you know what you are doing. Bernstein recommends use of the cliché "only with discrimination and sophistication." For example: "The delegates to the conference seem unable to see the disarmament forest for the weapons trees." The writer has made it clear to his readers that he knows what he is doing in using a stereotype.

The sports writer and the police reporter must exercise extra caution in this regard, because stereotypes abound in their departments. The sports writer must learn to avoid such words and expressions as these:

pill	rifled the ball
apple	sent to the showers
horsehide	battled furiously
pellet	charity toss
pigskin	a brilliant 70
hoghide	chalked up a victory
tangle with	in the shadow of their own goal posts

The police reporter must beware of such expressions as these:

grilled	hail of bullets
angry mob	fusillade of bullets
brutal murder	a shot rang out
reign of terror	miraculous escape
lodged in jail	caught red-handed
pitched battle	shrouded in mystery
pool of blood	struck with a blunt instrument

Writers in other fields of reporting must avoid the use of expressions which have been overworked. A few examples of expressions to be avoided are given below. There are hundreds of others.

acid test	goes without saying
admiring friends	grim reaper
at long last	host of friends
avenging justice	in our midst
blanket of snow	iron out (their troubles)
bolt from the blue	large and enthusiastic audience
bonds of matrimony	lingering illness
bone of contention	long-felt want
breakneck speed	met head-on
breathless silence	mourned their loss
colorful display	in the nick of time
dashed the hopes of	nipped in the bud
deadly earnest	pale as death
devouring (hungry) flames	paramount issue
enjoyable occasion	point with pride
fair sex	proud father (parent)
feathered songster	proud possessor

reigns supreme	tender mercies
riot of color	time immemorial
ripe old age	too numerous to mention
rode roughshod over	took (him) to task
round of applause	untiring efforts
saw the light of day	view with alarm
second to none	weaker sex
select few	worse for wear
soul of honor	wreathed in smiles
supreme sacrifice	

2. Generally, the use of *slang* in journalistic writing should be avoided. *Slang* is defined as words or phrases which have been invented or which have been altered from their standard meanings. Such words and phrases have popular currency, but most of them are short-lived. Here are a few worn examples:

the bee's knees	glad rags	Says you!	confab
the cat's whiskers	a dreamy dress	Do you dig me?	Natch!

You will note that we said the journalist must avoid the *unnecessary* use of slang. Newspaper editors try to keep their papers comparatively free of slang, but most editors permit their writers to follow a middle-of-the-road policy. They recognize that many words and expressions which originated as slang have been accepted as good usage by the compilers of dictionaries, and that more such words and expressions will become good English in the future. In fact, we must recognize that slang has played an important role in enriching the English language. Most editors would approve the use of these expressions today:

mob (of gangsters)	yes man	debunk
fortune-telling racket	gob (sailor)	bamboozle
razzle-dazzle	roughneck	highbrow
big house (penitentiary)	gobbledygook	stooge
rubberneck	blurb	cold feet

If a slang word or expression can be used to give a more specific or clearer idea, use it; but learn early that most publications avoid the use of slang because there is usually an acceptable word or expression which will better convey the idea.

One of the best discussions on the use of slang by the journalist is found in William E. Hall's *Reporting News*. Hall gives the journalist this pertinent advice:

> There is bobbing up here and there some slang that has humor, point and sparkle to it. It has enough quality and meaning to add zest to expression by its occasional use. When a news writer comes upon any slang which has that much merit, he should not hesitate to use it where it may fit in appropriately.[2]

But make sure that any slang word or expression you use is appropriate—and that there is not a better dictionary word to express the idea.

Use of slang may no longer be the No. 1 question for editors and writers. The big debate today is over the use of gobbledygook and jargon.

After former President John F. Kennedy used the word *finalize* in a press conference and was criticized by some for using slang, Dr. Phillip B. Grove, the editor in chief of the Merriam Webster dictionaries, came to his defense by stating that *finalize* had been in use "by a wide variety of erudite publications and personages" since World War I.

In *The American Language*, H. L. Mencken noted a vast coinage of similar verbs in recent years from adjectives, common nouns and proper names: slenderize, tenderize, permanentize, pressurize, hospitalize, routinize, moisturize, winterize, Texanize and Sovietize.

Criticism of using such a word as *finalize,* declared Dr. Grove, would be "a typical reaction by those who shudder over the use of particular words they don't like and who refuse to

[2] *Reporting News* (Boston: D. C. Heath & Co., 1936), p. 136.

recognize the obligation of a dictionary to report the language as it is spoken and written by educated people."

Remarked one newspaper editorial writer, after reading Dr. Grove's statement: "Such criticism, Dr. Groves means, should be *funeralized.*

Recently the author heard this usage in a TV sermon: "You must *positionize* yourself in the right relationship with God." Really, to what ridiculous lengths can we go in creating "new verbs" by adding *ize* to adjectives and nouns?

Although *finalize* and some similar "new verbs" are accepted in the new Webster's International Dictionary, you will find that most newspaper editors, at least, will frown upon such usage. And, you will find authorities such as Copperud stating: "*Finalize,* like *implement* as a verb, is hopelessly associated with gobbledygook, and its user may bring scorn upon himself." And even Rudolf Flesch, a liberal in English usage, calls *finalize* jargon.

Before using such jargon or gobbledygook, then, you certainly should consult the stylebook or your editor.

3. *Wordiness* is a common fault of many writers. Do not use more words than are necessary to express the intended meaning. Editors, who demand concise writing, complain that many cub reporters are wordy.

There are many forms of wordiness, and they go under such names as tautology, circumlocution, verbosity, verbiage, redundancy, prolixity and euphemism. This book cannot attempt to explain these terms and discuss them. If you wish to know more about them, consult any good book on rhetoric or look in the various reference books on language. Just remember that the journalist must avoid wordiness. He must not be long-winded. He must write in a style that is not only accurate and clear but also terse. Learn to "boil down" your writing.

A partial list of wordy expressions is all that can be given here. The words that can be omitted are in italics. The word that could be used for a phrase is given in parentheses.

rest *up*	half a hundred (fifty)
passed away (died)	25 acres *of land*
refer *back*	made his home (resided)
check *up on*	made his escape (escaped)
jumped off *of*	effected his entrance (entered)
end *up*	downy couch (bed)
lift *up*	kind of (rather) rattled
inside *of*	all of a sudden (suddenly)
all *of*	devoured by flames (burned)
fold *up*	*totally* destroyed
paid *out*	*present* incumbent
high noon	as a *general* rule
noon luncheon	*invited* guest
summer *months*	55 *guests* attended
true facts	10 a.m. *in the morning*
continue *on*	met *in regular session* ·
feel *of*	made a statement (stated)
later *on*	was in possession of (had)
over *with*	was in receipt of (received)
large *in size*	the issue *in question*
many *in number*	acted as chairman (presided)
eye witness	was the speaker (spoke)
quite unique	quite a few (several)
pair of (or *two*) twins	a number of (several)
visible *to the eye*	*both* the two sons
final outcome	widow *woman*
regular meeting of	widow *of the late*
ugly *in appearance*	*general* public
consensus *of opinion*	*There are* many *who* recommend

You see that wordiness often results from the use of unnecessary prepositions and adverbs, unnecessary adjectives, unnecessary prepositional phrases, and faulty repetition. Watch your writing for these errors.

The bad practice of adding unnecessary particles to verbs is considered in the discussion of *idioms* on page 273.

PROVINCIALISMS, COLLOQUIALISMS, IDIOMS

If a newspaper circulates in only a limited section of the country, the journalist may be warranted in using expressions that are native to the section. If you expect to write for publications that cover the nation, however, you must limit your use of expressions that will not be understood outside the region of their origin.

1. *Provincialisms* are words or expressions that are used and understood in a limited section of the country. For instance, you will hear such a sentence as this in some parts of our country: "She *carried* her husband to work in the station wagon." Another part of the country would say *took* instead of *carried*, and still others would use *drove*. Would you know what was meant if you heard someone say, "He's *fixing* to go," or "I *reckon* that's right"? Use such expressions as these only if they give color to a story or are used by the person you are quoting.

2. *Colloquialisms* are informal words used in conversation. They are regarded as unacceptable in formal writing, and many of them are not suitable in newspaper writing. With the emphasis on readability, however, and on writing as you would talk, many colloquialisms are finding their way into newspaper articles and stories. Certainly the reporter need not hesitate to use such acceptable contractions as *isn't, don't, doesn't, I'll* and such common words as *phone* and *auto*.

Here are some colloquialisms which you should watch out for:

It's a *deal* (bargain).
I'll be there *around* (about) ten o'clock.
I *guess* (believe) it's true.
Jones *located* (settled) here in 1895.
Smith *runs* (manages) a barber shop.
I *sure* (surely) would like to go.

She wears the *pants* (trousers) in that family.
He hasn't enough *gumption* (sense) to come in out of the rain.
They were all *mighty* (very) tired.

Colloquialisms may be used effectively in newspaper writing that is conversational in style, particularly in feature stories. And they are appropriate in direct quotations, of course.

And in electronic journalism, as may be expected, frequent use of colloquialisms is accepted. Example: The high is expected to be *around* (about) 80 degrees.

What was said about the use of slang applies also to the use of colloquialisms: Use colloquialisms where they are appropriate and where their use will keep your writing from sounding artificial. Remember that you can refer to the dictionary to determine what words are considered colloquial.

3. *Idioms* are words or expressions that are peculiar to a particular language, and they often have some grammatical irregularity. Perhaps the majority of idioms in the English language which may be regarded as correct are idioms in which a verb is modified by one or more prepositions used adverbially. Using the preposition as an adverb to modify the verb radically alters the meaning of the verb. Some examples of correct idioms are given below. Note that most of these include one or more prepositions used adverbially.

to make good	Let's don't
to catch a cold	fall in
to put up with	hold up
to be up against	drop in

However, the writer certainly must recognize that there is a trend toward adding unnecessary particles to verbs, and you will find that most editors condemn such usage. Examples: *face up to* for *face; paid off* for *paid; meet up with* for *meet; lose out* for *lose, heat up* for *heat; continue on* for *continue, merged together* for *merged; postponed until later* for *postponed, or reduced down* for *reduce.*

The *use of prepositions* is one of the most delicate and tricky problems in English. Here are some incorrectly used phrases and the correct idiomatic forms:

INCORRECT	CORRECT
comply to	comply *with*
die with	die *of*
free of disease	free *from* disease
pleased with an idea	pleased *at* or *by* an idea
pleased by a toy	pleased *with* a toy
speak *or* talk to him	speak or talk *with* him
identical to	identical *with*
different than	different *from*
plan on going	plan *to go*
sort of a person	sort *of* person

There are hundreds of English words which may be followed by any one of several prepositions, according to the meaning to be conveyed. An unabridged dictionary gives the correct phrases and their meaning, and there is an excellent list of correct prepositions in the chapter on use of words in Skillin and Gay's *Words into Type*. You can make use also of Funk & Wagnall's *Standard Handbook of Prepositions, Conjunctions, Relative Pronouns and Adverbs*.

AVOIDING SOLECISMS AND VULGARISMS

Solecisms are words or expressions that violate good idiomatic usage in speech or writing. Here are some examples, with the correct form in parentheses.

It looks like snow (*as if* it will snow).
This is a very healthy (healthful) climate.
I have the last (latest) issue of *Life* magazine.
We drove along real slow (*very slow* or *slowly*).
He suspicioned (suspected) that Fagan was a thief.
The team liked (lacked) $95 of reaching its goal.
Advertisement: We have sold 90,000 pair (pairs) of hose.

You will not be guilty of using improprieties if you know how to use the parts of speech correctly.

Vulgarisms, sometimes called *barbarisms,* are words or expressions which are not approved or which are not standard in a language. The only time a journalist might use such expressions would be in quoting someone literally. Even then he will do well to eliminate them unless they are needed to present an accurate picture of the person quoted.

Here are some examples of words and expressions you should avoid using:

ain't	enthuse	anywheres	hadn't ought
hisself	couldn't of done it	towards town	lousy with money
can't hardly	should of done it	to orate	dark-complected

Quiz Answers

1. It was about 1898 when he and his small family settled in the village of Wilton. 2. His outlook on life is quite different from his partner's (or, from that of his partner). 3. Delete *first.* 4. One would never have (or never would have) suspected that his Brigham Young team had finished at the bottom (or, in the cellar) in the 1967 conference race. 5. Suddenly the walls caved in, and despite the efforts of the firemen, the flames destroyed the warehouse. 6. With the agreement signed, the two firms will now be merged. 7. The average tuberculosis patient has a very good (or, excellent) chance today to recuperate in a healthful climate. 8. He lurched drunkenly toward the man who held a knife. 9. It was plain (or clear or evident) that she was going (or, about) to raise a ruckus. 10. He had one car in front of and one behind two new Lincolns. May set off *and one behind* for clarity. 11. The police quickly began a search of the area and caught the drunk (drunken) hit-and-run driver about an hour later. He had a half-emptied bottle of whiskey in his car. He (or, the man) was promptly booked and jailed (or placed in jail). 12. Declaring (that) they had the cabs necessary to public operation, directors of the GI Transportation Company announced they would continue. . . 13. Understanding people is Juan Mason's business. 14. To bring the home

and the school closer together has become the PTA's chief goal. 15. Although the number of deaths from Hong Kong influenza may rise sharply this week, City Health Officer Tav Lupton feels that the epidemic is now under control.

PART 3

PUNCTUATION AND SPELLING

17

Punctuation
To Make the
Meaning Clear

If you have been convinced that clarity in writing must
be a primary objective of the journalist, you recognize the fact
that correct, effective punctuation is essential to clear writing.
An understanding of sentence structure should enable you to
grasp, with a minimum of effort, all the rules of punctuation
which you need to know. For, in your study of sentence structure, you could not fail to observe that correct punctuation is
closely related to correct sentences.

You cannot punctuate a sentence correctly unless you know
the proper relationship of the parts of the sentence. Once you
have learned how to put a sentence together and to understand why you put it together that way, you will see that punctuation serves the primary purpose of making the meaning of
the sentence clear to the reader.

Punctuation marks are not to be used like ornaments on a
Christmas tree, to dress up the sentence. To a certain degree
they are used for emphasis, but punctuation is functional
rather than ornamental. Its purpose is to make reading easier
and to bring out the meaning intended by the writer.

The Associated Press, with which Rudolf Flesch worked for several years on a program to improve readability of copy, gives in its style book this excellent definition of punctuation and its purpose: "Punctuation is the visual inflection. The marks should clarify meaning and, like shouting, should be employed sparingly. Skillful phrasing avoids ambiguity, insures interpretation and lessens need for punctuation."

In other words, the only reason for using punctuation marks is to convey the exact thought and the desired tone to the reader. Punctuate for clarity and for emphasis, and in all instances use as few punctuation marks as possible. The author of *The Dallas News Style Book* makes this trenchant comment: "Avoid necessity of involved punctuation by avoiding long and intricate sentences." Felsch, Gunning and other readability experts say "Amen" to that.

But remember that, fundamentally, punctuation is determined by the grammatical construction. Learn the rules, and make your punctuation consistent.

THE PERIOD

WHEN TO USE THE PERIOD

1. Use a period at the end of a declarative sentence or an imperative sentence that is not exclamatory.

The thief was caught two hours later.
Put the books on that desk in the corner.

2. Use a period after most abbreviations.

Mr.	Jr.	LL.D.	etc.	*ibid.*	Lt.	a.m.
Mrs.	Sr.	Ph.D.	i.e.	Feb.	Sgt.	p.m.
Dr.	B.A.	c.o.d.	e.g.	Oct.	E. Elm St.	ft.
the Rev.	M.A.	f.o.b.	o.k.	Dec.	N. Dak.	vol.

Months are abbreviated only when used with an exact date: Feb. 5, Dec. 21. Months with short names, such as April, May and July, are never abbreviated, even when used with a date.

3. Use a period as a decimal point.

$15.75   101.5 degrees
25.5 per cent   a .325 batting average

4. Use three periods to indicate omission of words.

He told his audience, "I will . . . see that wages are raised."
Webster defines ellipse as "Omission of one or more words . . .
necessary to make the expression grammatically complete."

When Not to Use the Period

1. Do not use a period after *per cent* "They received a 10 per cent increase."

2. Do not use a period after nicknames like *Tom, Dick* and *Sam.*

3. Do not use a period after initials or abbreviations that name well-known organizations.

FBI   AAF   UN   YMCA   Station WFAA   Texas Tech

4. Do not use a period after abbreviations of common words that are used in colloquial language, such as: *ad, bus, gas, phone, photo, exam, gym.*

THE COMMA

When to Use the Comma

1. A comma is used to separate two independent clauses joined by the coordinate conjunction *and, or, nor, but, yet* or *for.*

Note these sentences:

George James received money from Sam Jones in the transaction, and Dick White was paid $5,000 by James Black.
George James received money from Sam Jones in the transaction, but Dick White got nothing.

Grasshoppers descended upon the fields in huge waves, and the corn soon was stripped to the ground.

He will pay every cent of the money he owes, or he will surely go to jail.

He was unable to find anyone who would back him in the venture, yet he refused to give up the idea of producing the play.

Black simply must raise the $2,000, for his sister must pay off the mortgage by Saturday.

In general, the comma is used if the subjects of the two clauses are different. It is usually needed for clarity.

However, the trend is toward eliminating the comma when the clauses are short, thus:

He was tall but his brother was short.

You can play it safe by using the comma, leaving it to the editor to omit it if he considers it unnecessary.

The trend toward eliminating the comma before the coordinate conjunction *and* in compound sentences is much stronger than the trend toward eliminating the comma before the conjunction *but*.

Be sure to note that *so* is not listed with the coordinate conjunctions. The good journalist will avoid the use of *so* by changing one of the independent clauses to a dependent clause or a phrase.

POOR: The detectives knew that Smith still had a room at the Blotz boarding house, so they waited for him to return there for his clothes.

BETTER: As the detectives knew that Smith still had a room . . ., they waited. . . .

Or: Knowing that Smith still had a room . . ., they waited. . . .

2. Commas are used to separate words or figures which might be misunderstood.

What the major problem is, is not clear.

3. Commas are used to indicate the omission of a word common to both parts of the sentence and easily understood.

Talent is often inherited; genius, never.

4. Commas are used to separate words, phrases or clauses used in a series when the coordinating conjunction is omitted from the series.

When the conjunction, usually *and* or *or,* is used before the last word or phrase or clause in the series, no comma need be inserted before the conjunction. This is universal journalistic style.

A frank, blunt statement was made to the press by the city council.
South Dakota State College, Idaho State College, Oklahoma Baptist University and the University of New Mexico are members.
He had a pale face, shifty eyes and a battered right ear.
Mantle could cover center field capably, could bat from either side of the plate and could hit game-winning home runs consistently.
He wrapped a scarf around his neck, turned up his overcoat collar and hurried through the door.
In another hour he must decide whether to push on, to pause for a brief rest or to camp for the night.
Bigamy Jones was a first-rate man with a gun, with a horse or with the women.
He demanded to know immediately whether we would make the trip, if we could bring his wife and when we could arrive.

If the conjunction is omitted at the end, the comma must be used.

The injured man painfully made his way over the ridge, down the hill, through the shallow stream.

You note that when adjectives are used in a series, the comma is not placed after the last adjective: a *frank, blunt* statement. Make sure that the parts of the series are coordinate. Can they be joined by *and*'s? If not, the comma is not needed, for one word usually modifies the meaning of the second word, even if they are not joined by a hyphen: *a white brick* house; a *dull green* finish. Use of a comma in these expressions would be an error.

Sometimes the final adjective in a series is so closely associated with the noun that follows that the two appear to be a compound noun: an old *oaken bucket;* a sharp *steel blade;* her new *spring bonnet.* No comma is used in such constructions.

5. Commas are used to set off a nonrestrictive clause.

The *nonrestrictive* clause is not needed for one to understand fully and completely the meaning of the sentence in which such a clause occurs.

Ralph Wolfe, who has served two terms as mayor, announced today that he would not seek re-election.
John Thomas, the man who is standing on that corner, is my cousin.

Note that the identity of the subjects in the sentences above is made perfectly clear by giving their proper names, Ralph Wolfe and John Thomas. The clauses "who has served . . . as mayor" and "the man . . . on that corner" give additional information about the subjects, but are not needed to identify them. Nonrestrictive clauses, then, are enclosed by a pair of commas to show that these clauses are of secondary importance. You will do well to consider the pair of commas that enclose a nonrestrictive element as one punctuation mark: you cannot use one comma without the other. Don't fail to insert the second comma!

Note these additional examples of nonrestrictive clauses:

The latest entrant in the race for mayor is James West, who has served two terms in office.
Appearing in top form are Lyons and Thompson, upon whom the team is depending to win the game.
Cesar Tovar, who played all nine positions and pitched one hitless inning as the Twins beat Oakland, 2-1, made the headlines Sunday as he became only the second man in baseball history to make a complete tour of all nine positions.

charged that "nonunion student anarchists" took over the AFT picket lines.

They have elected a new man, John Town, to the presidency.

The Board of Trustees today elected a new president, Frank Williams.

Streaking farther and farther from earth Sunday toward man's first rendezvous with the moon was a lonely speck of life, Apollo 8.

The appositive, like the nonrestrictive clause, is not grammatically essential to the sentence, which is the reason for setting it off by commas. The only exception to this rule is the use of a single word as an appositive in such sentences as these:

Her daughter *Mary* has gone to England.
This occurred in the reign of Alexander *the Great*.
We *boys* will attend to the moving of the furniture.

7. Commas are used to set off parenthetical words and phrases. The journalist must occasionally use transition devices to guide the reader. These words and phrases contribute to the smoothness and clarity of the writing, but they are not grammatically essential to the sentences.

Be especially careful to set off an adverb or an adverbial phrase which modifies an entire clause or sentence.

However, the mother found it impossible to support the girl.
His story, *in the first place,* is inaccurate.
On the other hand, the story is plausible.
Their rival forces, *meanwhile,* prepared to meet Wednesday to patch up a peace.
Otherwise, we cannot avoid raising the tax rate.

8. Commas are used to set off the year in a date, and also to set off the month and the exact date following the day of the week.

The Soviet Union and four of its Warsaw Pact allies invaded Czechoslovakia Aug. 23, 1968, and seized virtual control of the government.

Floyd Addington and Tommy Towery, upon whom Coa
Bell relies to win the championship, appeared to be in

If the clause is *restrictive*—if it is necessary to the
of the sentence—no commas are used.

In the two sentences below, the subject "man" is no
identified without the *who* clauses. Note how these
point out a definite person.

The man who has served two terms as mayor has announ
he will not seek re-election.

The man who is standing on that corner is my cousin.

Try reading these sentences without the *who* clauses. Y
find that you do not know, in either sentence, which pa
man is being spoken about. The *who* clauses restrict or
the meaning of the vague subject *man*. Since the clau
essential to the meaning of the sentence, they are not ei
by a pair of commas.

Here is one more example of a restrictive clause:

The two men upon whom Coach Bell relies to win the cha
ship are Addington and Lowry.

6. Commas are used to set off words and phrases th
used as appositives.

The *appositive* is a phrase that means the same thing
explains the word it follows.

The man responsible for giving the experts red faces was
Hank Iba, the grand old man of U.S. college basketball,
team beat Yugoslavia, 65-50, to win America's seventh st
gold medal in Olympic basketball.

Eastman Kodak, the world's biggest photographic compan
records in both sales and earnings during the July-Sept
quarter.

He, the only heir, will inherit the entire fortune.

The sole heir, his son John, will inherit the entire fortune.

S. I. Hayakawa, acting president of San Francisco State Co

The ceremony took place on Friday, May 16, in Los Angeles.

9. Commas are used to set off the name of the state or country when it follows the name of a city.

He was caught and arrested in Bloomington, *Ill.*
Harry was born in Colorado, but his family moved to Tulsa, *Okla.,* when he was three.
She came here from Dublin, *Ireland,* when she was sixteen.

10. Commas are used to set off explanatory figures, such as the age of a person or his address.

The woman injured in the accident was Mrs. R. L. Hillinger, 22, of 690 Oak Street.
Mrs. R. L. Hillinger, 690 Oak Street, was injured.
She gave her telephone number, HA 4-9052, to the reporter.

11. Commas are used to set off titles or degrees given after a name.

The next head of the university may be Wayne A. Danielson, Ph.D.
We entertained Frank Yates, City Manager, at dinner last night.

Most newspapers do not use commas to set off *Jr.* or *Sr.* after a name. Find out what the practice is for the publication for which you work.

12. Commas are used to set off nominatives of direct address.

She said, "You know, *Joe,* Ruby is to be your tennis partner."
Susan, where did you put our raincoats?
Ladies and gentlemen, I am pleased to be with you this evening.
It is evident, *Mr. Chairman,* that the club must have more money for this project.

13. Commas are used to separate direct quotations from explanatory matter.

The mayor said, "I can't give you a statement now," but he promised to meet the reporters after the meeting.

The witness stammered, "I just can't remember."
"If I'm elected," he declared, "I'll clean up the city."

14. Commas are used to set off participial and infinitive phrases or long prepositional phrases which precede the main clause.

Remember that the participial phrase is used as an adjective or an adverb. The introductory infinitive phrase may be used as a noun or as an adverb.

PARTICIPIAL PHRASES:

Having suffered heavy losses, the troops withdrew.

The participial phrase modifies the noun *troops.*

Slowed by collapse today of a company negotiator, efforts to reach an agreement in the Lone Star Steel dispute made limited **headway.**

The participial phrase modifies the noun *efforts.*

You may need to be warned about confusing a gerund—which is always used as a noun—with the present participle. The gerund or gerund phrase is never set off by commas.

Swimming is excellent exercise.
Harvesting of a bumper wheat crop was in full swing Sunday throughout the Texas Panhandle.

INFINITIVE PHRASES:

To provide an incentive for raising higher-grade livestock, the Iowa State Fair next fall will offer livestock premiums totaling $60,000.

The infinitive phrase modifies the verb *will offer.*

To win ball games, a team must have high-grade pitching.

The infinitive phrase modifies the verb *must have.*

But note that no comma is needed in the following sentence, in which the infinitive phrase is used as a noun, subject of the verb *has become.*

To balance agriculture with industry has become a chief goal of the South.

PREPOSITIONAL PHRASES:

With a pinstriped railroad cap cocked on his blond head, young L. M. Crandall Jr. deftly engineered his way into the finals of the Texas Public Links Golf Association championship Saturday.

The prepositional phrase *With a . . . cap cocked on his blond head* modifies *Crandall*. Although it is used as an adjective, it is so long that it requires a comma.

After days of desperate filibustering, the Senate finally passed the bill late Friday night.

The prepositional phrase *After days of . . . filibustering* modifies *passed*. A comma is needed for clarity.

If the prepositional phrase is short, no comma is needed. Note these examples:

In his hat he stuck a feather.
Throughout the night they searched the forest for the lost boy.

NOTE: Although the length of the introductory prepositional phrase is the chief guide in determining whether or not to use a comma, remember that the main purpose of all punctuation is to make the meaning clear. If a short prepositional phrase needs a comma to make the meaning easily clear to the reader, use the comma. The comma contributes to clarity in the following constructions.

In Texas, weather prophets are difficult to find.

How confused the reader would be without a comma after *Texas!*

After his years in Washington, Nixon should be thoroughly initiated into politics.

Running the two proper nouns together would be confusing.

In the drowsy early-morning hours, passers-by and visitors to the Tulsa police station often stop and listen to the harmonizing of the department's first quartet to be organized in a decade.

Most editors would agree that the comma after *hours* helps to make the meaning clearer.

15. Commas are used to set off nominative absolutes.

The *nominative absolute* is another independent element of the sentence. It is not grammatically necessary to the sentence; hence it must be set off.

The inauguration (being) over, Washington began to return to normal Tuesday.

Her right hand paralyzed from the snake bite, the child could not lift the box.

16. Commas are used to set off introductory dependent clauses. This is one of the most important usages of the comma —and one which journalists too often violate. Unless the introductory clause is very short, the comma should be used to set it off.

Because so many young folks put aside schoolbooks and hobbies during the war to help with national defense, there is a tremendous shortage of researchers.

In the preceding sentence the long adverbial clause of cause is set off.

When Johnson leaves Washington to return to his ranch on the Perdenales River, he will devote his time to lecturing, writing— and just resting.

The long adverbial clause of time is set off.

If another widespread coal strike takes place in the next few weeks, the entire country will suffer.

The long adverbial clause of condition is set off.

If the introductory dependent clause is short, the comma may often be omitted.

When the actress arrived she greeted her mother first.
If he gets in late he will telephone.

However, you will not be in error if you place a comma after these clauses.

If the dependent adverbial clause comes in the middle of the sentence, it must be set off with commas, like the nonrestrictive clause.

The great Mickey Mantle, unless he can play for his nineteenth season, will not continue to wear the Yankee pin stripes, either as a coach or maybe in the front office.

If the dependent clause follows the independent clause, no comma is needed usually. Be governed by the sense of the sentence.

He said that the community would suffer unless there is an increase in the water supply.

WHEN NOT TO USE THE COMMA

1. No comma is used before an *of* phrase indicating place or position.

Senator Hugh Butler of *Nebraska* died at Bethesda Naval Hospital Thursday night.

2. No comma is used between two nouns that identify the same person.

The general is proud of his *son John.*

3. No comma is used in such phrases as: five feet three inches; 2 gallons 1 pint; 10 hours 20 minutes 8 seconds.

The fighter is only five feet three inches tall.

4. No comma is needed before a partial quotation—that is, a short quotation closely associated with the preceding word.

He declared that the result might be "utter confusion."

The maxim of "every man for himself" should not apply in this instance.

He swore that "everyone involved in the case will be prosecuted."

5. No comma is needed to set off restrictive clauses.

The car *which is stalled* is the one the colonel was using.
The man *who set the player's arm* is Dr. Benjamin Carroll.

6. No comma is used to separate the clauses of a complex sentence when the dependent clause follows the independent clause.

Morrall will be used at quarterback *if Unitas can't start.*
Morrall will be at quarterback *because Unitas is still ailing.*

7. No comma is used before the coordinate conjunction which connects the last two items in a series.

The flag is red, white *and* green.
A tall, dark-haired *and* handsome man was her companion.
He wanted to know how he could get there, what he was to bring *and* what he was expected to do on arrival.

8. No comma is needed between adjectives which could not be separated by *and* and make sense. The noun and its preceding adjective may often be considered as a compound noun: *race horse; cutting edge.*

That is a *beautiful race horse.*
The knife had a *sharp cutting edge.*
She wore a *bright red dress.*

THE SEMICOLON

The journalist should use the semicolon sparingly. Its chief use is in compound sentences, and the reporter will avoid using sentences in which the conjunction is omitted between two independent clauses.

1. Use a semicolon to separate independent clauses which are not connected by a coordinate conjunction.

He was lying in the ditch; he was dead drunk.

The breeze had died completely; there was not a ripple on the lake.

The Creighton center cannot stand; he is hurt.

The women are ready to leave; the men are not (ready to leave).

The top of the dog's head is often affected; it twitches in a most peculiar manner.

2. Use a semicolon between clauses of a compound sentence that are joined by adverbial conjunctions like *there, however, nevertheless, otherwise, furthermore.*

The Drake Bulldogs fought hard; nevertheless, they lost.

A new Peoria junior high school must be built; therefore, it is essential to vote favorably on the bond issue.

The company must submit detailed specifications with its bid; otherwise, it cannot be awarded the contract.

The disease will occur in the best regulated kennels; however, dogs which have been inoculated are less likely to contract the disease.

3. A semicolon is used to separate coordinate phrases and clauses which are punctuated internally with a comma or commas.

The new officers are: James Johnston, president; Raymond Nix, vice-president; Mrs. Melba Myrick, secretary; and Miss Jane Brown, treasurer.

A. M. Myrick, president of the company, is expected to arrive at noon; and Sam Katz, vice-president, should arrive this afternoon.

4. A semicolon is used to separate independent clauses which are joined by a coordinate conjunction if the clauses are long or have internal punctuation.

The youngster, who was a raw but willing recruit, found that brawn still helps; but he learned quickly that today's rookie cop must have a nimble mind, an even temper and mature personality—qualities which get the young applicant past the first hurdles of intelligence tests.

5. A semicolon is used to separate phrases which contain commas, particularly when the meaning otherwise would not be clear.

In the group were J. K. Thomas, the president of Wisconsin Service Company; Mrs. Jane Brown, his secretary; T. K. Thomas, his brother; Mrs. R. B. Thomas; two accountants; and a statistician.

THE COLON

1. The colon is used before a long, formal quotation, such as statements and excerpts from speeches or writings.

If the quotation is longer than one sentence, it should start a new paragraph.

In a fighting speech which clearly set forth the issues of the campaign, Governor Black said in part:

"When I ask you to vote for John Black in the Democratic primary on July 24, I do so with a feeling of gratitude and humility. I have tried with all my strength and with all my mind to be worthy of your trust.

"During my term of office, the state has prospered. . . ."

2. The colon is used to introduce an explanatory statement.

The question is: Where do we go from here?

We are here for just one purpose: we are going to drill, drill, drill.

3. The colon is used after a clause which introduces a list.

Try this menu: roast beef, mashed potatoes, carrots, apple pie and cheese.

The following officers were elected: A. P. Smith, Tallahassee; G. A. Morgan, Tucson; and Walter Cross, San Antonio.

If the words *the following* or *as follows* are not used, the colon need not be used, but it is correct to include it.

Among the delegates are Smith, Morgan and Cross.

The cities and their new populations are: Canterville, 50,500; Popplarside, 48,200; Sunnyvale, 43,500.

4. A colon is used between the numbers giving the chapter and verse of a Scripture passage.

You will find it in Genesis 1:1–5.

5. A colon is used in writing figures that show time and timed events in sports.

Martin is expected at 4:30 p.m. Thursday.
They won in 1:02:45.8 (one hour, two minutes and 45.8 seconds).

THE APOSTROPHE

The use of the apostrophe in possessives has been treated in detail in Chapter 6. Review that chapter if you need to.

Here are the chief uses of the apostrophe:

1. An apostrophe is used to form possessives.

Mr. Dale's house   the Dales' automobile
the baby's rattle   the children's toys

2. An apostrophe is used to form some plurals.

Use two m's.
All his 8's look like 3's.

3. An apostrophe is used to indicate omission of a letter or letters.

wasn't   they'd   o'clock
don't   hasn't   I'll

QUOTATION MARKS

1. Double quotation marks are used to enclose direct quotations.

"With the help of real Americans," said the senator, "we can rid the country of this totalitarian menace."

There are four rules to be remembered in connection with the use of direct quotations: (*a*) Set off explanatory expressions with commas. (*b*) Capitalize the first word of the quotation if it is a complete sentence. (*c*) Place a period or a comma within the quotation marks. (*d*) Place a question mark inside the quotation marks if the quotation is a question; otherwise, put the question mark outside the quotation marks. Note these examples of the four important rules:

a) "If we can have the support of every citizen," the governor declared, "we can solve this problem."
   Or: "If we have the support of every citizen, we can solve this problem," said the governor.

b) "Shortage of water is not our only problem," the governor reiterated. "Soil conservation is also important."
   But: The governor said that "we can solve this water-shortage problem." (Partial quotation not capitalized.)

c) Reread the preceding examples and note that the commas and periods are always placed inside the quotation marks regardless of the meaning.

d) "When will they be ready?" he asked.
   But would you accept his statement of being "always conscious of the importance of the position"?

When a quotation runs to two or more paragraphs in length, the quotation marks are placed at the beginning of each paragraph and at the end of the last paragraph of the quotation.

2. Single quotation marks are used to designate quoted matter that is given within a direct quotation.

The man testified, "I asked her, 'Did you find this copy of the book lying beside the body?' but she did not answer my question."

3. Double quotations are used to set off slang expressions or words that are used with another meaning than the usual one.

The blonde is that burglar's "gun moll," I believe.
He's just another "hippie."
The miser's "generosity" consisted of leaving two thousand dollars to his dog and cutting out the servants from his will.

In quoting two or more persons in the same story, put quotations of the separate individuals into separate paragraphs.

Most editors will insist that you do not mix one or more complete sentences of direct quotation with one or more complete sentences of non-quoted material within the same paragraph.

In newspapers, the names of papers, magazines, books and the like are not quoted, as: The New York Times. In printing, such names are often italicized. The general rule in most writing is to quote the names of poems and of articles in a publication, the titles of chapters in a book, of short stories, of one-act plays, and so on.

A common error of journalism students is the failure to close the quotation—to insert the second pair of quotation marks. Be alert to avoid this error.

PARENTHESES

1. Parentheses are used to set off material inserted by the writer to explain a term or to indicate an alternative choice.

The other point (made earlier) is that we need to increase the force.
Use synonyms for such common words as *walk* (*strode, limped, hurried,* etc.) and *said* (*declared, asserted, shouted,* etc.).

2. Parentheses are used to set off a phrase that is incidental to the meaning of the sentence. These are parenthetical expressions and may be set off by commas, as has been explained earlier.

That is the reason (and the only reason) for our selling the house.

3. Parentheses are used to give information about a person named, such as his political affiliation and his state or his degree and college.

John Harrison (Dem., Iowa) was elected chairman.
Dr. Warren K. Agee, Ph.D., Minnesota) was commencement speaker.

4. Parentheses are sometimes used to insert the name of the state after the name of a city named in the title of a newspaper or an organization.

The Stillwater (Okla.) News-Press was founded by his grandfather.

5. Parentheses are used to enclose a nickname in a given name.

The "Coach of the Year" is C. B. (Bear) Bryant.

Note that it would be correct to use quotation marks instead of parentheses in such cases: C. B. "Bear" Bryant.

If a parenthesis ends a sentence, the final mark of punctuation for the sentence is placed outside the parenthesis unless the statement in the parenthesis is a complete sentence in itself.

We believe there will be other occasions for the use of this device (and many more, at that).

The speaker used two quotations from the Bible (one from Genesis and one from Luke).

The speaker used the same quotation twice in his speech. (The quotation was from the first chapter of Genesis.)

BRACKETS

The journalist will not have much use for brackets in his writing, but he should know what they mean when he encounters them in his reading.

Brackets are used to enclose material that is not in the passage being quoted. The material is added by the editor to explain or comment on the quotation, or to make clear the connection of the quotation with the previous statement.

"At that time [1820] Mexico was ruled by the aristocracy," the historian stated.

His conclusion was that "they [the students] should read those authors in their own language."

THE DASH

Too many writers overwork the dash. Many newspaper editors will point out to you that a period, a semicolon or a colon may be used to better advantage. Learn to use the dash sparingly but effectively. In typing, be sure to strike the hyphen bar twice to make a dash.

1. A dash is used to indicate a sudden break in the thought or the speech.

She stammered, "But—but—I did not—"
David is tall, dark—and ugly.
The slaying of Floyd's son was mysterious—the most mysterious murder in the history of Texas, in fact.
Trigger man in the slaying—the other side does not deny it—is Juan Julio Perkins.
If the Terrorists win the election—God forbid!—right-thinking men and women will be driven from the country.

2. A dash is sometimes used before a repetition, for effect.

Men grow weary of life—weary of constant struggle for existence.
There is but one love common to all—the love of life.

3. A dash is sometimes used to set off a statement or a summary of particulars.

Wine, women, money—all make men falter.
She has left it all—love, money, fame—for a life devoted to the poor.

4. The dash is often used to indicate questions and answers in a verbatim report of testimony.

Q.—Did you see the man in the tavern?
A.—No, I did not.

THE HYPHEN

The hyphen is sometimes classed as a mark of spelling instead of as a mark of punctuation. Its greatest use is in compounds, but the journalist must know how to use it also in dividing words at the ends of lines.

1. The use of the hyphen in compound nouns is so varied that the student is advised to consult the dictionary when in doubt.

2. The hyphen is used in prepositional phrase combinations.

attorney-at-law   out-of-doors
mother-in-law   door-to-door (poll)

3. The hyphen is used to form compound adjectives that precede the noun.

well-known story   happy-go-lucky way
100-yard dash   ready-to-wear clothes
good-looking woman   matter-of-fact attitude
ten-year-old girl   terror-stricken face

You are reminded that the hyphen is not used between an adverb ending in *ly* and a participle (adjective) that precede a noun: the *brightly lighted* room. And remember that adjectives which follow the noun need not be hyphenated.

He is tall and good looking.
His mother is very gentle mannered.

4. The hyphen is used in compound numerals and fractions.

sixty-five years old   a three-fourths share

5. The hyphen is used in suspended compounds.

It will probably be a twelve- or sixteen-page booklet.

6. The hyphen is used to distinguish different meanings in words of like spelling.

The shoplifter eventually reformed.
The line was re-formed at the end of the field.
Without recreation, Jack becomes a dull boy.
They decided on the re-creation of certain rules they had abolished.

7. A hyphen is used between some prefixes and nouns or adjectives, and always between the prefix and a proper noun or proper adjective.

ex-governor	un-American	anti-Communist
ex-champion	pro-German	non-African

8. The hyphen is used to take the place of the preposition *to* in figures indicating an extension.

It was the April-July report of income.
Look on pages 130-158 for the information.
The concert lasted from 2-4 p.m.

9. The hyphen is used to divide a word at the end of a line of type or of writing.

Words are divided only between syllables. Most printers do not advocate dividing words of two syllables, and of course words of one syllable may not be divided. Most newspaper editors advise reporters to avoid all hyphenation of this kind, ignoring an uneven right margin. If you do divide a word at the end of the line, be sure to place the hyphen at the end of that line. Also, make sure that you follow the division of the word that is given in the dictionary. This does not always follow the division of the word as spoken. Notice these examples:

rec-om-men-da-tion	pref-er-ence	sup-po-si-tion
skill-ful-ness	pre-ferred	su-preme-ly

18

Correct Spelling
Is a "Must"
for the Journalist

Originality in style of writing has been stressed. One place, however, where the journalist must not display originality is in his spelling.

If you need special encouragement to improve your spelling, recall the findings of a survey in which almost two-thirds of 100 American newspaper editors rated deficiency in spelling as the second greatest fault of journalism graduates whom they have employed. Only deficiency in grammar was called a greater fault. This should convince you that correct spelling and good grammar are important assets for success in the field of journalism.

Knowledge of a few basic rules of spelling and the habit of using the dictionary when in doubt will see you through. You want to succeed at your first job, and you want to rise in the journalism ranks with maximum speed. Learn to spell correctly, then, and to use good reference books when you need to.

BASIC RULES OF SPELLING

There are five basic rules of spelling you need to know. You will use these largely in spelling verbs. However, note that the rules apply also to nouns, adjectives and adverbs.

Rule 1. Words of one syllable that end in a single consonant preceded by a single vowel double the consonant before adding a suffix that begins with a vowel.

The vowels are *a, e, i, o* and *u;* sometimes *y* is regarded as a vowel. All the other letters are consonants.

Take the verb *trap* and test it with the rule above. Is it a one-syllable verb? Yes. It ends in a single consonant, *p.* The consonant is preceded by a single vowel, *a.* The suffixes *ed* and *ing* begin with a vowel. Hence when one of these suffixes is added to *trap,* the *p* must be doubled: *trapped, trapping.* This is a foolproof rule you may follow for *all* one-syllable verbs.

Some of the suffixes to which this rule applies are: *-able, -ably, -age, -al, -ed, -ent, -est, -ing, -ish.* Try out the rule on the following words, thus: bag, bagged, bagging, baggage; beg, begged, begging, beggar; man, manned, manning, mannish; etc.

bag	dot	flip	jam	plot	slam
bar	drag	get	lag	put (in golf)	stop
beg	drop	grab	man	run	trip
brag	fan	hop	pin	ship	wet
dab	flit	knit	plan	sit	wrap

There are some exceptions to this rule, but you should have no trouble with these. Words that end in the consonants *k, v, w, x* and *y* do not double the consonant before a suffix with a vowel. Examples are:

box, boxing, boxed   row, rowing, rowed   play, playing, played

Rule 2. Words of more than one syllable that end in a consonant preceded by a single vowel double the final consonant before adding a suffix beginning with a vowel—*if* the word is accented on the last syllable.

Take the word *commit*. It ends in the consonant *t*. The final consonant is preceded by the single vowel *i*. The word is accented on the second syllable: com-mit'. The consonant *t* is doubled before adding a suffix like *ed* or *ing*: *committed, committing*.

Other words that follow this rule are:

admit	concur	deter	permit	recur	repel
allot	confer	excel	prefer	refer	submit
begin	control	infer	propel	regret	transfer
compel	defer	occur	rebel	remit	

The verb *equip* is considered as belonging under this rule because the *u* has the sound of *w*: *equip, equipping, equipped*.

You might note that many of the verbs listed above may add suffixes like *able, ably, al, ent, er*, etc., to form nouns, adjectives and adverbs. Note that the consonant is doubled, according to the rule, in these words: controller, controllable, regrettable, regrettably, concurrent, deterrent, referral, repellent. However, if the word you form must have the accent on the first syllable, don't double the consonant, as in the adjective pref'erable.

If the words are accented on any other syllable than the last syllable, the consonant is not doubled before adding a suffix beginning with a vowel.

hap'pen, happening	ben'e-fit, benefiting
o'pen, opened, opening	de-vel'op, developer
ex-hib'it, exhibitor	dif'fer, different
can'cel, canceled	pro-hib'it, prohibited
mod'el, modeling	sum'mon, summoning

There are a few words that may double the final consonant or not double it, either form being considered correct. The dictionary shows both forms, with the preferred form given first, thus: *trav' el, -eled* or *-elled, -eling* or *-elling*. Other examples are *counsel* and *kidnap*. Use the preferred form in your writing.

Rule 3. Words that end in silent *e* drop the *e* before adding a suffix beginning with a vowel.

advise, advising	move, moving	force, forcibly
change, changing	notice, noticing	love, lovable
come, coming	desire, desirable	use, usable
hope, hoping	guide, guidance	sale, salable
dine, dining	argue, arguing	judge, judging

The exceptions to this rule include words in which the dropping of the *e* would confuse the neaning, and words ending in *ce* or *ge* in which the *c* or the *g* has a soft sound, like *s* or *j*.

eye, eyeing	canoe, canoeing	change, changeable
dye, dyeing	peace, peaceable	courage, courageous
hoe, hoeing	notice, noticeable	manage, manageable

Note the difference between *die, dying,* and *dye, dyeing*.

Rule 4. (*a*) Verbs ending in *y* preceded by a consonant change the *y* to *i* before adding *es* to form the third-person singular, present tense, or before adding *ed* to form the past tense.

try, tries, tried	study, studies, studied
cry, cries, cried	reply, replies, replied
deny, denies, denied	carry, carries, carried
hurry, hurries, hurried	worry, worries, worried

The exception is for the ending *-ing*: try, trying, etc.

(*b*) Nouns and adjectives ending in *y* preceded by a consonant change the *y* to *i* before adding *es, est* and other suffixes that do *not* begin with an *i*.

lady, ladies	dry, drier, driest	busy, busily
city, cities	mercy, merciful	noisy, noisily
sky, skies	happy, happiness	theory, theories

But: gray*er*, gray*est*, etc.

Rule 5. When *i* and *e* occur together in a word, the *i* usually precedes the *e* except after the consonant *c*.

The journalist will do well to remember the old jingle:

Use *i* before *e*
Except after *c*
Or when sounded like *a*
As in *neighbor* and *weigh*.

True, there are more exceptions to this rule than to the others, but the rule is often helpful. The more important exceptions should be learned, and the dictionary should be consulted when there is any doubt.

Words that follow the rule are:

grieve	achieve	fierce	receipt
grief	frontier	thief	receive
piece	chief	relief	conceit
believe	yield	siege	conceive
friend	pierce	alien	deceive

The most common exceptions to the rule are:

foreign	inveigle	science
either	leisure	their
height	counterfeit	weird
financier	heifer	

You will see that there are several exceptions to Rule 5, but remember that the first four rules may be followed with few exceptions. You will save yourself many trips to the dictionary by using all five rules. But when there is no safe rule to use or whenever you have any doubt about the spelling of a word, the safest rule to follow is to look it up in the dictionary!

FORMING PLURALS AND POSSESSIVES

Journalism students have been found to be particularly weak in the correct use of the possessive case. A review of Chapter 6 will refresh your memory on many points.

FORMING PLURALS

The essential things to remember are the following:

1. Most nouns, particularly those ending in a consonant, form their plurals by adding *s* or *es*.

lens, lenses   point, points   gas, gases

2. Nouns ending in *o* preceded by a vowel add *s* to form the plural.

cameo, cameos   hoe, hoes   radio, radios

3. Nouns ending in *o* preceded by a consonant usually add *s* to form the plural, but sometimes add *es*.

halo, halos   buffalo, buffaloes
Eskimo, Eskimos   potato, potatoes

4. Nouns ending in *y* preceded by a vowel form the plural by adding *s*.

guy, guys   key, keys   alloy, alloys

5. Nouns ending in *y* preceded by a consonant form the plural by changing *y* to *i* and adding *es*.

baby, babies   army, armies   soliloquy, soliloquies

In *soliloquy* the *u* is pronounced like *w,* so the word follows this rule.

6. Some nouns form their plurals irregularly.

man, men   woman, women   child, children   foot, feet

7. The plurals of letters, figures, signs, abbreviations and

words named as words are formed by adding an apostrophe and *s*.

three r's   five B-29's   too many *and's*

8. Nouns ending in *f, fe* or *ff usually* form the plural by adding s.

proof, proofs   cuff, cuffs   handkerchief, handkerchiefs

A few of these nouns change the *f* to *v* and add *es* to form the plural

loaf, loaves   half, halves   thief, thieves   wife, wives

9. Foreign words sometimes retain their foreign plurals.

datum, data   crisis, crises

FORMING POSSESSIVES

You will do well to turn back to pages 90–92 to review the detailed discussion of Forming Possessives of Nouns. You will find below only a brief summary of the rules for forming possessives.

1. The possessive of singular nouns, with a few exceptions, is formed by adding *'s*.

child's toy   baby's crib   Charles's book (or Charles' book)

Remember, if a noun ends in *s*, and *'s* makes the word disagreeable to the ear or difficult to say, the apostrophe alone may be used. In fact, newspaper and wire service stylebooks now advise adding only the apostrophe in such cases: Charles' boat; Moses' tablet.

2. The possessive of plural nouns ending in *s* is formed by adding the apostrophe only.

the Blakes' car   my two sisters' home

3. The possessive of plural nouns not ending in *s* is formed by adding *'s*.

two men's reports   several children's parents

4. The possessive pronouns do not have an apostrophe.

mine   hers   his   its   yours   ours   theirs

THE HYPHEN IN COMPOUNDS

The journalist's use of the hyphen is largely in compounds. As far as dividing words at the end of lines is concerned, the rule is to avoid dividing any one-syllable or two-syllable word and to divide other words according to the syllabication given in the dictionary. A good style book to use in this connection is the University of Chicago's *Manual of Style*. Webster's Unabridged defines *compound* as:

> . . . a combination into a solid or hyphened form of two or more distinct words (*gatekeeper; passer-by; large-scale*), or of a word with one or more affixes or combining forms (*supergovernment; Anglophobe*), or a word phrase having a specialized or figurative sense not deducible from the meanings of the components, which serve grammatically as a single word and usually blend in pronunciation (*vice-admiral; post office; past master; billfold; all right*).[1]

The most difficult problem with English compounds is whether to write them as (1) hyphenated words or (2) solid words or (3) separate words. There are no mandatory rules which can be applied universally or mechanically in the forming of compounds. Follow the dictionary.

Anomalies in compounding are discussed expertly by George Summey Jr. in his book *American Punctuation*. Summey points out that "practice in the choice of solid, hyphened and open forms is a queer mixture." He defines the "open form" as the compound made up of two separate words: *gas engine, fishing rod*.

---

[1] *Webster's New International Dictionary* (2d ed.; Springfield, Mass.: G. & C. Merriam Co., 1954).

Practice in the choice of solid, hyphenated and open forms, according to Summey,

> . . . is based partly on the year-to-year and day-to-day decisions of copy editors (copyeditors) and proofreaders, who are necessarily guided by what they find in dictionaries and stylebooks, partly on the intelligent or mistaken personal choices of editors and writers, partly on fine-spun theories of what ought to be. Upon a superficial view, one is tempted to say that the name of our system of compounding is Chaos, and that this chaos is a disgrace to American typography and American lexicography.[2]

Summey continues:

> . . . certain it is that stylebooks do not always agree with each other or with the dictionaries, or the dictionaries with each other. For example, one finds *stepping stone* in the American College Dictionary, *steppingstone* in Webster's New International Dictionary and in the New College Standard Dictionary. Two of these dictionaries have *waiting room*; the other makes it *waiting-room*. And in three admirable books by professional printers one finds *foot-note* and *footnote*, *proof-reader* and *proofreader*, *galley-proofs*, and *galley proofs*, *title-page* and *title page*. It is not surprising to find John Benbow saying that consistent use of the hyphen is impossible and that "if you take hyphens seriously you will surely go mad."

What, then, is the journalist to do in using compounds? If he works for a newspaper or a magazine, he should check with his editor. If the publication has its own stylebook, the editor will refer the staff member to the section of general rules on compound words and phrases. In this section, the staff member should not be surprised to find this admonition: The sole guide in the compounding of words and phrases, as to whether separated, hyphenated or solid, shall be Webster's New International Dictionary. If the publication for which you work does not have its own stylebook, the editor will tell you which dic-

---

[2] *American Punctuation* (New York: The Ronald Press Co., 1949), pp. 128–29.

tionary to use as your guide in compounding words and phrases.

In addition to the dictionary, there are several style manuals to which you may refer, such as *A Manual of Style* of the University of Chicago Press and the *Style Manual* of the Government Printing Office. For an excellent treatment of compound words and open compounds, refer to *American Punctuation* by George Summey Jr.

Review the brief treatment of the use of the hyphen given on pages 300–301.

SPELLING HINTS FOR THE JOURNALIST

The pages that follow have a list of the words most commonly misspelled by journalists. You should make it a "must" to learn to spell these words correctly. Concentrate on the words that give you trouble. The so-called "spelling demons" are designated by asterisks (*).

You are urged to follow these nine steps with any words you misspell regularly:

1. Look up the word in the dictionary.
2. Study the spelling of the word and its meaning.
3. Fix in your mind the exact appearance of the word, paying particular attention to the sequence of letters and to the division of the word into syllables. (Many words are misspelled because the writer has failed to divide them into their correct syllables. Example: *in/ci/dent/ly* for *in/ci/den/tal/ly.*)

You may find that you have been misspelling a word because you mispronounced it. You may have been inserting an unnecessary consonant in a word, as in saying "drownded" for *drowned.* On the other hand, you may have been adding an unnecessary vowel to the word in writing it, as in writing "athelete" for *athlete.* Do you make the mistake of using an unnecessary *i* in writing *similar?* It is not spelled "similiar." You may be omitting a necessary vowel in some words. The word *sophomore* is often misspelled "sophmore." Or you may be omitting a consonant, as in gover(n)ment.

Another fact you may have failed to learn is that many English words contain silent letters. You must learn to spell these words correctly. Note the following words. The letters in parentheses are not sounded, but they must be included when you write the words:

(p)neumonia   kil(n)   (w)rapped   tho(ugh)   thoro(ugh)

4. Pronounce the word aloud several times, syllable by syllable.

5. Type or write the word ten times to fix it in your mind.

6. Now study the word again. Take a pencil and write the word divided into syllables with a slant line between each two syllables, like this: in/ci/den/tal/ly.

7. Underline the parts of the word that give you trouble, thus:

embarrass	fiery	separate	familiar	picnicking
disappoint	weird	believable	similar	questionnaire
judgment	arctic	recommend	marshal	cemetery

8. Devote as much time as you feel is necessary to reviewing the words that give you trouble.

9. Make sure that you can now spell the word correctly without using the dictionary.

However, whenever you are in doubt about the spelling or the syllabication of a word, *look it up in the dictionary.*

WORDS COMMONLY MISSPELLED

The asterisks (*) indicate the "spelling demons."

abandon	aberration	abreast
abbreviate	abet	abridg(e)ment
abdomen	abeyance	abscess
abduct	abhorrence	abscond

absence
absorb
absorption
absurd
abundance
abysmal
abyss
academy
academic
accelerator
acceptable
accessibility
accessory (ies)
*accidentally
*accommodate
accompanying
accompanist
accomplish
accumulate
accurate
accustomed
acetylene
ache
achievement
acknowledge
acknowledgment
acoustics
acquaintance
acquiesce
acquire
acquitted
acrid
*across
acumen
adaptability
additionally
addressed
adjacent

adjutant
administrator
admirable
admissible
admitted
admittance
adolescent
advantageous
advertise (ment)
advice (*noun*)
advise (*verb*)
advisable
adviser
advisory
aeronautics
affidavit
affiliate
agenda
aggravate
aggregate
aggressive
aggressor
agreeing
alias
alienate
align
allege
allegiance
alleys
allies
allied
allocate
allotted
allotment
*all right
almanac
almost
already

although
altogether
aluminum
always
amateur
ambidextrous
ambiguous
ammonia
amnesia
among
analogous
analysis
analyze
animosity
ankle
annihilated
annual
answer
antarctic
antecedent
anticipate
anticlimax
antidote
antiseptic
antitoxin
anxiety
anxious
apartment
aperture
apology
*apologize
appalling
apparatus
apparel
apparent
apparition
appealed
appearance

appellate
appetite
appraise
appreciate
approaching
appropriate
apropos
architect
arctic
arguing
argument
arising
arithmetic(al)
armament
arouse
arousing
arrangement
arranging
arrival
arthritis
article
artificial
artillery
ascend
ascent
ascertain
asinine
asked
aspirin
assassin
assassinate
assault
assessment
assistance
association
astronaut
*athlete
*athletic(s)

atmosphere
attacked
attendance
attitude
attorney
auctioneer
audible
audience
authentic
author
authoritative
authorities
authorize
autumn
auxiliary
awkward

baccalaureate
bachelor
bacteriology
bailiff
balance
ballad
ballet
ballistic(s)
balloon
ballot
bananas
bankruptcy
Baptist
*baptize
barbarous
bargain
baring
barricade
barring
basically
battalion

bearing
becoming
beggar
begging
beginning
behavior
believable
*believe
believable
believing
belligerent
beneficial
*benefit(ed)
benign
beverage
bicycle
biennial
bigoted
binoculars
biscuit
boisterous
bookkeeper
boulevard
boundary(ies)
bouquet
breath (*noun*)
breathe (*verb*)
brethren
brief
brilliant
bristle
Britain
Briton
broccoli
brochure
brogue
bronchitis
built

bulletin
buoyant
bureau
burglar
buries
bury
bus
bus(s)es
business
bustle

cache
cadaver
cafeteria
caffeine
calendar
caliber
calm
calumny
camouflage
campaign
cancel
cancel(l)ed
cancellation
*candidate
*can't (cannot)
cantaloupe
*captain
carburetor
career
careful
carriage
carrying
cartridge
cashier
catalog(ue)
catastrophe
catechism

category
categorically
caucus
cauliflower
cavalry
ceiling
*cemetery
census
*certain
champagne
*changeable
changing
chaperon
characteristic
characterize
chargeable
chassis
chatter
chauffeur
chief
chiffonier
chili *or* chilli, chile
chimney
chocolate
choir
choose
choosing
chord (in music)
chose
chosen
chronology
circuit
circular
circumstantial
cite
cities
clientele
climactic

climatic
clique
civilize
cloth (*noun*)
clothe (*verb*)
clothes (*plural*)
coconut
coincide
coincidence
collar
collateral
collegiate
collide
collision
colloquial
cologne
colonel
*color
colossal
column
combatant
combat(t)ing
coming
commemorate
commentator
commercial
commission
commissioner
committed
*committee
communication
community
comparable
comparatively
compatible
compel
compelled
competent

competition
competitive
complexioned [3]
complimentary
comprise
compulsory
comrade
comradeship
concede
conceit
conceive
conceivable
concentration
concerned
concession
conciliation
concise
condemn
confectionery
confer
conferred
confident (*adj.*)
confidentially
connoisseur
conqueror
conscience (*noun*)
conscientious (*adj.*)
conscious (*adj.*)
consciousness (*noun*)
consensus
consider
consistency
consonant
conspicuous
consul
consumer
contagious

[3] Not "complected."

contemporary
contemptible
contemptuous
contentious
continually
continuously
contradictory
control
controlled
controversy
convalescent
convene
convenience
convenient
conveyed
coolly (*adv.*)
cooperate
copies
copyright
*corner
corps
corpus delicti
correlate
correspondence
correspondent
corroborate
corsage
cosmic
costume
cough
countenance
counterfeit
countries
courageous
courteous
courtesies
courtesy
*cried

cries
criticism
*criticize
crochet
cruelty
curiosity
curriculum
customary
cylinder
czar

data (*plural*)
datum (*sing.*)
dealt (*past of* deal)
debatable
debater
debris
debtor
deceased
deceitful
deceive
decide
*decided
decision
defendant
defense *or* defence
defer
deferred
defiance
deficiency
deficit
*definite
demagogue
deny
denied
denying
dependent
depositary (person)

depository (place)
depth
deprivation
derived
descendant
descend
descent
*describe
description
*desirable
desirous
despair
desperate
desperation
despicable
destroy
deteriorate
detriment
devastating
*develop
developed
development
dexterous
diagnose
diagonally
dialog(ue)
dictatorial
dictionary
dietitian
difference
diffidence
digestible
dilapidated
dilemma
diligent
diminish
*dining
dining-room

diocese
diphtheria
dirigible
disability
*disappear
*disappoint(ed)
disastrous
disavowal
disavowed
discernible
disciple
discipline
discuss(ed)
discussion
disease
disinfectant
dissatisfied
dissect
dissension
dissipate
dissipation
distinction
distinguish
distribute
distributor
*divide
*divine
division
doctor
*doesn't
dominant
*don't
dormitories
dormitory
drastically
drowned
drudgery
drunkenness

dullness
dumbbell
dumfounded
durable
dyeing
dying (expiring)

easily
eccentric
economically
economize
ecstasy
effect
effective
efficiency
*eighth
eligible
eliminate
eloquence
emanate
*embarrass
embed(ded)
emergencies
emergency
emotionally
emphasis (*noun*)
*emphasize (*verb*)
emphatic
employe(e)
encourage
encouragement
encouraging
encyclical
endeavor
endurance
enemies
enemy
enough

enthusiastic
entirely
entrance
enunciate
envelop (*verb*)
envelop(e) (*noun*)
envelopment
environment
epidemic
epoch
equable
equilibrium
equip
equipment
equipped
*equivalent
erroneous
escape
especially
espionage
essence
essential
etc.
ever
every
everybody
evidently
exaggerate
examine
examination
exceed
excel
excelled
excellent
except
exceptional
exceptionally
excess

excessive
excitable
excitement
exercise
exhaust(ed)
exhibit
exhibition
exhilarate
*existence
exorbitant
expense
experience
experiment
explanation
explicit
extension
extraordinary
extravagance
extremely
eyeing

facilitate
facilities
fallacies
*familiar
familiarity
famous
fascinate
fascinating
feasible
*February
fictitious
field
fierce
*fiery
fifth
finally

financial
financially
financier
flier *or* flyer
fluoridation
focal
forehead
*foreign
foremost
foresee
foreword
forfeit
fortieth
*forty
forty-four
forward
fourth
fragrant
frantically
fraternity
fraudulent
freight
frequency
*freshman (*adj.*)
friend
friendliness
frivolous
frontier
fulfil(l)
fulfilled
ful(l)ness
fundamental
furniture
further
fusillade

gage *or* gauge
gaging *or* gauging

gagging
  (obstructing)
gaiety *or* gayety
gallant
gamble
gambling
gases
gelatin
generally
generous
genius
genuine
ghost
gipsy *or* gypsy
glycerin
gnawing
goddess
goodby(e)
*government
*governor
*grammar
grammatical
grandeur
grandiose
grateful
grief
grievous
gruesome
guarantee
guard
guardian
gubernatorial
guess
guidance
guillotine

Halloween
handful

handkerchief
handle
handling
handsome
haphazard
harass
hardening
hastily
haul(led)
haven't
hazardous
*height
helpfulness
hemorrhage
herald
hereditary
heresy
heroes
heroine
hesitancy
hesitantly
hindrance
hearse
hope
hopeless
hoping
hopping (leaping)
hospitable
huge
humidity
humorous
hundred
hundredths
hurried
hurriedly
hurrying
hygiene
hygienic

hymn
hymnal
hypnosis
hypnotize
hypocrisy
hysterical

icicle
identity
ideologies
idiocy
idiomatic
idiosyncrasies
illicit
illiterate
illogical
illustrate
imaginary
imagination
imagining
imitation
immaculate
*immediately
immensely
immigrate
immigration
immovable
impetuous(ity)
impostor
imprisonment
impromptu
impugn
inaccessible
inaccuracy
inadequate
inaugurate
incalculable
incentive

incessant
*incidentally
incipient
incomparable
incompetent
incorrigible
incredible
incredibly
incredulous
incur(red)
incurable
indefinitely
independence
*independent
Indian
indict(ment)
indigestible
indiscreet
indispensable
induce
inebriated
inefficiency
inescapable
inevitable
inexhaustible
infectious
inferred
infinite(ly)
inflammable
influence
influential
infuriate
ingredient
inherent
initiation
initiative
innocence
innocuous

innuendo
inoculate
inseparable
insignia
insistence
instance
instantaneous
instead
instil(l)
insulin
intellectual
intelligence
intelligent
intelligible
intentionally
intercede
intercepted
interested
*interesting
interfere
intermittent
interpret
interpretation
interrupt(ion)
intolerable
intricacies
introduce
invariably
inveigle
iridescent
irrelevant
irreligious
irresistible
irresponsible
island
isthmus
itemize
itinerary

*its (pron.)
*it's (it is)
itself

January
jaundice
jealous
jeopardize
jewelry
jodhpurs
*judgment
ju-jitsu
judicial
kaleidoscope
keenness
khaki
kidnap(p)ed
kidnap(p)er
kimono
kindergarten
knack
knowledge(able)
knuckle

label
*laboratory
ladies
*laid (past of lay)
laryngitis
larynx
later
latter
laundered
lavender
*led (past of lead)
leggings
legible
legislative

legislator
legitimate
leisure
leisurely
*length
lenses
lethargic
liable
liaison
*libel
library
license
lieutenant
likelihood
likable
likely
lilies
lingerie
liquefy
liqueur
liquidate
liquor
listener
literary
literature
livable
livelihood
liveliness
loneliness
loose (to untie)
*lose
*losing
*lovable
loveliness
loyalty
lucid
luminous
luscious

luxurious
*lying

macaroni
machinery
magazine
magnificence
mahogany
maintain
maintenance
malfeasance
manageable
managing
mandatory
maneuver
manual
manufacturer
many
marriage
marries
*marshal
Massachusetts
material
mathematics
mattress
maximum
*meanness
*meant
medicine
medieval
mediocre
menu
mercenary
merciful
messenger
mileage
militia
millinery

millionaire
mimicking
miniature
minimum
minutely
miscegenation
miscellaneous
mischievous
mislead (*present*)
*misled (*past*)
Mississippi
missile
*misspell(ed)
mobilize
model(ed)
modifying
momentous
monopolize
monotonous
monsignor
monstrous
*morale
mortgage
mosquitoes
mountainous
movable
municipal
murmur(ing)
muscle
museum
musical(e)
mustache
myriad
mysterious

naive
naphtha
natural(ly)

nearby
nebulous
*necessary
necessarily
necessity
necessitate
necessities
Negroes
neighbor
*neither
neutral
nevertheless
nickel
niece
nineteen
nineteenth
ninety
ninth
nomenclature
nominative
nonagenarian
notable
noticeable
notoriety
nowadays
nucleus
nuisance
nullify
nutritionist

obedience
obeisance
obligation
oblige
obliging
obscene
observer
obsolete

obstacle
obstreperous
*occasion
*occasionally
occur
*occurred
occurrence
o'clock
oculist
odor
offense
offered
official
omission
omit
*omitted
oneself
operate
opinion
opponent
*opportunity
oppressive
optimism
optimistic
optimistically
ordinarily
organization
origin
*original(ly)
outrageous
overrun

pageant
*paid (*past of* pay)
pamphlet
pantomime
paraffin
parallel

paralysis
paralyzed
paraphernalia
pari-mutuel
parishioner
parley
parliamentary
participle
*particularly
partner
passed (*past of* pass)
past (*adj.*)
passenger
pasteurization
pastime
pathos
patronize
pavilion
peaceable
peasant
peculiar(ly)
peculiarity
pendulum
perceive
perceptible
perception
*per cent
peremptory
perform
perhaps
permanent
permissible
perpendicular
per se
perseverance
persistence
persistent
personal (*adj.*)

personally (*adv.*)
personnel (*noun*)
*perspiration
persuade
persuasion
pertain
pertinent
pervade
pessimistic
phenomenal
Philippines
philosophy
physically
physician
pianist
picnic
*picnicked
*picnicker
pilgrim
pimiento
pitiful
plainness
plaintiff
*planned (*past of plan*)
platoon
playwright
pleasant
pleasure
plurality
pneumonia
poignant
politician
politics
polluted
portray(ed)
positively
*possess(ion)

possessive
possibility
possible
possibly
potato(es)
practicable
practical(ly)
practice *or* practise (*verb*)
practice (*noun*)
prairie
*precede
precedence
precedent(s)
preceding
precious
predecessor
predicament
predominant
preferable
preference
prefer(red)
prejudice
preliminary
premonition
preparation
preparatory
prepare
preposterous
pressure
pretend
pretense
prevalence
prevalent
primitive
prisoner
*privilege
probably

*procedure
*proceed
process
prodigy
profess(ed)
profession
*professor
profligate
proffered
proficiency
program
prohibition
promenade
prominence
promissory
promptness
pronunciation
propel(led)
propeller
proportion
prosperous
protrude
prove
proving
prudence
psalm
pseudonym
psychic
psychology
ptomaine
publicize
puerile
purchase
purchasing
pursue
pursuing
pursuit
putting

quandary
quantity
quarantine
quarrel(ed)
quarter
quartet
*questionnaire
quietly
quiz(zed)
quizzes

raccoon
racial
racketeer
radiator
rapid(ly)
rarefy
rarity
readiness
ready
realistically
realize
*really
rearrangement
rebellious
recede
receipt
*receive
reciprocate
*recognize
*recommend(ation)
reconcile
reconciliation
recur(red)
recurrence
reference
referred
regard

region
rehearsal
reign
reimburse
reinforced
relapse
relevant
reliable
relief
relieve
religious
remarkable
*remembrance
reminiscences
reminiscent
remittance
remuneration
renaissance
repair(ed)
repellent
repentance
repetition
repetitious
*replied
replies
representative
reptile
requirement
rescind
resemblance
reservoir
resistance
*respectfully
*respectively
responsible
restaurant
restaurateur
retaliate

revelation
reverence
rheumatic
rheumatism
rhyme
rhythm
rhythmical
ricochet(ed or ted)
ridiculous
riding
running
rural
rutabaga

sacrifice
sacrificing
sacrilegious
safety
*salable
sandwich
sarcastically
Saturday
sauerkraut
saxophone
scarcely
scarcity
schedule
scheme
science
scion
scissors
scream(ed)
scrupulous
secede
secession
secondary
secretary
seize(d)

*sensible
*separate
*sergeant
serviceable
several
severely
shepherd
*sheriff
shiftless
*shining
shoulder
shriek
siege
signature
significance
significant
silhouette
*similar(ly)
*similarity
simile
simplify
simulate
simultaneous
sincerely
siphon
sirup *or* syrup
sizable
skeleton
skier
skiing
skilful(ly) *or*
   skillful(ly)
smooth
sobriquet
solemn
soliloquy (-quies)
soluble
somber

sophisticated
*sophomore
sororities
sovereign
souvenir
spaghetti
specially
specialty
specifically
specimen
specter
speech
spoonful(s)
step(ped)
*stop(ping)
*stopped
*stopper
stories
*straight
strait jacket
strategic
strategy
*strength(en)
strenuous
*stretch
strictly
studious
studying
subscription
substantial
subtle
succeed
success(ful)
succession
suddenness
sufficient
suffrage
suite (of rooms)

*summarize
*superintendent
supersede
superstitious
supervision
supervisor
supine
suppress
sure(ly)
*surprise
surveillance
*suspicious
swimming
switch
syllable
symmetrical
symmetry
sympathize
synonymous

taciturn
tactfully
taking
tantamount
tariff
temblor
temperament(al)
temperance
temperature
temporarily
tenant
tendency
tentacles
tentative
*theater
their (*pron.*)
there (*adverb*)
therefore (*conj.*)

they're (they are)
*thorough
thousandth(s)
*tied
till
toe(ing)
together
tomato(es)
toward
traceable
tragedy
tranquillity
transfer(red)
transient
transmission
transmitter
travel(l)ed
treacherous
treasure
treasurer
tries
trolley
trouble
trousseau
truant
*truly
tuberculosis
Tuesday
twelfth
tying
typical
typify
typing
typography
tyrannically
tyranny

ulterior

ultimatum(s)
unanimous
unconscious
uncontrollable
undesirable
undoubtedly
universally
*unnecessary
unparalleled
unprecedented
*until
unusual(ly)
usable
usage
useful(ly)
*using
*usual(ly)
utility
utilize
utterance

vacancy
vaccinate
vacuum
valiant
valleys
valuable
valves
varicose
vaudeville
vegetable
vehicle
vender or vendor
vengeance
verified
verbatim
vermilion
vertebra

vertebras or
    vertebrae (pl.)
*veteran
veterinarian
vexatious
vice versa
vicinity
vigilance
vignette
vilify
*village
*villain
*villainy
virile
virtuous
visa
visible
visibly
vitreous (of glass)
volume
voluntary

warrant
wasteful(ly)
weakness(es)
weather(ed)
*Wednesday
weigh(ed)
weird
welcome
welfare
wherever
*whether
whir(red)
whistle
wholly
whose
who's

wield	*writing	your (*poss.*)
*wiener	written	you're (you are)
*wil(l)ful	wrought	yourself
wintry		
wiry	X ray (*noun*)	zeal
wizard	X-ray (*adj.*)	zealot
wo(e)ful	xylography	zealous
*woman	xylophone	zephyr
*women (*pl.*)		zinc
won't	yacht	zodiac
wool(l)y	yield	zoning
writer	yokel	zoology

TROUBLESOME HOMONYMS

Homonyms are words which sound alike but which are spelled differently and have different meanings.

There are hundreds of such words in the English language, but the ones that will give you the most trouble are listed below. Study the list carefully. Concentrate on the words with which you have difficulty. Your objective is to ground yourself thoroughly in the correct spelling and meaning of each word. Remember always to use the dictionary if you do not know what a word means or how it should be used in a sentence. For example, make sure you can use *principle* and *principal* correctly.

A List of Homonyms; and Other Words Easily Confused

accept	aid	all ready	alumna
except	aide	already	alumnae
			alumnus
access	aisle	allusion	alumni
excess	isle	illusion	
			anecdote
affect	alleys	altar	antidote
effect	allies	alter	

angel
angle

area
aria

ascent
assent

auger
augur

bail
bale

baring
barring
bearing

bath
bathe

berth
birth

beside
besides

better
bettor

blond
blonde

border
boarder

bolder

boulder

born
borne

brake
break

breach
breech

breath
breathe

brunet
brunette

cannon
canon
canyon (cañon)

canvas
canvass

capital
capitol

carton
cartoon

cast
caste

cavalry
Calvary

censor
censure

choose
chose

chord
cord

cite
site
sight

clamber
clamor

clench
clinch

climactic
climatic

cloth
clothe

coarse
course

complement
compliment

conscience
conscious

consul
council
councilor
counsel
counselor

corespondent

correspondent

decent
descent
dissent

deprecate
depreciate

desert
dessert

device
devise

disapprove
disprove

draft
draught
drought
drouth

dual
duel

dyeing
dying

emigrate
immigrate
emigrant
immigrant

eminent
imminent

envelop

envelope

ever
every

faint
feint

flaunt
flout

foreword
forward

fiancé
fiancée

forego
forgo

formally
formerly

forth
fourth

foul
fowl

farther
further

guarantee
guaranty

hair
hare
heir

hangar
hanger

healthful
healthy

hoard
horde

hoping
hopping

human
humane

idle
idol

idyl

indict
indite

inflammable
inflammatory

ingenious
ingenuous

instance
instant

its
it's

later
latter

lead

led

lessen
lesson

liable
libel

lightening
lightning

likely
liable

loose
lose

luxuriant
luxurious

magnate
magnet

mantel
mantle

manual
Manuel

marshal
martial

miner
minor

moral
morale

oneself
one's self

ordinance
ordnance

partition
petition

passed
past

peace
piece

peak
peek
pique

peal
peel

peer
pier

personal
personnel

plain
plane
planed
planned

pole
poll

pore
pour

practicable	rite	stationery	too
practical	write		two
		statue	
pray	rout	stature	track
prey	route	statute	tract
precede	sanitarium	steal	troop
proceed	sanitorium	steel	troupe
prescribe	scene	straight	turban
proscribe	seen	strait	turbine
principal	sense	surely	vain
principle	since	surly	vane
			vein
prophecy	sensual	than	
prophesy	sensuous	then	vale
			veil
quiet	serge	tenants	
quite	surge	tenets	vice
			vise
rain	sew	their	(vice versa)
reign	so	there	
rein	sow	they're	waive
			wave
raise	shone	therefor	
raze	shown	therefore	waiver
			waver
rapped	soar	thrash	
wrapped	sore	thresh	wander
			wonder
respectfully	sole	threw	
respectively	soul	through	weather
			whether
rhyme	stair	throne	
rime	stare	thrown	weighed
			weighted
right	stationary	to	

whole	holey	who's	your
hole	holy		you're
		woman	
wholly	whose	women	

Bibliography

Works of reference most often consulted and cited by the author in this revision of GRAMMAR FOR JOURNALISTS were mentioned in Chapter 1. They are:

BERNSTEIN, THEODORE M. *The Careful Writer: A Modern Guide to English Usage.* New York: Atheneum, 1965.

COPPERUD, ROY H. *A Dictionary of Usage and Style.* New York and London: Hawthorn Books, Inc., 1964.

FLESCH, RUDOLF. *The ABC of Style: A Guide to Plain English.* New York, Evanston, and London: Harper & Row, 1964.

Although the following books were not used as primary references in the process of revising this text, the author can recommend them as helpful books of reference for the journalism student and the practicing journalist:

BERNSTEIN, THEODORE M. *Watch Your Language.* Great Neck, N.Y.: Channel Press, 1958.

————. *More Language That Needs Watching.* Manhasset, N.Y.: Channel Press, 1962.

BOGUE, JESSE C. (ed.) *United Press International Stylebook.* Revised Edition. N.Y., N.Y., United Press International (1968)

CURME, GEORGE O. *Principles and Practice of English Grammar.* New York: Barnes & Noble, Inc., 1947.

FLESCH, RUDOLF. *The Art of Readable Writing.* New York: Harper & Brothers, 1949.

——, and A. H. LASS. *The Way to Write.* New York: McGraw-Hill, 1955.

FOWLER, H. W. (See listing for Nicholson, Margaret.)

FUNK & WAGNALLS EDITORIAL STAFF. *Standard Handbook of Prepositions, Conjunctions, Relative Pronouns and Adverbs.* New York: Funk & Wagnalls Co., 1953.

GUNNING, ROBERT. *The Technique of Clear Writing.* New York: McGraw-Hill Book Co., Inc., 1952.

McCORKLE, JULIA N. *Learning to Spell.* Boston: D. C. Heath & Co., 1953.

MENCKEN, H. L. *The American Language.* 3 vols. New York: Alfred A. Knopf, Inc., 1936–1948.

NICHOLSON, MARGARET. *A Dictionary of American-English Usage: Based on Fowler's Modern English Usage.* N.Y., N.Y.: Signet Books, published by The New American Library of World Literature, Inc., by arrangement with Oxford University Press, Inc. (Paperback)

OPDYCKE, JOHN B. *Get It Right.* New York: Funk & Wagnalls Co., 1941.

PARTRIDGE, ERIC. *Usage and Abusage.* Baltimore: Penguin Books, 1963.

SKILLIN, MARJORIE E., and ROBERT M. GAY. *Words Into Type.* New York: Appleton-Century-Crofts, Inc., 1948.

SUMMEY, GEORGE. *American Punctuation.* New York: The Ronald Press Co., 1949.

WEBSTER'S NEW INTERNATIONAL DICTIONARY OF THE ENGLISH LANGUAGE, Second Edition, Springfield, Mass.: G & C. Merriam Co., 1954.

WEBSTER'S THIRD NEW INTERNATIONAL DICTIONARY OF THE ENGLISH LANGUAGE, Springfield, Mass.: G. & C. Merriam Co., 1961.

WINKLER, G. P. (ed.) *The Associated Press Stylebook.* N.Y., N.Y.: The Associated Press, 1967. (The first joint AP-UPI stylebook was published in 1960. This is the second edition issued, obtainable from either The Associated Press or the United Press International.)

Index